D0583967

Frank Bridge. *Courtesy of the Frank Bridge Trust.*

FRANK BRIDGE

FRANK BRIDGE

A Bio-Bibliography

KAREN R. LITTLE

Bio-Bibliographies in Music, Number 36
Donald L. Hixon, Series Adviser

Greenwood Press
New York • Westport, Connecticut • London

Library of Congress Cataloging-in-Publication Data

Little, Karen R.
Frank Bridge : a bio-bibliography / Karen R. Little.
p. cm.—(Bio-bibliographies in music, ISSN 0742-6968 ; no. 36)
Discography: p.
Includes bibliographical references and index.
ISBN 0-313-26232-2 (alk. paper)
1. Bridge, Frank, 1879-1941—Bibliography. 2. Bridge, Frank, 1879-1941—Discography. I. Title. II. Series.
ML134.B84L5 1991
016.785 '0092—dc20 90-23779

British Library Cataloguing in Publication Data is available.

Library of Congress Catalog Card Number: 90-23779
ISBN: 0-313-26232-2
ISSN: 0742-6968

First published in 1991

Greenwood Press, 88 Post Road West, Westport, CT 06881
An imprint of Greenwood Publishing Group, Inc.

Printed in the United States of America

The paper used in this book complies with the Permanent Paper Standard issued by the National Information Standards Organization (Z39.48-1984).

10 9 8 7 6 5 4 3 2 1

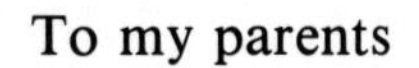

To my parents

Contents

Preface

This book is divided into four major sections followed by two appendices and an index. The major sections are as follows:

(1) a *biography* providing an overview of Bridge's life;

(2) a list of *works and performances*, including arrangments and orchestrations, classified by genre and then arranged alphabetically by title. This list includes the date of composition, publisher and date of publication, duration, instrumentation, commission and dedication (when applicable), as well as references to related versions where appropriate. Following many titles is a listing of the premiere and other selected performances. References are made to reviews of performances in the *Bibliography*. Each work is preceded by the mnemonic "W" (W1, W2, etc.) and each performance of that work is identified by successive lowercase letters (W1a, W1b, W1c, etc.);

(3) a *discography* of commercially-produced sound recordings, arranged alphabetically by title. Performers, album title, recording location and date, and contents are listed. Reissue information is included where appropriate. All entries are assumed to be 33⅓ rpm, stereophonic recordings unless otherwise indicated. References are made to reviews of recordings in the *Bibliography*. Each entry is preceded by the mnemonic "D";

(4) an annotated *bibliography* of writings by and about Frank Bridge. This section is divided into sub-sections entitled "Books and Articles" and "Reviews." The numbering is consecutive throughout. References refer the user back to *Works and Performances* and to the *Discography*. Each citation is preceded by the mnemonic "B".

The two *appendices* provide alphabetical and chronological listings of Bridge's works. A complete *index* of names, titles, and selected subjects concludes the volume. Use of the *index* precludes the need to consult cross-referenced entries within the book.

Despite careful research, it was not possible to provide premiere information for all works believed to have been performed. Readers able to supply this information are encouraged to contact the author through Greenwood Press.

Acknowledgments

I wish to express my gratitude to the great number of persons and institutions who assisted in the compilation of this work. Without their generous assistance, this book would not have been possible. In particular I would like to thank the following:

For providing specialized bibliographical assistance:

John Bishop, Secretary, Frank Bridge Trust;
Paul Hindmarsh, BBC Radio 3 Music Producer, and author;
Roderic M. Keating, Wuppertal, Federal Republic of Germany;
Rosamund Strode, Keeper of Manuscripts and Archivist, Britten-Pears Library;
Staffs of the British Library Reading Room, the British Library's Newspaper Library, and the Royal College of Music Library.

For providing institutional support:

Doug Hurd, Document Delivery Coordinator, University of Virginia, and his staff, in particular, Peggy Holley, Mark Irwin, and Mary Ramsey;
Ljilja Kuftinec, Interlibrary Loan Department Head, University of Louisville;
Southern Regional Education Board Small Grants Program;
University of Louisville Graduate School Research Committee;
University of Virginia Library Faculty Research Committee.

For providing editorial assistance:

Mary M. Blair, Acquisitions Editor, Music, Greenwood Press;
Donald L. Hixon, Fine Arts Librarian, University of California, Irvine and Series Advisor, Bio-Bibliographies in Music, Greenwood Press;
Donald W. Krummel, Professor of Library and Information Science and of Music, University of Illinois.

I would also like to thank the staffs of the following publishing houses who kindly took the time to respond to my correspondence: Boosey & Hawkes, Warner Chappell, Chester Music, William Elkin, EMI Music Publishing, Faber Music, Novello, Oxford University Press, Stainer & Bell, and Thames Publishing. In addition, I would like to express my appreciation to Richard Griscom and C. Martin Rosen for their valuable suggestions, particularly in the final stages of the book. And finally, my special thanks goes to my husband, Hoyt, for his encouragement and patience.

FRANK BRIDGE

Biography

Frank Bridge's life was one of a well-rounded, complete musician. As a violist, he performed for years as a member of the English String Quartet and was in demand at the Royal College of Music long after receiving his degree. As a conductor, he was trusted to direct major ensembles with little or no rehearsal. He was, for some time, best known as a teacher of Benjamin Britten, a composer who revered and respected his instructor. But his most remarkable legacy is as a composer; a composer whose achievements have been acknowledged only in the past two decades.

Bridge was born in Brighton on February 26, 1879. His father, William Henry Bridge (1845–1928), was, by training, a lithographer. William Bridge's real calling, however, was music and eventually he turned to violin teaching and conducting. From his home in Brighton, he traveled to boarding schools in neighboring towns to instruct his pupils. In addition to teaching, William Bridge took employment as musical director of the Empire Theatre, a position that involved conducting the orchestra of this music hall in Brighton.

Frank Bridge's mother, Elizabeth Warbrick (1848–1899), was William's third wife. Of his eleven siblings, Frank was closest to Nellie (1881–1965) and William (1883–1956). Both Nellie and William shared Bridge's interest in music. Nellie was a fine vocalist and William was a professional cellist in London.

Bridge attended school at York Place while taking violin lessons, from age twelve, at the Brighton School of Music. Once having mastered basic violin technique, Bridge was allowed to perform in his father's orchestra. He also had the occasion to perform on other instruments as the need arose, to arrange music when necessary, and to conduct. In 1896, at age seventeen, Bridge was accepted as a violin student at the Royal College of Music in London.

Two particularly noteworthy members of the Royal College of Music's teaching staff at the time of Bridge's acceptance were Sir C. Hubert H. Parry, instructor of music history, and Sir Charles Villiers Stanford, teacher of composition and conducting. Bridge's early responsibility at the College was as a performer in the orchestra where, early in his college days, he sat toward the back of the second violins. However, he soon became a regular, strong member of the second violins and by the summer of 1899 Bridge was leading the seconds, a position he retained until graduation. Bridge's initial appearance as a chamber music player was on November 14, 1900 when he played the violin for the first performance of his Piano trio in D minor (1900). From that time on, his name appeared regularly on College programs as a chamber music performer, most often as a violist. Since the chamber music repertoire most frequently performed at the College was works by Brahms and Dvořák, Bridge received significant exposure to these composers' styles.

In addition to playing the violin, Bridge also had the opportunity to conduct while at the College. Having gained considerable experience conducting his father's orchestra, Bridge was allowed to conduct the first performances of his *Berceuse* (1901) and *The Hag* (1902).

In 1899, Bridge was awarded a scholarship from the College that enabled him to study composition under Stanford for four years. Stanford's list of pupils at that time included Thomas Dunhill, Gustav Holst, and John Ireland. Hiawatha Coleridge-Taylor and Ralph Vaughan Williams had studied with Stanford earlier and Eugene Goossens, Herbert Howells, and E. J. Morean were to become Stanford students in the years after Bridge's graduation. Stanford was remembered by his students as a rigorous and highly critical instructor. He insisted that his pupils have a thorough understanding of counterpoint prior to moving on to original composition. He stressed that compositions were above all written to suit the medium for which they were composed. Stanford's admiration of the classics was seen in his choice of music for orchestral performance during Bridge's years at the College. Most of the music was by Romantic composers; relatively few Mozart or Haydn works were performed. Brahms's symphonies were performed more often than Beethoven's while first performances of works by Parry, William Hurlstone, Vaughan Williams, and Edward Elgar took place during Bridge's attendance at the College. This conservative outlook is seen in Stanford's own compositions as well. His conservatism is also reflected in the music Bridge wrote while at the College.

By his own choosing, Bridge's composing during his college years consisted primarily of chamber music. His Piano trio in D minor, String quartet in B-flat major (1900), String quintet in E minor (1901), and Piano quartet in C minor (1902) were all given first performances at the College. A wealth of performers were available for these performances. Pianists Harold Samuel and James Friskin were listed repeatedly in programs as were string players Ernest Tomlinson, Arthur Trew, Thomas Morris, Herbert Kinsey, and Ivor James. Along with Bridge, the latter three were to form the English String Quartet in 1908.

Another important event during Bridge's time at the Royal College of Music was his introduction and subsequent relationship with Ethel Elmore

Sinclair. Born near Melbourne in Australia on July 10, 1881 she was to become Bridge's wife in 1908. As a violinist, she won a scholarship in her native Australia which allowed her to travel to London in May 1899 to study at the College. She played in the College orchestra and performed in chamber ensembles. On one such occasion she played the violin for the first performance of Bridge's Piano quartet in C minor. Sinclair was awarded the ARCM (violin) and the Hill and Sons violin prize in 1903. Bridge's ARCM, also granted in 1903, was in composition. He also won two awards: the Arthur Sullivan prize for composition in March 1901 and the 'Tagore' Gold Medal in 1903.

After graduation, Bridge continued performing. He played in several theater orchestras but was primarily involved with smaller chamber ensembles. He played second violin in the Grimson Quartet and viola in the Motto and English String Quartets. A large number of these groups' performances were in London but performances were given in the provinces as well. The Grimson Quartet performed even farther afield, touring Belgium and France in the Autumn of 1907. Bridge's reputation as a violist grew when he was called to perform with the well-known and highly respected Joachim String Quartet in 1906.

One series of concerts for which Bridge performed, either as a member of one of these quartets or on a free-lance basis, was a series arranged by Dunhill beginning in 1907. These concerts were devoted to second and third performances of contemporary works. Another reputable series for which the English String Quartet frequently performed was the Classical Concert Society. Edward Speyer founded this society upon the death of Joseph Joachim and the subsequent end of his quartet society and it was Speyer who was responsible for the program selections for these concerts. The works most frequently selected were from the Classic and Romantic repertoires. Occasionally, a work by Bridge was performed. Bridge also had the opportunity to perform in the Northlands Chamber Music Concerts, a concert series arranged by Sir Donald Tovey beginning in 1893. Bridge's name first appeared as a performer for these concerts in 1906.

Even with all these outside performing opportunities, Bridge performed regularly in student chamber music concerts at the Royal College of Music until 1910. He was particularly active in the Royal College of Music Student Union. The Union frequently held evening events at members' houses. These "At Homes," as they were called, were intended as a time during which members could socialize with their friends as well as hear a variety of different works performed. The evening's program typically included at least one work by a student at the College. Bridge's Piano quintet (1905) and its 1912 revision were first performed at two such musical evenings.

The College Quartet, of which Bridge was a member, was often called to perform at these "At Homes." The College Quartet came to be known as the Chips Quartet. The 'chips' portion of the title referred to the improvised, somewhat amusing musical snippets often performed by the group. Ivor James told of one such event:

> We played tunes on four wood-winds, on four brass instruments, and *Sweet and Low* on four double basses, also a passionate love duet for two violins accompanied by viola and 'cello, in which one of the violinists became so enraptured that he was unable to hold his instrument, which slipped over his shoulder and shot up into the air behind him; we all rushed to save it, but down it dropped on the floor. In our anxiety to pick it up someone trod on it. I shall never forget the sound of that scrunch, nor the sight of the faces in the audience, all of which paled with horror. It was only later they discovered that it was a toy fiddle![1]

Also performed at this particular "At Home" was Bridge's *Scherzo phantastick* (1901). This work also proved highly entertaining.

Bridge was also in demand as a conductor and upon graduation he conducted whenever the opportunity arose. One such opportunity came after the founding of the New Symphony Orchestra in 1905 when he accepted the responsibility of presiding over its repertory rehearsals. Henry Wood, impressed with Bridge's abilities, felt confident in calling him in at the last minute to conduct for him at a Promenade Concert, an opportunity which helped create for Bridge his title and reputation as an "ambulance conductor." Bridge also conducted opera performances. His first was as principal conductor of Marie Brema's 1910–1911 opera season at the Savoy Theatre. Works performed during this season included Handel's *L'Allegro ed il Pensieroso* and Gluck's *Orfeo ed Euridice*. Bridge received positive reviews for his conducting of the *Orfeo*.

Bridge's ability as a composer, however, outpaces that of his other roles as a musician. The first twelve years of the twentieth-century were his most prolific and these were the years that Bridge showed himself a master at writing with both the taste of his audience and the capabilities of his performers in mind.

Bridge's style during this early mature period was largely that of Brahms and Stanford. Under Stanford, he had learned his craft as a craftsman would and this approach was apparent in his early compositions. A traditional four movement structure was typically employed. His harmonic language was less than adventuresome and his songs, in particular, were little more than straightforward salon pieces. This conservative style resulted in a fair following and positive support from both the competition judges and the critics of first performances.

A portion of Bridge's early works were written for competitions. While still a student at the Royal College of Music, Bridge had composed *Coronation March* (1901) for a competition sponsored by the Worshipful Company of Musicians. *Music when soft voices die* (1904), also an early work, was written for a competition announced by *The Musical Times* in 1904. Bridge's success with competitions began in 1905, when he composed his Capriccio no. 1 in A minor (1905) for a competition arranged by pianist Mark Hambourg. Bridge won this competition and its prize of ten guineas. His Capriccio was performed by Hambourg in Bechstein Hall on May 20, 1905.

A series of competitions in which Bridge was particularly successful was begun in 1905 by Walter Willson Cobbett (1847–1937) with the cooperation of the Worshipful Company of Musicians. The aim of these competitions was to encourage the composition of British chamber music through monetary awards, and the performance and publishing of winning works. Specifically, Cobbett stipulated that works for this competition be written in the form of a phantasy. The work was

> to be performed without a break, and to consist of sections varying in tempo and rhythm; in short to be (like the Fancies) in one-movement form and not to last more than twelve minutes. The parts were to be of equal importance.[2]

Cobbett specified that the entered works for the first competition be a string quartet in this form. Hurlstone won the first prize of Ł50 for his work. Bridge's Phantasie in F minor (1905) placed second and a quartet by Haydn Wood placed third. The first six phantasies were performed on June 22, 1906 in Bechstein Hall. The second Cobbett competition was for a piano trio in the form of a phantasy. This competition was won by Bridge for his Phantasy in C minor (1907). Friskin and Ireland placed second and third. The third Cobbett competition, for which Bridge did not send an entry, was for a work in sonata form. In addition to sponsoring this series of competitions Cobbett also provided outright commissions to young British composers. Bridge's Phantasy in F-sharp minor (1910) was one such commission. It was completed in 1910.

Another contest entered by Bridge was an international competition sponsored by the Accademica Filarmonica in Bologna. In 1906 Bridge entered his String quartet no. 1 in E minor (1906). For this entry, his 'Italian' quartet, Bridge received honorable mention.

In addition to the experience gained by writing for competitions, Bridge was also fortunate to have a large number of his works performed at Patron's Fund concerts. This source of patronage, administered by the Royal College of Music, was intended to promote the first performance of compositions by young British composers, to provide traveling funds to young musicians, and to allow British performers an opportunity to perform in public. Bridge's *The Hag* was performed in 1904 at the first Patron's Fund concert. A few of the other Bridge works performed at later Patron's Fund concerts include his *Night lies on the silent highways* (1904), *A Dead violet* (1904), *A Dirge* (1903), and *I praise the tender flower* (1906).

In 1909, Bridge was selected as one of the composers represented at the first festival of the Musical League Festival at Liverpool. His *Dance rhapsody* (1908) was performed as part of the festival on September 25, 1909. Other rising talents of the day selected for the first festival were Arnold Bax, Havergal Brian, Vaughan Williams, and Joseph Holbrooke.

Public sentiment toward Bridge's works during the first decade of his mature writing was positive, as reviews of performances prove. His *Three Idylls* (1906), dedicated to "E.E.S.", was described as "delicate impressionist sketches of a light and fantastic nature."[3] His Phantasy in F-sharp minor, commissioned by Cobbett, was described as a work of "singular beauty."[4] His orchestral works fared even better. *Dance rhapsody* and *Isabella* (1907) both received a fair number of performances early in their life although they did not become repertoire standards. *Dance rhapsody* was described, after its performance at the Musical League Festival, as "clever, and of light character."[5] Bridge's *The Sea* (1911), his only orchestral work to really find its way into the orchestra repertoire, was described as "among the most individual, imaginative and pleasing of the works"[6] performed during the 1912 Promenade season. As Bridge's style gradually changed over the next ten or eleven years, so did public acceptance of his works.

The years 1913 through 1924 were years of transition for Bridge, not to mention the world at large. Bridge's career as a violist and a conductor, and his compositional output were to be affected by World War I and the new world that emerged.

As violist in the English String Quartet during these years, Bridge performed in public less often than previously although the group continued to perform at private concerts. The Quartet's personnel changed slightly when Marjorie Hayward replaced Morris upon his departure for the Royal Flying Corps.

It was around this time that Bridge joined the Ridgehurst Quartet. Formed purely for private performances, the typical personnel consisted of Edward Speyer's son, Ferdinand, Ethel and Frank Bridge, and Ivor James. The quartet was named after the location of these private performances: Edward Speyer's home, Ridgehurst, at Shenley in Hertfordshire. Edward Speyer recalled Bridge and the quartet's performances in his home:

> Frank's name recalls to me many of the happiest hours of our life at Ridgehurst, spent in listening to chamber music. By reason of his great qualities as a musician, he dominated and guided the various London quartets with which he was associated from time to time. At Ridgehurst he was always ready not only to do music but to ensure the utmost possible perfection of performance. He has the conscience of the true artist.[7]

Although Bridge's appearances in public as a violist declined, his conducting engagements did not. It was to Bridge's disappointment, however, that a permanent conducting position did not materialize. His friend, Ivor James, explained that Bridge's personality may have been a contributing factor:

> He had an exceptional sense of standard... But this sense of standard made him intensely impatient of any shortcomings in others, either actual or imaginary, and being a bundle of

> sensitiveness, out would come some remark which probably the players would resent. If only they could have understood that it was impossible for Bridge to wrap his pills in sugar, his recognition as a really fine conductor would have been assured.[8]

Though he was never offered a permanent position, Bridge continued to deputize for indisposed conductors. Among others, Bridged stepped in for Sir Henry Wood, Raymond Rôze, Goossens, and Sir Landon Ronald. Bridge gained quite a reputation through these emergency conducting stints. Of a 1922 concert which Bridge conducted on short notice, a reviewer said, "It was a night that Mr. Frank Bridge will remember; one also for which he deserves to be held in remembrance."[9] Not all conducting was done with short notice, however. Bridge conducted Rôze's opera season at Covent Garden in 1913 and, in 1923, he conducted several of his own orchestral works in Boston, Cleveland, Detroit, and New York City.

Bridge also supplemented his income by teaching, as often as twice a week at times. As composing became a slower, more difficult task with his change in style, the time he had for composing seemed less and less and the burden of the time spent teaching greater and greater. A sponsor was what Bridge needed and, in Elizabeth Sprague Coolidge, what he received.

American Elizabeth Sprague Coolidge (1864–1953) was a wealthy patron of music with a special interest in chamber music. She inaugurated, in 1918, the Berkshire Chamber Music Festival, a festival held annually at Pittsfield, Massachusetts. This festival, lasting three days each September, was devoted to chamber music, particularly modern chamber music.

Bridge's chamber music was an appropriate choice for performance at such a festival and his String quartet no. 1 in E minor was the first of his works to appear there. It was performed at the Berkshire Festival in 1920. In 1922, Mrs. Coolidge chose Bridge, along with Goossens and Rebecca Clarke, to participate in the 1923 Festival. Bridge's String sextet in E-flat major (1912) was selected for performance and Bridge and his wife, Ethel, were asked to attend.

The Bridge's left for New York and the Berkshire Festival in August of 1923. The String sextet in E-flat major was performed at the Festival on September 27. Following the performance the Bridge's toured portions of Pennsylvania, Delaware, New Jersey, and Washington, D.C. In October, Bridge began a conducting tour to Cleveland, Detroit, Boston, and New York City. The successful tour was followed by more sightseeing and additional performances of Bridge's works. The Bridge's returned to England in December of 1923.

Mrs. Coolidge and the Bridge's became close friends through this and other encounters and often vacationed together. Through the Berkshire Festival and Mrs. Coolidge's patronage—she was to support him with a generous allowance for the rest of his life—Bridge was soon able to reduce his teaching load and concentrate on composing.

In addition to their trip to the United States in 1923, the Bridge's moved from central London to a home built for them at Friston, near Eastbourne. In frequent visits to the home of their friend Marjorie Fass, they had been intrigued by the beauty of the scenery there and the proximity of that area to the sea. This new home at Friston provided a place of beauty and quiet from which Bridge was to compose his most important works.

Even though Bridge's appearances with student chamber ensembles at the Royal College of Music decreased greatly after 1910, his association with the school, particularly when he lived in London, remained strong. In 1918, Bridge composed an organ work, *Lento (In memoriam C.H.H.P.)* (1918), as a tribute to his former College teacher, Parry. It was performed at Parry's funeral on October 16 of that year. Bridge also performed with the English String Quartet at the College in December of 1918 for Parry's memorial service. In 1919 Bridge conducted an orchestral arrangement of *Blow out you bugles* (1918) at the first of three concerts held to commemorate the 25th anniversary of the opening of the new College building.

While Bridge had gained wide recognition in the musical community, a reputation that grew in the 1920's in large part due to Mrs. Coolidge's efforts, the public at large remained generally unaware of his music due to his few published works. Only two of nearly forty Bridge songs were published prior to 1913. They were *The Primrose* (1901) and *If I could choose* (1901). By 1913, his only important published chamber works had been the three Cobbett works and *Three Idylls*. Fortunately, this was to change over the next ten years as Augener began printing some new works and some earlier works, such as the songs *Adoration* (1905) and *Come to me in my dreams* (1906) that had remained in manuscript. However, Augener did not take up the publishing of orchestral works. Bridge's first published orchestral work was *The Sea*. It was published in 1920 by Stainer & Bell, a result of having been chosen in the music publication scheme sponsored by the Carnegie United Kingdom Trust in 1917.

It was during the years 1913 through 1924 that Bridge's compositional style began to shift away from the tight restraints of Stanford's teaching to a more adventuresome, dissonant style which culminated with the Piano sonata of 1924. The shift was to a much more intense, difficult post-war style. The genre which experienced the smallest amount of this experimentation was song. With the exception of the Piano sonata, only slightly more experimentation is seen is Bridge's works for piano, where he continued largely in the Romantic tradition of the miniature until 1924. Also, fewer works appeared during the war years. Perhaps this was a result of his change in style to one which was more difficult to compose.

Bridge's greatest, although gradual, shift in style is seen most easily in his chamber and orchestral works of the period. In brief, Bridge's works exhibited a new harmonic language, one with increasing dissonance and an increasingly sensuous sound.

Some of the works which most clearly demonstrated Bridge's experimentation at this time were his *Dance poem* (1913), *Summer* (1915), and his Violoncello sonata in D minor (1917). Public opinion of these works varied and seemed to depend, at least to some extent, on the degree of dissonance Bridge employed. Of *Dance poem* the reviewer of the first performance had this to say:

> As to Mr. Frank Bridge's new *Dance Poem*—which, as the programme stated, is intended to depict the emotions which a dancer feels in her movements—with great regret we find it impossible to say that it afforded any pleasure. It is bizarre, and both as regards its form and material it is designed apparently to amaze and startle. No doubt this is to be well in the fashion, but all the same the friends of the composer will hope that he will revert to the style in which he has distinguished himself.[10]

Summer fared somewhat better. An more tame example of Bridge's increasing maturity, it was described as a "charmingly coloured mood-picture."[11] The Violoncello sonata's harmonic language was less severe as well and its music was more immediately attractive. Its reviews were generally more positive.

Bridge's reaction to the more frequent negative criticism his works received is observed in an interview he gave in 1923. The interviewer quotes Bridge:

> The true artist writes to express his own honest views, not to please the public... The self-criticism to which the artist subjects himself will prevent him from fostering an ill-prepared work upon the public. The true artist may be trusted to take that care, and the greater the artist he is, the greater the care he takes. After that, the truth of his message must make itself known. If he is sincere, then all is well. It is the sincerity of his work which is the real test.[12]

It is fortunate that Bridge held this view since criticism directed toward his Piano sonata, the piece to which his harmonic experimentation ultimately would lead, was even more biting.

The Piano Sonata was the third of three works visibly influenced by the war. The first was *Lament* (1915) whose dedication read "to Catherine, aged 9, Lusitania." Catherine was a friend of Bridge who drowned with her family in the Lusitania disaster in June of 1915. The second work was *Three Improvisations* (1918) for left hand only. This work was composed for Douglas Fox, a young organist and pianist at the Royal College of Music who lost his right arm in the war. Bridge's Piano Sonata was similarly dedicated. His friend, Ernest Bristow Farrar, to whom the sonata was dedicated, was killed in action in France.

The Piano sonata, written between 1921 and 1924, is Bridge's first attempt to compose a large scale work using his new style. Many of the characteristics first used individually in the experimental works composed just prior to the 1920's are combined here in a unified whole. Of the work, critical opinion varied but it was particularly sharp in its negative criticism. The work, which "uses no key signature and would no doubt be described by the new theorists as 'polytonal'"[13] is described in one review as a "disappointment" with the reviewer lamenting Bridge's move to composing in a "hard-minded, clashing, atonal style."[14] But Bridge was to continue to refine this style and, as a result, to continue to lose favor in the public eye.

After the mid-1920's, Bridge's conducting activity was limited primarily to his own works. In the late 1920's, essentially retiring from public chamber music performing, Bridge relinquished his position in the English String Quartet.

Although teaching was, after the mid-1920's, not as economically necessary as it had been prior to Mrs. Coolidge's patronage, Bridge continued to do some teaching through the decade of the twenties. Benjamin Britten, his most famous student, began his studies with Bridge in 1927. Of his instruction, Britten recounted the following:

> Even though I was barely in my teens, this was immensely serious and professional study; and the lessons were mammoth. I remember one that started at half past ten, and at tea-time Mrs. Bridge came in and said, "Really, you must give the boy a break." Often I used to end these marathons in tears; not that he was beastly to me, but the concentrated strain was too much for me. I was perhaps too young to take in so much at the time, but I found later that a good deal of it had stuck firmly.
>
> This strictness was the product of nothing but professionalism. Bridge insisted on the absolutely clear relationship of what was in my mind to what was on the paper. I used to get sent to the other side of the room; Bridge would play what I'd written and demand if it was what I'd really meant...
>
> I badly needed his kind of strictness: it was just the right treatment for me. His loathing of all sloppiness and amateurishness set me standards to aim for that I've never forgotten. He taught me to think and feel through the instruments I was writing for: he was most naturally an instrumental composer, and as a superb viola player he thought instrumentally.[15]

Of his relationship outside of composition instruction, Britten recalled the following:

> He also drove me around the south of England (though to my hypercritical juvenile standards he was never a good driver) and opened my eyes to the beauty of the Downs, with their tucked-away little villages, and to the magnificence of English ecclesiastical architecture. I can also remember a gay trip to Paris with him and Mrs. Bridge. Opportunity for travel had never much

> come my way—I was the fourth child who had had to be expensively educated—so it can be imagined what I owe to Bridge's guidance at this particularly impressionable time of life. I repaid him a little by helping him with his tennis, which was wild and unconventional; I considered mine rather good and stylish.[16]

Britten also discussed Bridge's gentle pacifism. Britten's *War requiem* may have been composed partly as a result of discussions on this topic with Bridge.

In 1926, Bridge traveled to the United States for the second time. This journey's purpose was to serve on the jury of the first Coolidge prize competition and to attend a performance of his String quartet no. 2 in G minor (1915) at the Ojai Valley Festival in California. Sightseeing trips were taken as well.

Although throughout the 1920's Bridge's compositions continued to fall from public favor, two encouraging events did occur. In 1924 Bridge was named as a Fellow of the Royal College of Music and in 1929 he was awarded the Cobbett medal for "services to chamber music."

Bridge's chamber music composed between 1925 and 1932 continued in the style first presented in its complete form in the Piano sonata. In his String quartet no. 3 (1925–1927) his new harmonic style is central, appearing refined and developed. Mrs. Coolidge was instrumental in getting this work performed as part of a traveling series of concerts that she sponsored. The work premiered in Vienna and Paris late in 1927 and its American debut was on October 30, 1928 for Mrs. Coolidge's 64th birthday. The reaction of the reviewer for the first performance was strikingly positive. He said, "Probably Bridge has written nothing better."[17]

Bridge's Piano trio (1929), however, was strongly criticized; it was perhaps the most negatively received of all his works composed during this period. A reviewer said this about the first performance:

> Mr. Bridge's trio was a proposition of a different order. This was patently 1929—owing a good deal to Scriabin and more to Schoenberg. As it proceeded one wondered whether Mr. Bridge had not somewhat forced upon himself this style of writing, whether the greater part of this trio had any real meaning, even superficial, to the composer himself. We are, or so it seems to me, faced today, in this present international vogue of atonalism, with a new species of *Kapellmeistermusik*. Mr. Bridge is not the only instance of a composer on this side of the Channel having suddenly adopted a manner (as he did in his recent piano sonata) that bears no recognizable relationship to his own natural development.[18]

Even as late as 1966, Bridge's music written in the late 1920's was discussed with disapproval:

> Born in 1879, he [Bridge] was one of the first generation to benefit from the influence of Parry and Stanford, which meant that he grew up at the end of the Romantic period and spoke its harmonic language naturally, but lived on into the reaction against it after the First World War and became aware of finding himself being shelved at the height of his career. To meet this galling situation he did what Bax, who was an even more conspicuous victim of the *Zeitgeist*, refused to do: he began to uglify his music to keep it up to date.[19]

While Bridge viewed his stylistic development as an exploration of possible expressions rather than a deliberate attempt to up-date his music, his critics obviously believed otherwise. The distaste for the European avant-garde of composers such as Schoenberg and Berg was clear and the preference for nationalism in music was strong. Bridge's view of the nationalistic attitude of the day is revealed in a interview conducted in 1923:

> You really cannot speak of nationality in music, since art is world-wide. If there is to be any expression of national spirit, it must be the expression of the composer's own thoughts and feelings, and must come from the promptings of his own inspiration; he cannot seek it, and any effort on his part to aim at it, as a national expression must end in failure.[20]

Clearly, Bridge was at odds with the sentiment of the musical community in England at the time. Additional reactions to his compositions further demonstrated this.

Bridge's *There is a willow grows aslant a brook* (1927), composed for that year's Prom season, was one work for which a negative reception was repeatedly received. One of the first comments received illustrated the reviewer's opinion that the work "did not strike one either as a tremendously important contribution to modern British music or as a work likely to figure prominently among that fine musician's output."[21] Additional comments on the work argue that Bridge "fails to communicate his emotion when he sets out to express it."[22] *Enter spring* (1927), one of Bridge's longer works and one of few composed for large orchestra, was also received with comments expressing the audience's dislike of its the harmonic system. In the words of one reviewer, "Spring not only enters, but comes to stay an unconscionably long time."[23]

Although not performed until the mid-1930's, Bridge's *Phantasm* (1931) and his *Oration, concerto elegiaco* (1930) were also composed during this time. *Phantasm*, a one movement work for piano and orchestra, is described as "undistinguished and its treatment turgid."[24] *Oration*, while described again as difficult to listen to and understand on first hearing, fairs a little better in the critical reviews.

A late chamber piece that received its share of negative reviews was Bridge's Violin sonata (1932). In comparing the work to others in Bridge's earlier style, one reviewer felt the sonata lacked spontaneity and charm. He explained further:

> It is of the species of music which is called 'contemporary,' and only a brilliantly constructed Scherzo movement condescended to immediate attractiveness. After this the return of the tortuous manner of the first *Allegro* produced a laboured climax. Save for the *Scherzo* the two instruments seemed to be given very little of that opportunity for playing into one another's hands which is the essence of the duet Sonata.[25]

On the other hand, Bridge's earlier works, such as *Two Poems* (1915), *Sir Roger de Coverely* (1922), and *The Sea* continued to be performed and admired.

The years 1932 to 1941 saw Bridge traveling twice more to the United States. His fourth visit—the third had been in 1930 to attend performances of his Piano trio—took place in 1934 when he traveled to Massachusetts to attend performances of his Violin sonata at the Berkshire Festival. His last visit to the States was in 1938; this time with his wife Ethel who had accompanied him only on his first visit in 1923. This trip was planned so that Bridge would be present for the first performance, again at Pittsfield, Massachusetts, of his String quartet no. 4 (1937). Also during this trip Bridge was awarded the E. S. Coolidge Foundation Medal.

Bridge's String quartet no. 4 was finished while recovering from a serious illness suffered in 1936. This was the second time that Bridge had had to reduce his work load for health reasons. In 1932 he was forced to slow his pace after being diagnosed with high blood pressure. The heart attack in October of 1936 was to result in six months limited activity which slowed progress on the quartet. The quartet, written in the style of Berg and Schoenberg with a high degree of chromaticism, is dedicated to Mrs. Coolidge and is described as "difficult to assimilate."[26] This description is similar to that given *Phantasm* and *Oration, concerto elegiaco* in the early 1930's.

At his death Bridge was composing an *allegro moderato* movement of a work for string orchestra. The movement has elements of Bridge's chromatic style as well as a strong developmental emphasis. The movement was completed by Anthony Pople.

Bridge died in the afternoon of January 10, 1941 at age sixty-one of a heart attack. His ashes were buried in Friston churchyard. Obituaries were numerous but by and large very brief.

Several tributes were given in Bridge's memory. They include a memorial concert in Mrs. Coolidge's auditorium at the Library of Congress in March. and a BBC program devoted to Bridge's orchestral works. In addition, a Frank Bridge Society was formed by Coleridge-Taylor. The Society, formed to promote a concert series of chamber music at the Brighton Art Gallery in his memory, gave a series of fourteen concerts but was abandoned in 1942, a victim of the War.

Bridge was in all endeavors an accomplished musician. To have begun a career in composition with recognition and renown was justified. To have spent the latter half receiving negative reviews was a case of being in the wrong place at the wrong time. England, with its narrow, ultra-conservative view of music between the wars, is largely to blame. Now the recognition which his works deserve is being bestowed on his memory. Writings on Bridge beginning in the 1970's present a new appraisal of his works. This has been further encouraged by several record companies and publishers and especially the work of the Frank Bridge Trust. Words used to describe his works today, particularly his chamber music, include 'outstanding' and 'brilliant' and his last two string quartets are considered among the finest works of 20th-century English chamber music. His extraordinary stylistic development will be studied for years to come.

NOTES

1. Ivor James, "Obiturary: Frank Bridge," *RCM Magazine* 37, no. 1 (1941): 24.

2. "British Chamber Music," *The Musical Times* 52 (April 1911): 242.

3. "Yesterday's Concerts: The Grimson Quartet," *Morning Post* (London), 9 March 1907, p. 5c.

4. "London Concerts: Henkel Pianoforte Quartet," *The Musical Times* 52 (February 1911): 117.

5. "Musical League Festival at Liverpool," *The Musical Times* 50 (November 1909): 724.

6. "The Promenade Concerts," *The Musical Times* 53 (November 1912): 737.

7. Edward Speyer, *My Life and Friends* (London: Cobden-Sanderson, 1937), p. 221.

8. Ivor James, "Obituary: Frank Bridge," *RCM Magazine* 37, no. 1 (1941): 23.

9. C. "Mr. Frank Bridge and the Philharmonic," *The Musical Times* 63 (April 1922): 251.

10. "London Concerts: Royal Philharmonic Society," *The Musical Times* 55 (April 1914): 256-57.

11. "Music and Musicians: Royal Philharmonic Society," *Sunday Times* (London), 19 March 1916, p. 4d.

12. P.J. Nolan, "American Methods will Create Ideal Audiences," *Musical America* 39 (November 17, 1923): 3.

13. "Recitals of the Week: Miss Myra Hess and New Piano Sonata," *Times* (London), 16 October 1925, p. 12b.

14. "Piano Recital - New Sonata by Mr. Frank Bridge," *Morning Post* (London), 16 October 1925, p. 6e.

15. Benjamin Britten, "Britten Looking Back," *Musical America* 84 (February 1964): 4.

16. Ibid, p. 5.

17. Edwin Evans, "The Coolidge Chamber Music Concerts: Vienna," *The Musical Times* 68 (November 1927): 996.

18. Herbert Hughes, "New Chamber Music: Mr. Bridge's Trio," *Daily Telegraph* (London), 5 November 1929, p. 8f.

19. Frank Howes, *The English Musical Renaissance* (New York: Stein and Day, 1966), p. 160.

20. P.J. Nolan, "American Methods will Create Ideal Audiences," *Musical America* 39 (November 17, 1923): 3.

21. E.B., "The Promenade Concerts: Season's First Novelty," *Manchester Guardian*, 22 August 1927, p. 8d.

22. "New Orchestral Work - Mr. Bridge's Composition at the 'Proms,'" *Morning Post* (London), 22 August 1927, p. 5f.

23. E.B., "London Promenade Concerts: New Work by Frank Bridge," *Manchester Guardian*, 26 September 1930, p. 16d.

24. "British Music: BBC Orchestra's Concerts," *Times* (London), 11 January 1934, p. 8c.

25. "Royal Philharmonic Society: Chamber Concerts," *Times* (London), 19 January 1934, p. 12b.

26. Jay C. Rosenfeld, "Berkshire Festival," *New York Times*, 2 October 1938, p. 7X, col. a.

Works and Performances

"See" references, e.g., *See*: B61d or *See*: W144, identify citations in the "Bibliography" section or related citations in the "Works and Performances" section.

CHAMBER MUSIC

W1. **Allegretto** ca. May 1905; Thames Publishing (1980)

Incomplete.
For viola and piano.
Completed by Paul Hindmarsh.

Premiere

W1a. British Music Information Centre; Michael Ponder, viola.

W2. **Allegro appassionato** ca. 1907–1908; Stainer & Bell (1908)

Duration: 2'30"
For viola and piano.
Written for Lionel Tertis.

Premiere

W2a. November 24, 1909; Royal College of Music; Audrey ffolkes, viola, Harold Smith, piano.

W3. **Amaryllis** 1905 (yr. on printed edition); Winthrop Rogers (1919), Boosey & Hawkes, Thames Publishing (forthcoming)

Duration: 2'30"
For violin and piano.

W4. **Berceuse** August 18, 1901; Keith Prowse (1902), Faber (1982)

Duration: 2'30"
For violin or violoncello and piano.
Also in versions for piano, for small orchestra, for violin and strings, and for large orchestra. *See*: W96, W140, W141, W253

W5. **Con moto** April 16, 1903 (ms); unpublished

Duration: 1'
For violin and piano.

W6. **Country dance** ca. 1912 (yr. of publication); Augener (1912), Stainer & Bell, Thames Publishing (forthcoming)

Duration: 2'30"
For violin and piano.
Dedicated to Cynthia Lubbock.

W7. **Cradle song** 1910 (yr. on printed edition); Goodwin Taub (1911), Faber Music (1982)

Duration: 2'30"
For violin or violoncello and piano.
Dedicated to Phyllis Compton.

W8. **Three Dances** 1900 (yr. on printed edition); Goodwin Taub (1911), Augener (1925), Stainer & Bell: 3 only, Thames Publishing: 3 only (forthcoming)

1: Adagio ben sostenuto e con tristezza
2: Allegretto
3: Moto perpetuo: Allegro

Duration: 6'
For violin and piano.

Premiere (Movement 3 only)

W8a. November 24, 1909; King's Room, Broadwood; Audrey ffolkes, violin.

W9. **Divertimenti** 1934-1938 (dates encompassing original and revised versions); Boosey & Hawkes (1940), Hawkes & Sons (London) Ltd. (1942), Boosey & Hawkes

1: Prelude
2: Nocturne
3: Scherzetto
4: Bagatelle

Duration: 15'30"
For flute, oboe, clarinet, and bassoon.
Precise dates of original version: June and July 1934.
Dates of individual movements (revised version): July 27, 1937, August 31, 1937, November 6, 1937, and February 27, 1938.

Premiere

W9a. April 14, 1940; Coolidge Festival of Chamber Music, Washington, D.C. *See*: B394

Other Selected Performances

W9b. 1950; Aldeburgh Festival.
W9c. 1979; Aldeburgh Festival.

W10. **Elégie** 1904 (yr. on printed edition); Goodwin Taub (1911), Faber Music (1982)

Duration: 4'30"
For violoncello and piano.
Dedicated to Ivor James.
Also exists in version for violoncello and orchestra. *See*: W256

Premiere

W10a. March 6, 1908; Kensington Town Hall; Ivor James, violoncello.

Other Selected Performances

W10b. 1979; Aldeburgh Festival.

W11. **Gondoliera** 1907 (yr. on printed edition); Augener (1915), Stainer & Bell (revised version), Thames Publishing (forthcoming)

Duration: 5'
For violin and piano.
Revisions done presumably nearer the publication date.

Premiere

W11a. April 6, 1908; Bechstein Hall; May Harrison, violin, Hamilton Harty, piano. *See*: B276

W12. **Heart's ease** Between April 1921 and 1930 (yr. of printed edition); Augener (1930), Thames Publishing (forthcoming)

Duration: 1'50"
For violin and piano.
Also exists in version for piano and in an orchestrated version. *See*: W114, W257

W13. **Three Idylls** May 6, 1906 (ms); Augener (1911), Stainer & Bell

1: Adagio molto espressivo - Allegretto moderato e rubato
2: Allegretto poco lento
3: Allegro con moto

Duration: 12'
For 2 violins, viola, and violoncello.
Dates of individual movements: April 18, 1906, April 26, 1906, and May 6, 1906.
Dedicated to E. E. S. (Ethel Elmore Sinclair), later to become Bridge's wife.

Premiere

W13a. March 8, 1907; Bechstein Hall; Grimson Quartet. *See*: B160, B180, B264, B424

Other Selected Performances

W13b. 1911/1912; Aeolian Hall; Motto Quartet. *See*: B378
W13c. December 2, 1919; Royal Society of Artists' Gallery; Catterall Quartet. *See*: B302

W14. **An Irish melody** September 8–October 6, 1908 (ms); Augener (1915) - parts, Augener (1915) - miniature score, Stainer & Bell

Duration: 7'
For string quartet.
Commissioned by the Hambourg family.
Written as the first movement of a string quartet written jointly by Hamilton Harty, J. D. Davis, Eric Coates, and York Bowen.
Composite work known as The Hambourg Quartet.
Also exists in version for string orchestra. *See*: W149

Premiere

W14a. 1908; Aeolian Hall; Hambourg String Quartet.

Other Selected Performances

W14b. 1915; Aeolian Hall; London String Quartet.
W14c. November 26, 1921; Boston; London String Quartet.

W15. **Une Lamentatione d'amour** August 17, 1900 (ms); unpublished

Duration: 5'
For violin and piano.

W16. **Lullaby** ca. 1912 (yr. of publication); Augener (1912), Stainer & Bell, Thames Publishing (forthcoming)

Duration: 3'
For violin and piano.
Dedicated to Cynthia Lubbock.

W17. **Mazurka** December 19, 1903 (ms); Thames Publishing (forthcoming)

Duration: 4'
For violoncello and piano.

W18. **Meditation** ca. 1912 (yr. of publication); Augener (1912), Stainer & Bell

Duration: 2'30"
For violin or violoncello and piano.
Dedicated to Cynthia Lubbock.

W19. **Mélodie** May 12, 1911 (ms) - violin version; Goodwin Taub (1911), Faber Music (1982)

Duration: 4'
For violin or violoncello and piano.
Violoncello version dedicated to cellist Felix Salmond.

Premiere

W19a. November 21, 1918; Royal College of Music; Elsa Ivimey-Martin, violoncello.

Other Selected Performances

W19b. March 1, 1922; Royal College of Music Students' Union "At Home" Concert; Ivor James, violoncello, Angus Morrison, piano.
W19c. November 9, 1937; Patron's Fund Concert; Vera Canning, Charles Grove, piano.
W19d. July 12, 1939; Ivor James, violoncello.

W20. **A Merry, merry xmas** December 1934 (ms); unpublished

Duration: 2'
For oboe, clarinet, trombone, and piano.
Written as a gift for Elizabeth Sprague Coolidge and her family to play during their Christmas festivities.

W21. **Miniatures, set 1** ca. 1908; Goodwin Taub (1909), Augener, Stainer & Bell

1: Minuet
2: Gavotte
3: Allegretto con moto

Duration: 5'50"
For violin, violoncello, and piano.
Durations of individual movements: 2'10", 2'30", and 1'10".
Written for Rachael and Betty Hanbury, as were Miniatures, sets 2 and 3.

Premiere

W21a. November 7, 1913; Exeter.

Other Selected Performances

W21b. August 9, 1941; Frank Bridge Society.

W22. **Miniatures, set 2** ca. 1908; Goodwin Taub (1911), Augener, Stainer & Bell

1: Romance
2: Intermezzo
3: Salterello

Duration: 9'20"
For violin, violoncello, and piano.
Durations of individual movements: 5'40", 1'20", and 2'20".
Written for Rachael and Betty Hanbury, as were Miniatures, sets 1 and 3.

Premiere

W22a. November 7, 1913; Exeter.

W23. **Miniatures, set 3** ca. 1908; Goodwin Taub (1915), Augener, Stainer & Bell

1: Valse russe
2: Hornpipe
3: March militaire

Duration: 8'
For violin, violoncello, and piano.
Durations of individual movements: 3', 2'30", and 2'30".
Written for Rachael and Betty Hanbury, as were Miniatures, sets 1 and 2.

Premiere

W23a. November 7, 1913; Exeter.

W24. **Morceau characteristique** ca. 1907–1908; unpublished

For violin and piano.

Premiere

W24a. April 6, 1908; Bechstein Hall; May Harrison, violin, Hamilton Harty, piano. *See*: B276

W25. **Morning song** April 1918 (yr. on printed edition); Winthrop Rogers (1919), Boosey & Hawkes

Duration: 3'50"
For violoncello and piano.
Also exists in version for violoncello and orchestra. *See*: W258

Premiere

W25a. January 22, 1920; Royal College of Music; Edward J. Robinson, soloist.

W26. **Norse legend** 1905 (yr. on printed edition); Winthrop Rogers (1919), Boosey & Hawkes, Thames Publishing (forthcoming)

Duration: 4'
For violin and piano.
Also exists in versions for piano and for orchestra. *See*: W121, W153

W27. **Novelletten** September 1904 (ms); Augener (1915) - parts, Augener (1915) - miniature score, Stainer & Bell

1: Andante moderato
2: Presto
3: Allegro vivo

Duration: 11'
For 2 violins, viola, and cello.

Premiere

W27a. November 24, 1904; Royal College of Music student's concert; English String Quartet. *See*: B176

Other Selected Performances

W27b. 1906; Bechstein Hall; Rose Quartet.
W27c. November 28, 1910; Bechstein Hall; Motto Quartet. *See*: B172
W27d. Fall 1915; Aeolian Hall; Philharmonic String Quartet.

W28. **Two Old English songs** May 1916; Schirmer (1916), Winthrop Rogers, Boosey & Hawkes

1: Sally in our alley
2: Cherry ripe

Duration: 7'50"
Durations of individual movements: 4'20", 3'30".
For string quartet.
Completion dates for each movement given on printed edition: May 9, 1916 and May 30, 1916.
Also in versions for piano duet and for string orchestra. *See*: W122, W154

Premiere

W28a. June 17, 1916; Aeolian Hall; London String Quartet. *See*: B139, B183, B261, B306

W29. **Oration, concerto elegiaco** May 21, 1930 (ms); Faber Music (1986)

Duration: 28'
For violoncello and piano.
Also exists in version for violoncello and orchestra. *See*: W155

W30. **Pensiero** May 23, 1905 (ms); Stainer & Bell (1908)

Duration: 2'30"
For viola and piano.
Substantial revisions made probably just before publication.
Title before revision: *Andante e sostenuto*.
Written for Lionel Tertis.

Premiere

W30a. November 24, 1909; Royal College of Music; Audrey ffolkes, viola, Harold Smith, piano. (original version)

Other Selected Performances

W30b. British Music Information Centre; Michael Ponder, viola.

W31. **Phantasie in F minor** ca. July–September 1905; Novello (1906) – parts, Stainer & Bell

Duration: 12'
For 2 violins, viola, and violoncello.

Premiere

W31a. June 22, 1906; Bechstein Hall; Saunders String Quartet. *See*: B179, B185, B268

W32. **Phantasy in C minor** After June 1907; Novello (1909), Augener, Stainer & Bell

Duration: 16'
For violin, violoncello, and piano.

Premiere

W32a. April 27, 1909; at a Banquet of the Incorporated Society of Musicians; London Piano Trio.

Other Selected Performances

W32b. April 7, 1922; Cambridge, Mass. at the Harvard Musical Association.
W32c. September 19, 1923; private performance for Mrs. Coolidge.

W33. **Phantasy in F-sharp minor** June 2, 1910 (ms); Goodwin Taub (1911), Augener (1911), Stainer & Bell

Duration: 12'
For violin, viola, violoncello, and piano.
Commissioned by and dedicated to W. W. Cobbett.

Premiere

W33a. January 21, 1911; Steinway Hall; Henkel Piano Quartet. *See*: B260, B301, B307, B377, B387

Other Selected Performances

W33b. February 1, 1911; Royal Academy of Music, Concert-Goers Club. *See*: B166, B377
W33c. September 19, 1923; private performance for Mrs. Coolidge.
W33d. October 4, 1941; Brighton; Frank Bridge Society.
W33e. 1948; Aldeburgh Festival.
W33f. 1967; Aldeburgh Festival.

W34. **Piano quartet in C minor** July 14, 1902 (ms); unpublished

1: Allegro ma non troppo
2: Scherzo: Presto
3: Poco adagio
4: Presto

Duration: 30'
For violin, viola, violoncello, and piano.

Premiere

W34a. January 23, 1903; Royal College of Music; Ethel Sinclair, violin, Frank Bridge, viola, Arthur Trew, violoncello, Harold Samuel, piano. *See*: B254

W35. **Piano quintet** April 4, 1905 (ms); unpublished

1: Allegro energico
2: Adagio ma non troppo
3: Allegro con brio
4: Adagio - Allegro con fuoco

Duration: 32'
For 2 violins, viola, violoncello, and piano.
Dates of individual movements: December 26, 1904, January 31, 1905, February 15, 1905, and April 4, 1905.
Exists in a revised version. *See*: W36

Premiere

W35a. May 28, 1907; Royal College of Music Students' Union "At Home" Concert; Thomas Morris and Ethel Sinclair, violins, Frank Bridge, viola, Ivor James, violoncello, Harold Samuel, piano.

W36. **Piano quintet (1912)** 1912 (ms); Augener (1919), Stainer & Bell

1: Adagio – Allegro moderato
2: Adagio ma non troppo – Allegro con brio
3: Allegro energico

Duration: 28'
For 2 violins, viola, violoncello, and piano.
A revised version of Piano quintet. *See*: W35

Premiere

W36a. May 29, 1912; Royal College of Music Students' Union "At Home" Concert; English String Quartet with Harold Samuel, piano.

Other Selected Performances

W36b. October 30, 1918; Wigmore Hall. *See*: B215
W36c. February 18, 1919; Wigmore Hall; English String Quartet with William Murdoch, piano.
W36d. June 1921; Worchester, Mass.
W36e. April 7, 1922; Harvard Musical Association.
W36f. September 19, 1923; Private performance for Mrs. Coolidge.
W36g. 1951; Aldeburgh Festival.

W37. **Piano trio in D minor** Before November 1900; unpublished

1: Allegro moderato
2: Scherzo: Allegretto
3: Andante
4: Allegro

For violin, violoncello, and piano.

Premiere

W37a. November 14, 1900; Alexandra House, Royal College of Music; Frank Bridge, violin, Arthur Trew, violoncello, Florence Smith, piano

W38. **Piano trio (1929)** October 1928–January 1929 (ms); Augener (1930), Stainer & Bell

1: Allegretto ben moderato
2: Molto allegro
3: Andante molto moderato
4: Allegro ma non troppo

Duration: 29'
For violin, violoncello, and piano.
Three of the movements are dated individually: 1) October 10, 1928, 2) November 17, 1928, and 3) January 31, 1929.
Dedicated to Elizabeth Sprague Coolidge.

See: B148, B198

Premiere

W38a. November 4, 1929; Langham Hotel; Antonio Brosa, violin, Anthony Pini, violoncello, Harriet Cohen, piano. *See*: B241

Other Selected Performances

W38b. October 13, 1930; Simpson Theater, Chicago, Coolidge Festival of Chamber Music; Antonio Brosa, violin, Anthony Pini, violoncello, Harriet Cohen, piano. *See*: B293, B346, B388
W38c. October 26, 1930; Colony Club (NY); Antonio Brosa, violin, Anthony Pini, violoncello, Harriet Cohen, piano.
W38d. October 30, 1930; Coolidge Hall, Washington, D.C.; Antonio Brosa, violin, Anthony Pini, violoncello, Harriet Cohen, piano. *See*: B279, B390
W38e. 1963; Aldeburgh Festival.
W38f. 1981; Aldeburgh Festival.

W39. **Two Pieces** 1911-1912; Thames Publishing (1981) - mvmt. 2 only

1: Caprice
2: Lament

For 2 violas.
Written for Lionel Tertis.

Premiere

W39a. March 18, 1912; Aeolian Hall; Lionel Tertis and Frank Bridge, violas. *See*: B256

Other Selected Performances (Movement 2 only)

W39b. February 12, 1980; British Music Information Centre; Michael Ponder and Tomas Tichauer, violas.

W40. **Three Pieces for string quartet (1904)** August 31, 1904 (ms for mvmt. 1); unpublished

1: Allegro marcato

2: Moderato
3: Allegretto

Duration: 2'25"
For 2 violins, viola, and violoncello.
Durations for individual pieces: 45", 40", and 1'.

W41. **Three Pieces for string quartet (1905)** ca. 1905; unpublished

1: Pizzicati
2: (untitled)
3: Adagio

Incomplete.
For 2 violins, viola, and violoncello.

W42. **The Pneu world** ca. March–April 1925; unpublished

For violoncello and piano.
"A parody sketch of the first four bars of 'The Star-Spangled Banner', written for Elizabeth Sprague Coolidge (piano) and her son Sprague (cello)."

W43. **The Rag** After June 1906; unpublished

Duration: ca. 4'
For 2 violins, viola, and violoncello.

W44. **Rhapsody** March 1928 (ms); Faber Music (1965)

Duration: 17'
For 2 violins and viola.

Premiere

W44a. June 24, 1965; Jubilee Hall, Aldeburgh, as part of the Eighth Aldeburgh Festival; members of the Alberni String Quartet.

W45. **Romanze** Christmas 1904 (ms); unpublished

Duration: 3'
For violin and piano.

W46. **Scherzetto** ca. 1901–1902; unpublished

Duration: 3'
For violoncello and piano.
Also in version for violoncello and orchestra. *See*: W259

Premiere

W46a. April 28, 1979; Snape Maltings; Julian Lloyd Webber, violoncello, Simon Nicholls, piano.

Other Selected Performances

W46b. November 20, 1980; Wigmore Hall; Julian Lloyd Webber, violoncello, Eric Parkin, piano.

W47. **Scherzo** After ca. 1902; Faber Music (1982)

Duration: 4'
For violoncello and piano.

Premiere

W47a. March 6, 1908; Kensington Town Hall; Ivor James, violoncello.

W48. **Scherzo phantastick** July 8, 1901 (ms); unpublished

Duration: 5'30"
For 2 violins, viola, and violoncello.

Premiere

W48a. June 27, 1907; Royal College of Music Students' Union "At Home" Concert; English String Quartet.

W49. **Serenade** April 1903 (yr. on printed edition); Reid Bros Ltd. (1906), Chappell, Faber Music (1982)

Duration: 2'
For violin or violoncello and piano.
Also in versions for piano and for orchestra. *See*: W134, W161

W50. **Sir Roger de Coverley** June 30, 1922 (ms); Augener (1922) - parts, Augener (1923) - miniature score

Duration: 4'30"
For string quartet.
Also exists in versions for string orchestra and orchestra. *See*: W162, W163

W51. **Souvenir** 1904 (yr. on printed edition); Winthrop Rogers (1919), Boosey & Hawkes, Thames Publishing (forthcoming)

Duration: 3'
For violin and piano.

W52. **Spring song** ca. 1912 (yr. of publication); Augener (1912), Stainer & Bell, Thames Publishing (forthcoming)

Duration: 2'
For violin or violoncello and piano.
Dedicated to Cynthia Lubbock.

W53. **String quartet in B-flat major** December 1900 (ms); unpublished

1: Adagio - Allegro
2: Scherzo: Allegro
3: Andante
4: Presto

Duration: ca. 30'
For 2 violins, viola, and piano.

Premiere

W53a. March 14, 1901; Alexandra House, Royal College of Music; Haydn Wood, Thomas Morris, Ernest Tomlinson, Edward Mason.

W54. **String quartet movement** ca. 1936; unpublished

Incomplete.
For 2 violins, viola, and violoncello.

W55. **String quartet no. 1 in E minor** Before October 31, 1906; Cary & Co. (1916), Augener (1920), Stainer & Bell

1: Adagio – Allegro appassionato
2: Adagio molto
3: Allegretto grazioso
4: Allegro agitato

Duration: 33'
For 2 violins, viola, and violoncello.

Premiere

W55a. June 16, 1909; Bechstein Hall; English String Quartet. *See*: B161, B203, B259, B300, B376

Other Selected Performances

W55b. December 13, 1910; Motto Quartet.
W55c. October 20, 1916; Aeolian Hall; London String Quartet. *See*: B262
W55d. February 18, 1919; Wigmore Hall; English String Quartet.
W55e. 1920; Berkshire Festival, Pittsfield, Mass.; London String Quartet.
W55f. 1979; Aldeburgh Festival.

W56. **String quartet no. 2 in G minor** Summer 1914–March 30, 1915 (ms); Novello (1915); Augener, Stainer & Bell

Duration: 25'
For 2 violins, viola, and violoncello.
Dedicated to W. W. Cobbett.

Premiere

W56a. November 4, 1915; Aeolian Hall; London String Quartet. *See*: B138, B296, B313, B314

Other Selected Performances

W56b. December 9, 1915; London String Quartet. *See*: B258
W56c. October 28, 1923; Colony Club (NY); London String Quartet.
W56d. November 4, 1923; Detroit; London String Quartet.
W56e. November 13, 1923; Aeolian Hall (NY); London String Quartet.
W56f. April 1926; Ojai (California) Festival; London String Quartet.
W56g. January 1939; Washington, D.C.; Coolidge Quartet.
W56h. March 11, 1941; Memorial Concert, Washington, D.C.; Coolidge Quartet.

W57. **String quartet no. 3** 1925–1927; Augener (1928), Galliard (1972), Stainer & Bell

1: Andante moderato - allegro moderato
2: Andante con moto
3: Allegro energico

Duration: 28'
For 2 violins, viola, and violoncello.
Dates of individual movements of original version (not the version published): April 17, 1925, May 21, 1925, and May 17, 1926.
Dedicated to Elizabeth Sprague Coolidge.

Premiere

W57a. September 17, 1927; Vienna; Kolisch Quartet. *See*: B207

Other Selected Performances

W57b. October 16, 1927; Paris; Pro Arte Quartet.
W57c. November 6, 1927; London; Pro Arte Quartet. *See*: B308
W57d. November 9, 1927; BBC Broadcast; Pro Arte Quartet.
W57e. September 17, 1928; Berkshire Festival, Pittsfield, Mass.; Roth Quartet.
W57f. Early October 1928; Siena Music Festival; Brosa Quartet. *See*: B199, B305

W57g. October 30, 1928; Founder's Day Concert, Washington, D.C.; Roth Quartet.

W57h. 1955; Aldeburgh Festival.

W57i. May 6, 1981; Purcell Room, London; Hanson String Quartet. *See*: B247

W58. **String quartet no. 4** July–November 1937 (ms); Augener (1939), Galliard (1972), Stainer & Bell

1: Allegro energico
2: Quasi minuetto
3: Adagio ma non troppo-allegro con brio

Duration: 22'
For 2 violins, viola, and violoncello.
Dedicated to Elizabeth Sprague Coolidge.
See: B150

Premiere

W58a. September 23, 1938; Berkshire Festival, Pittsfield, Mass.; Gordon String Quartet. *See*: B163, B368

Other Selected Performances

W58b. October 30, 1938; Founder's Day Concert, Washington, D.C.; Gordon String Quartet.

W59. **String quintet in E minor** May 6, 1901–July 21, 1901 (ms); unpublished

1: Allegro appassionato
2: Andante ma non troppo
3: Presto
4: Allegro molto vivace

Duration: 28'
For 2 violins, 2 violas, and violoncello.

Premiere

W59a. December 4, 1901; Royal College of Music; Thomas Morris, Haydn Wood, Ernest Tomlinson, Edward Behr, Arthur Trew.

W60. **String sextet in E-flat major** 1906–1912 (ms); Augener (1920), Stainer & Bell

1: Allegro moderato
2: Andante con moto - Allegro giusto
3: Allegro ben moderato

Duration: 27'
For 2 violins, 2 violas, and 2 violoncellos.
See: B152

Premiere

W60a. June 18, 1913; Bechstein Hall; English String Quartet with Ernest Tomlinson, viola and Felix Salmond, violoncello. *See*: B162, B204, B257

Other Selected Performances

W60b. December 8, 1915; Classical Concert Society, London; English String Quartet with Alfred Hobday, viola and Felix Salmond, violoncello. *See*: B258
W60c. October 30, 1918; Wigmore Hall. *See*: B215
W60d. September 27, 1923; Berkshire Festival, Pittsfield, Mass.; London String Quartet with Edward Kreiner, viola and Willem Willeke, violoncello. *See*: B140, B367
W60e. September 1930; Bradford Music Festival. *See*: B219
W60f. October 17, 1935; Wigmore Hall; Isolde Menges Quartet with Frank Bridge and Helen Just.
W60g. March 11, 1941; Memorial Concert, Washington, D.C.; Coolidge Quartet with Rebecca Clarke, viola.
W60h. 1949; Aldeburgh Festival.
W60i. 1976; Aldeburgh Festival.
W60j. 1983; Hanson String Quartet. *See*: B331

W61. **Valse Fernholt** ca. 1904–1906; unpublished

For strings and piano.

W62. **Viola sonata** ca. 1935–1936; unpublished

Incomplete.
For viola and piano.

W63. **Violin sonata** April 13, 1904 (ms); unpublished

1: Allegro
2: Andante ed espressivo

Incomplete.
For violin and piano.

W64. **Violin sonata (1932)** November 21, 1932 (ms); Augener (1933), Stainer & Bell

Duration: 24'
For violin and piano.
See: B149

Premiere

W64a. January 18, 1934; Aeolian Hall, Royal Philharmonic Society Chamber Concert; Antonio Brosa, violin, Harold Samuel, piano. *See*: B165, B380, B382, B392

Other Selected Performances

W64b. September 21, 1934; Berkshire Festival, Pittsfield, Mass; William Kroll, violin, Frank Sheriden, piano.
W64c. May 1938; Washington, D.C.; William Kroll, violin, Frank Sheriden, piano.
W64d. March 11, 1941; Memorial Concert, Washington, D.C.

W65. **Violoncello sonata in D minor** 1913–1917 (ms); Winthrop Rogers (1918), Boosey & Hawkes (1977)

1: Allegro ben moderato
2: Adagio ma non troppo – Andante con moto – Molto allegro e agitato

Duration: 23'
For violoncello and piano.

Premiere

W65a. July 13, 1917; Wigmore Hall; Felix Salmond, violoncello, William Murdoch, piano. *See*: B274, B275, B423

Other Selected Performances

W65b. October 12, 1917; Aeolian Hall.
W65c. 1921; Amsterdam; Felix Salmond, violoncello.
W65d. November 13, 1923; Aeolian Hall (NY); Felix Salmond, violoncello.
W65e. 1965; Aldeburgh Festival.

CHORAL MUSIC

W66. **Autumn** Before August 1903 (yr. of publication); Novello (*The Musical Times*, supplement, August 1903), Thames Publishing (1979)

Duration: 3'10"
For mixed chorus (SATB).
Words by Shelley.

W67. **The Bee** April 1913 (ms); Thames Publishing (1979)

Duration: 1'20"
For SATB.
Words by Tennyson.

Premiere

W67a. October 20, 1979; London College of Music; Exaltate Singers, Garrett O'Brien, director.

W68. **Easter hymn** ca. 1912 (yr. of publication of voice and piano version); Chappell (1930)

Duration: 2'30"
For SATB.
Arrangement of 17th century German hymn, *Laßt uns erfreuen herzlich sehr*, with English words by Hans Wagemann.
Also exists in versions for voice and piano and for flute, string quartet, bells, and organ. *See*: W189, W249

W69. **Evening primrose** Probably October or November 1922; Oxford University Press (1923), Thames Publishing (forthcoming)

Duration: 1'30"
For SS with piano accompaniment.
Words by John Clare.

W70. **The Fairy ring** October 14, 1922; Oxford University Press (1923)

Duration: 1'15"
For SSA with optional piano accompaniment.
Words: anon.

W71. **For God and king and right** July 1916 (yr. on printed edition); Schirmer (1916), Winthrop Rogers, Boosey & Hawkes

Duration: 3'30"
For unison voices and piano.
Words by Veronica Mason.
Also exists in version for voices and orchestra. *See*: W72

W72. **For God and king and right** After March 1919; Winthrop Rogers, Boosey & Hawkes

Duration: 3'30"
For voices and orchestra.
Request made in March 1919 for this orchestral version of the original unison voices and piano version.
Words by Veronica Mason.
Also exists in original version for unison voices and piano. *See*: W71

W73. **Golden slumbers** May 22, 1922 (ms); Augener (1928), Stainer & Bell, Thames Publishing (forthcoming)

Duration: 3'
For SSA unaccompanied.
Dedicated to Victor Harris and the St. Cecilia Club, New York.
Words by Thomas Dekker.

W74. **The Graceful swaying wattle** Probably July 1916; Schirmer (1916), Winthrop Rogers, Boosey & Hawkes

Duration: 2'30"
For two-part chorus and piano.
Words by Veronica Mason.
Also exists in version for two-part chorus and string orchestra.
See: W75

W75. **The Graceful swaying wattle** After March 1919; Winthrop Rogers, Boosey & Hawkes

Duration: 2'30"
For two-part chorus and string orchestra.
Request made in March 1919 for this orchestral version of the original two-part chorus and piano version.
Words by Veronica Mason.
Also exists in original version for two-part chorus and piano.
See: W74

W76. **Hence care** May 23, 1922 (ms); Augener (1923), Stainer & Bell, Thames Publishing (forthcoming)

Duration: 1'30"
For SSA unaccompanied.
Dedicated to Victor Harris and the St. Cecilia Club, New York.
Words: anon. (1595).

W77. **Hilli-ho! Hilli-ho!** March 1909 (ms); Thames Publishing (1979)

Duration: 1'30"
For SATB unaccompanied.
Words by Thomas Moore.

Premiere

W77a. October 20, 1979; London College of Music; Exaltate Singers, Garrett O'Brien, director.

W78. **Lantido dilly** May 8, 1919 (ms); Winthrop Rogers (1919), Boosey & Hawkes, Thames Publishing (forthcoming)

Duration: 1'30"
For SSA with piano accompaniment.
Words: anon. (17th century).

W79. **Lay a garland on my hearse** September 27, 1918 (ms); Winthrop Rogers (1919), Boosey & Hawkes, Thames Publishing (forthcoming)

Duration: 1'40"
For 2-part vocal canon with piano accompaniment.
Words by Beaumont and Fletcher (17th century).

W80. **A Litany** September 17, 1918 (ms); Winthrop Rogers (1919), Boosey & Hawkes, Thames Publishing (forthcoming)

Duration: 1'30"
For SSA with ad lib organ.
Words by Phineas Fletcher.

W81. **Lullaby** July 1916 (yr. on printed edition); Schirmer (1916), Winthrop Rogers, Boosey & Hawkes

Duration: 2'30"
For SSA and piano.
Words by Veronica Mason.
Also exists in version for SSA and string orchestra. *See*: W82

W82. **Lullaby** After March 1919; Winthrop Rogers, Boosey & Hawkes

Duration: 2'30"
For SSA and string orchestra.
Request made in March 1919 for this orchestral version of the original SSA version.
Words by Veronica Mason.
Also exists in original version for SSA and piano. *See*: W81

W83. **Music when soft voices die** 1904 (ms); Thames Publishing (1979)

Duration: 2'

For mixed chorus (SATB).
Words by Shelley.

Premiere

W83a. October 20, 1979; London College of Music; Exaltate Singers; Garrett O'Brien, director.

W84. **O weary hearts** March 1909 (ms); Thames Publishing (1979)

Duration: 2'30"
For SATB unaccompanied.
Words by Longfellow.

Premiere

W84a. October 20, 1979; London College of Music; Exaltate Singers, Garrett O'Brien, director.

W85. **Pan's holiday** November 4, 1922; Oxford University Press (1923), William Elkin, Thames Publishing (forthcoming)

Duration: 1'30"
For SS and piano.
Words by James Shirley.
Also exists in version for SS with piano and string orchestra. *See*: W86

W86. **Pan's holiday** November 4, 1922, scored March 21, 1924; Oxford University Press, William Elkin

Duration: 1'30"
For SS with piano and string orchestra.
Words by James Shirley.
Also exists in original version for SS and piano. *See*: W85

Premiere

W86a. May 5, 1924; Petersfield Musical Festival, Drill Hall, Petersfield; Petersfield Festival Orchestra.

W87. **Peter Piper** Probably 1916; Schirmer (1916), Winthrop Rogers, Boosey & Hawkes, Thames Publishing (forthcoming)

Duration: 1'
For unaccompanied chorus of three equal voices.
Words: traditional.

W88. **A Prayer** March 1916 (ms); Augener (1925), Stainer & Bell

Duration: 20'
For SATB chorus and organ.
Words by Thomas à Kempis.
Also exists in version for SATB chorus and orchestra. *See*: W89

W89. **A Prayer** March 1916 (ms), scored October 1–18, 1918; Augener (1918) - vocal score, Augener (1919) - string parts, Stainer & Bell

Duration: 20'
For SATB chorus and orchestra
Words by Thomas à Kempis.
Also exists in version for SATB chorus and organ. *See*: W88

Premiere

W89a. January 1919; Royal Albert Hall; Frank Bridge, conducting.

Other Selected Performances

W89b. December 3, 1919; Bristol; Bristol Philharmonic. *See*: B303
W89c. March 15, 1921; Liverpool; Liverpool Philharmonic. *See*: B304
W89d. February 2, 1935; Royal Albert Hall, Royal Choral Society; Frank Bridge, conducting.

W90. **Sister, awake** September 26, 1918 (ms); Winthrop Rogers (1919), Boosey & Hawkes, Thames Publishing (forthcoming)

Duration: 1'20"
For SS and piano.
Words by Thomas Bateson (17th century).

W91. **A Spring song** October 21, 1922; Oxford University Press (1923)

Duration: 1'20"
For unison voices and piano.
Words by M. Howitt.
Also exists in version for unison voices and string orchestra.
See: W92

W92. **A Spring song** October 21, 1922, scored February 1930; Oxford University Press (1923)

Duration: 1'20"
For unison voices and string orchestra.
Words by M. Howitt.
Also exists in version for unison voices and piano. *See*: W91

KEYBOARD MUSIC

W93. **"?"** ca. 1906-1908; unpublished

Duration: 1'
For piano.
Written for Florence Smith.

W94. **Adagio ma non troppo** ca. 1901; unpublished

Duration: 1'30"
For organ.

W95. **Arabesque** April 23, 1914 (ms); Augener (1916), Stainer & Bell

Duration: 2'30"
For piano.

W96. **Berceuse** August 18, 1901 (ms); Keith Prowse (1929), EMI Music

Duration: 2'30"

For piano.
Also in versions for violin or violoncello and piano, for small orchestra, for violin and strings, and for large orchestra. *See*: W4, W140, W141, W253

W97. **Canzonetta** July 7, 1926 (ms); Winthrop Rogers (1927), Boosey & Hawkes

Duration: 2'30"
For piano.
Two autograph mss. exist, one with title *Canzonetta* and one with the title *Happy South*.
Also exists in version for small orchestra. *See*: W142

W98. **Capriccio no. 1 in A minor** April 1905 (ms); Augener (1905), Stainer & Bell

Duration: 3'
For piano.
Original work entitled *Caprice*.

Premiere

W98a. May 20, 1905; Queen's Hall; Mark Hambourg, piano. *See*: B178, B297, B347

Other Selected Performances

W98b. June 15, 1905; Bechstein Hall; Harold Samuel, piano. *See*: B159

W99. **Capriccio no. 2 in F-sharp minor** July 1905 (yr. on printed edition); Houghton & Co. (1906), Augener (1917), Stainer & Bell

Duration: 4'
For piano.

Premiere

W99a. March 11, 1909; Bechstein Hall; Auriol Jones, piano.

W100. **Four Characteristic pieces** May–April 1917; Winthrop Rogers (1917), Boosey & Hawkes

1: Water nymphs
2: Fragrance
3: Bittersweet
4: Fireflies

Duration: 10'
For piano.
Durations of individual pieces: 2'30", 1'20", 3'10", and 3'.
Dates of individual pieces: May 1917, May 1917, May 5, 1917, and April 1917.
Piece #2, "Fragrance," is dedicated to E.E.B. (Ethel Elmore Bridge).
See: B363

Premiere (Movements 1, 2, and 4)

W100a. February 19, 1920; Royal College of Music; Cicely M. Morat, piano.

W101. **Columbine** 1912 (yr. on printed edition); Augener (1913), Stainer & Bell

Duration: 2'30"
For piano.

W102. **A Dedication** September 1926 (ms); Augener (1928), Stainer & Bell

Duration: 3'20"
For piano.

W103. **Dramatic fantasia** January 1906 (ms); Thames Publishing (1990)

Duration: 10'
For piano.

Premiere

W103a. June 2, 1979; Wigmore Hall; Peter Jacobs, piano.

W104. **Etude rhapsodique** November 1905 (ms); Thames Publishing (forthcoming)

Duration: 2'15"
For piano.

W105. **A Fairy tale** September 1917–October 1917; Augener (1918), Stainer & Bell

1: The Princess
2: The Orge
3: The Spell
4: The Prince

Duration: 10'40"
For piano.
Durations of individual movements: 3'30", 1'20", 3'20", and 2'30".
Dates of individual movements: September 1917, September 1917, September 1917, and October 1917.

W106. **Gargoyle** July 1928 (ms); Thames Publishing (1977)

Duration: 3'15"
For piano.

Premiere

W106a. December 21, 1975; Glasgow University; Isobel Woods, piano.

Other Selected Performances

W106b. January 31, 1977; Queen Elizabeth Hall, Redcliffe Chamber Music Concert; Richard Rodney Bennett, piano.

W107. **Graziella** July 26, 1926 (ms); Winthrop Rogers (1927), Boosey & Hawkes

Duration: 3'30"
For piano.

W108. **Hidden fires** ca. 1926; Winthrop Rogers (1927), Boosey & Hawkes

Duration: 2'50"
For piano.

W109. **The Hour glass** September 1919–April 1920; Augener (1920), Stainer & Bell

1: Dusk
2: The Dew fairy
3: The Midnight tide

Duration: 11'20"
For piano.
Durations of individual movements: 3'50", 3'20", and 4'10".
Dates of individual movements: September 1919, February 28, 1920, and April 1920.

Premiere (Movement 2 only)

W109a. June 23, 1936; British Music Movement Concert #2.

Premiere (Movement 3 only)

W109b. March 6, 1923; Royal College of Music; Evelyn Tyson, piano.

W110. **Three Improvisations** May–July 1918; Winthrop Rogers (1919), Boosey & Hawkes, Thames Publishing (1990)

1: At dawn
2: A Vigil
3: A Revel

Duration: 5'30"
For piano, left hand.
Durations of individual movements: 2',1'30", and 2'.
Written for pianist Douglas Fox who lost his right arm during WWI.
Dates of individual movements: May 1918, June 24, 1918, and July 22, 1918.

W111. **In autumn** April–June 1924; Augener (1925), Stainer & Bell

1: Retrospect
2: Through the eaves

Duration: 7'
For piano.
Durations of individual movements: 4'30" and 2'30".
Dates of individual movements: April 29, 1924 and June 30, 1924.
See: B222

W112. **Lament** June 14, 1915; Goodwin Taub (1915), Thames Publishing

Duration: 6'
For piano.
Composed in memory of Catherine, a friend who was drowned with her family in the Lusitania disaster.
Also exists in version for string orchestra. *See*: W151

W113. **Lento (In memoriam C.H.H.P.)** October 15, 1918 (ms) – original, October (ms) - revised version; H.F.W. Deane & Sons (1924) – revised version

Duration: 2'30"
For organ.
Original version was written for funeral service of Sir Hubert Parry.
Revision made for publication in *The Little Organ Book*.

Premiere

W113a. October 16, 1918; St. Paul's Cathedral; Sir Walford Davies, organ.

W114. **Three Lyrics** April 1921–June 1924; Augener (1922) – mvmts. 1 and 2, Augener (1925) – mvmt. 3, Stainer & Bell

1: Heart's ease
2: Dainty rogue
3: The Hedgerow

Duration: 6'10"

For piano.
Durations of individual movements: 1'50", 1'50", and 2'30".
Dates of individual movements: April 26, 1921, June 1922, and June 10, 1924.
Movement 1, Heart's ease, also exists in a version for violin and piano and in a version for orchestra. *See*: W12, W257
See: B222

W115. **Miniature pastorals, set 1** July 1917 (yr. on printed edition); Winthrop Rogers (1917), Boosey & Hawkes

1: Allegretto con moto
2: Tempo di valse
3: Allegretto ben moderato

Duration: 5'30"
For piano.
Durations of individual movements: 1'30", 2', and 2'.
Original edition included line drawings by Margaret Kemp-Welch.

Premiere

W115a. February 17, 1937; Royal College of Music; Joyce Nugent, piano.

W116. **Miniature pastorals, set 2** February 1921–March 1921; Winthrop Rogers (1921)

1: Allegro giusto
2: Andante con moto
3: Allegro ma non troppo

Duration: 6'50"
For piano.
Durations of individual movements: 2'10", 2'30", and 2'10".
1921 edition included drawings by Margaret Kemp-Welch.
Dates of individual movements: February 1921, February 1921, and March 1921.

Premiere

W116a. February 17, 1937; Royal College of Music; Joyce Nugent, piano.

W117. **Miniature pastorals, set 3** April 1921; Thames Publishing (1978) - movements 1-3 only

1: Andante molto tranquillo
2: Allegro con moto
3: Allegretto vivace
4: Marziale e ben marcato

Duration: 5'45"
For piano.
Durations of individual movements: 2', 1'40", 1'20", and 45".
Dates of individual movements: April 21, 1921, April 25, 1921, April 27, 1921, and April 22, 1921.

W118. **Miniature suite** Thames Publishing (forthcoming)

For piano.

W119. **Minuet** 1901; substantial revisions - 1912 (yr. on printed edition); Augener (1913), Stainer & Bell

Duration: 1'30"
For piano.

W120. **Moderato** September 5, 1903 (ms); unpublished

Duration: 2'30"
For piano.

W121. **Norse legend** 1905 (yr. on printed edition); Winthrop Rogers (1919), Boosey & Hawkes

Duration: 4'
For piano.
Also exists in versions for violin and piano and for orchestra. *See*: W26, W153

W122. **Two Old English songs** May 1916; Schirmer (1916), Winthrop Rogers, Boosey & Hawkes

1: Sally in our alley

2: Cherry ripe

Duration: 7'50"
For piano duet.
Durations of individual movements: 4'20", 3'30".
Completion dates of movements given in printed edition: May 9, 1916 and May 30, 1916.
Also exists in versions for string quartet and for string orchestra. *See*: W28, W154

W123. **Organ pieces, book 1** September–October 1905 (yr. on printed edition); Winthrop Rogers (1919), Boosey & Hawkes

1: Allegretto grazioso
2: Allegro comodo
3: Allegro marziale e ben marcato

Duration: 15'30"
For organ.
Durations of individual movements: 4', 3', and 3'30".
Dates of individual movements: September 1905, October 1905, and October 1905.
Revisions made probably done just prior to publication.

Premiere (Movement 3 only)

W123a. 1941; Ewell Parish Church.

W124. **Organ pieces, book 2** ca. 1901 - mvmts. 1 and 3, 1912 - mvmt. 2 (yr. on printed edition); *The Organ Loft*, book 105 (1901) - mvmt. 3 only, Winthrop Rogers (1914), Boosey & Hawkes

1: Andante con moto
2: Andantino
3: Allegro ben moderato

Duration: 9'50"
For organ.
Durations of individual movements: 4', 3'30", and 2'20".

W125. **Pensees fugitives I** Summer 1902 (ms); unpublished

Duration: 2'30"
For piano.

W126. **Phantasm** July 27, 1931 (ms); Augener (1941)

Duration: 25'
For two pianos.
Dedicated to Elizabeth Sprague Coolidge (probably in piano and orchestra version).
Also exists in version for piano and orchestra. *See*: W156

W127. **Piano sonata** March 3, 1924 (ms); Augener (1925), Stainer & Bell

1: Lento ma non troppo – Andante ben moderato
2: Andante ben moderato
3: Lento – Allegro ma non troppo

Duration: 32'
For piano.
Dedicated to Ernest Bristow Farrar, composer and friend killed in action in 1917.
See: B137, B311

Premiere

W127a. October 15, 1925; Wigmore Hall; Myra Hess, piano. *See*: B263, B319, B332, B354

Other Selected Performances

W127b. February 18, 1926; Aeolian Hall (NY); Myra Hess, piano. *See*: B197
W127c. December 1, 1927; Wigmore Hall; Alan Bush, piano. *See*: B144
W127d. January 29, 1931; Berlin; Alan Bush, piano. *See*: B187
W127e. 1985; Aldeburgh Festival.

W128. **Three Pieces for organ** ca. 1905 (yr. copyright assigned); Novello (1905) – separately, (1974) – collectively

1: Andante moderato in C minor

2: Adagio in E major
3: Allegro con spirito in B-flat major

Duration: 14'30"
For organ.

Selected Performances

W128a. 1979; Aldeburgh Festival.

Premiere (Movement 2 only)

W128b. October 9, November 12, and December 11, 1914; Twrgwyn Chapel; Olwen Rowlands, organ.

Other Selected Performances

W128c. January 24, 1925; H. F. Ellingford, organ.
W128d. 1953; Aldeburgh Festival.

W129. **Three Pieces for organ (1939)** October–December 1939; Curwen (1940), Thames Publishing (1982)

1: Prelude
2: Minuet
3: Processional

Duration: 13'30"
For organ.
Durations of individual movements: 2'20", 4'15", and 3'30".
Dates of individual movements: October 1939, November 1939, and November/December 1939.
Dedications: Movement 1, Prelude: John Alston; Movement 2, Minuet: Arthur M. Goodhart; Movement 3, Processional: Archibald M. Henderson.
See: B221

Selected Performances

W129a. 1979; Aldeburgh Festival.

W130. **Three Poems** December 26, 1913–April 25, 1914 (ms); Augener (1915), Stainer & Bell

1: Solitude
2: Ecstasy
3: Sunset

Duration: 9'30"
For piano.
Durations of individual movements: 3'20", 3'40", and 2'30".
Dates of individual movements: December 26, 1913, January 1914, and April 25, 1914.

Premiere (Movement 3 only)

W130a. July 9, 1923; Royal College of Music; Evelyn Willis, piano.

W131. **Romance** 1912 (yr. on printed edition); Augener (1913), Stainer & Bell

Duration: 2'40"
For piano.

W132. **Scherzettino** ca. 1901–1902; unpublished

Duration: 3'30"
For piano.

W133. **A Sea idyll** June 1905 (yr. on printed edition); Houghton & Co. (1906), Augener (1917), Stainer & Bell

Duration: 4'
For piano.

Premiere

W133a. June 15, 1905; Bechstein Hall; Harold Samuel, piano. *See*: B159

W134. **Serenade** April 1903 (yr. on printed edition); Reid Bros Ltd. (1906), Chappell, Faber Music

Duration: 2'
For piano.
Also in versions for violin or violoncello and piano and for orchestra. *See*: W49, W161

W135. **Three Sketches** 1906 (yr. on printed edition); Winthrop Rogers (1915), Boosey & Hawkes

1: April
2: Rosemary
3: Valse capricieuse

Duration: 6'20"
For piano.
Durations of individual movements: 2'2", 2'30", and 1'30".
Date on ms. of first movement: May 12, 1906.
Movement 2, "Rosemary," also in version for orchestra. *See*: W159

Premiere

W135a. November 4, 1910; Bechstein Hall; Ellen Edwards, piano. *See*: B267

W136. **Todessehnsucht (Come sweet death)** June 1931 (ms); Oxford University Press (1932)

Duration: 2'
For piano.
Commissioned by Harriet Cohen for inclusion in an album of Bach transcriptions entitled *A Bach Book* for Harriet Cohen.
An arrangement of a piece by J. S. Bach.
Also exists in version for string orchestra. *See*: W168

Premiere

W136a. October 17, 1932; Queen's Hall; Harriet Cohen, piano.

W137. **The Turtle's retort** ca. 1919; Winthrop Rogers (1919), Boosey & Hawkes

Duration: 4'30"
For piano.
Also exists in version for orchestra. *See*: W260

W138. **Vignettes de Marseille** October–November 1925 (ms); Thames Publishing (1979)

1: Carmelita
2: Nicolette
3: Zoraida
4: En Fete

Duration: 12'45"
For piano.
Durations of individual movements: 4', 3', 3'30", and 2'15".
Dates of individual movements: October 8, 1925, October 14, 1925, November 13, 1925, and November 16, 1925.
Nos. 1–3 also exist in version for small orchestra under the title *Vignettes de danse*. *See*: W171

Premiere

W138a. March 12, 1978; Broadcast performance from BBC Radio Scotland; Kathleen Renilson, piano.

W139. **Winter pastoral** December 4, 1925 (ms); Augener (1928), Stainer & Bell

Duration: 3'
For piano.

ORCHESTRAL MUSIC

W140. **Berceuse for orchestra** August 18, 1901 (ms); Keith Prowse (1929), EMI Music

Duration: 2'30"
For small orchestra.

Also in versions for violin or violoncello and piano, for piano, for violin and strings, and for large orchestra. *See*: W4, W96, W141, W253

W141. **Berceuse for violin and strings** August 18, 1901 (ms); Keith Prowse (1902), EMI Music

Duration: 2'30"
For violin and strings.
Also in versions for violin or violoncello and piano, for piano, for small orchestra, and for large orchestra. *See*: W4, W96, W140, W253

Premiere

W141a. June 20, 1902; Royal College of Music; Delia Mason, violin, C. Villiers Stanford, conducting.

W142. **Canzonetta** July 7, 1926 (ms); Winthrop Rogers (1927), Hawkes & Son, Boosey & Hawkes

Duration: 2'30"
For small orchestra.
Also exists in version for piano. *See*: W97

W143. **Coronation march** November 1901 (ms); unpublished

Duration: 8'
For orchestra.

W144. **Coronation march (1911)** Before May 1, 1911; Thames Publishing

Duration: 7'30"
For large orchestra.
Published title: *Coronation march*. Title on autograph: *March*.
Also issued in edition for symphonic wind orchestra by Thames Publishing.

Premiere

W144a. September 1977; Kensington Symphony Orchestra, Leslie Head, conducting.

W145. **Dance poem** July 30, 1913 (ms); Faber Music (1978)

Duration: 15'
For orchestra

Premiere

W145a. March 16, 1914; Royal Philharmonic Society Concert, Queen's Hall; Frank Bridge, conducting. *See*: B184, B273, B298

Other Selected Performances

W145b. July 25, 1933; BBC Broadcast.
W145c. August 27, 1935; Queen's Hall Promenade Concert; Frank Bridge, conducting.
W145d. August 1939; Queen's Hall Promenade Concert; Frank Bridge, conducting.
W145e. September 1, 1939; Frank Bridge, conducting.

W146. **Dance rhapsody** May 20, 1908 (ms); Faber Music (after 1977)

Duration: 15'
For orchestra.

Premiere

W146a. July 21, 1908; Royal College of Music; Frank Bridge, conducting. *See*: B369, B370

Other Selected Performances

W146b. September 25, 1909; Liverpool Festival of British Music, Philharmonic Hall. *See*: B310
W146c. October 15, 1914; Queen's Hall Promenade Concert; Frank Bridge, conducting.
W146d. December 1, 1918; Royal Albert Hall; Frank Bridge, conducting.

W147. **Dramatic overture** ca. 1906; unpublished

For orchestra.

W148. **Enter spring** Sketched January 5, 1927, scored May 27, 1927; Faber Music (1977) - study score, Faber Music - full score and parts

Duration: 17'
For large orchestra.
Commissioned by the Norwich Festival.

Premiere

W148a. October 27, 1927; Norwich Triennial Festival; Queen's Hall Orchestra, Frank Bridge, conducting. *See*: B141, B154, B271, B316, B320, B321, B396

Other Selected Performances

W148b. September 25, 1930; Queen's Hall Promenade Concert; Frank Bridge, conducting. *See*: B142, B153, B277, B317, B338
W148c. 1931; BBC Broadcast; Frank Bridge, conducting.
W148d. October 26, 1932; Queen's Hall Concert.
W148e. 1932; BBC Broadcast; Frank Bridge, conducting.
W148f. April 9, 1967; Aldeburgh Festival, Royal Festival Hall; New Philharmonia, Benjamin Britten, conducting. *See*: B239

W149. **An Irish melody** September 8–October 6, 1908 (ms), scored 1938; Augener (1915) - miniature score, Stainer & Bell - parts

Duration: 7'
For string orchestra (optional bass part added to original string quartet).
Also exists in version for string quartet. *See*: W14

W150. **Isabella** January 1907 (ms); Faber Music (1978)

Duration: 18'
For orchestra.

Premiere

W150a. October 3, 1907; Queen's Hall Promenade Concert; Queen's Hall Orchestra, Sir Henry Wood, conducting. *See*: B269, B341, B350

Other Selected Performances

W150b. February 25, 1908; Royal College of Music; Frank Bridge, conducting. *See*: B181
W150c. February 12, 1911; Queen's Hall; London Symphony Orchestra, Frank Bridge, conducting.
W150d. May 6, 1915; Queen's Hall; Frank Bridge, conducting.
W150e. May 14, 1935; BBC Orchestra; Frank Bridge, conducting.

W151. **Lament** June 14, 1915; Goodwin Taub (1915), Curwen, Faber Music

Duration: 6'
For string orchestra.
Composed in memory of Catherine, a friend who was drowned with her family in the Lusitania disaster.
Also exists in version for piano. *See*: W112

Premiere

W151a. September 15, 1915; Queen's Hall Promenade Concert; Frank Bridge, conducting. *See*: B339, B343

Other Selected Performances

W151b. October 14, 1916; Queen's Hall Symphony Concert; Frank Bridge, conducting. *See*: B404
W151c. 1974; Aldeburgh Festival.
W151d. 1979; Aldeburgh Festival.

W152. **Trois Morceaux d'orchestre** September 9, 1902 (ms); unpublished

1: Chant de Tristesse
2: Chant d'Esperance
3: Chant de Gaiete

Duration: 12'
For orchestra.
Dates of individual movements: April 1902, April 11, 1902, and September 9, 1902.

W153. **Norse legend** 1905, January 1938 (orchestral version); Hawkes & Son (Concert Edition, 1939), Boosey & Hawkes

Duration: 4'
For orchestra.
Also exists in versions for violin and piano and for piano. *See*: W26, W121

W154. **Two Old English songs** May 1916; Schirmer (1916), Winthrop Rogers, Boosey & Hawkes

1: Sally in our alley
2: Cherry ripe

Duration: 7'50"
For string orchestra.
Durations of individual movements: 4'20", 3'30".
Completion dates of each movement given on printed edition: May 9, 1916 and May 30, 1916.
Also exist in versions for string quartet and piano duet. *See*: W28, W122

Premiere

W154a. September 26, 1916; Queen's Hall Promenade Concert, Frank Bridge, conducting. *See*: B270, B356

Other Selected Performances

W154b. October 24, 1934; Bournemouth; Bournemouth Municipal Orchestra.
W154c. 1974; Aldeburgh Festival.

W155. **Oration, concerto elegiaco** Sketched March 25, 1930, scored May 9, 1930; Faber Music (1979)

Duration: 28'
For violoncello and orchestra.
Also exists in version for violoncello and piano. *See*: W29

Premiere

W155a. January 16, 1936; BBC Contemporary Music Concert, broadcast performance; BBC Orchestra, Florence Hooten, violoncello, Frank Bridge, conducting. *See*: B208, B251, B284, B309, B318, B419

Other Selected Performances

W155b. December 6, 1936; BBC Broadcast; Sir Adrian Boult, conducting.

W156. **Phantasm** July 31, 1931 (ms); Stainer & Bell

Duration: 25'
For piano and orchestra.
Dedicated to Elizabeth Sprague Coolidge.
Also exists in version for two pianos. *See*: W126

Premiere

W156a. January 10, 1934; Queen's Hall, BBC British Music Festival; BBC Orchestra, Kathleen Long, piano, Frank Bridge, conducting. *See*: B164, B167, B209, B283

W157. **Two Poems** October 20, 1915 - movement 1, October 29, 1915 - movement 2 (ms); Augener (1923), Stainer & Bell

1: Andante moderato e semplice
2: Allegro con brio

Duration: 11'
For orchestra.
Durations of individual movements: 5' and 6'.

Premiere

W157a. January 1, 1917; Queen's Hall; Queen's Hall Orchestra, Frank Bridge, conducting. *See*: B272, B315, B348

Other Selected Performances

W157b. November 16, 1921; Queen's Hall; London Symphony Orchestra, Frank Bridge, conducting. *See*: B292
W157c. November 11, 1923; Aeolian Hall (NY); New York Symphony Society Orchestra, Frank Bridge, conducting.
W157d. April 23, 1925; Queen's Hall; Frank Bridge, conducting.
W157e. September 18, 1936; Queen's Hall Promenade Concert.

W158. **Rebus** August 2, 1940 (ms); Boosey & Hawkes (1978)

Duration: 8'30"
For orchestra.

Premiere

W158a. February 23, 1941; Queen's Hall; London Philharmonic Orchestra; Sir Henry Wood, conducting. *See*: B147, B205, B223, B265

W159. **Rosemary** 1906 (yr. on printed edition); Hawkes & Sons (Concert Edition, 1939), Boosey & Hawkes

Duration: 2'30"
For orchestra.
Orchestration dates from 1936.
Also exists in original version for piano. *See*: W135

W160. **The Sea** July 5, 1911 (ms); Stainer & Bell (1920) (for the Carnegie Trust)

1: Seascape
2: Sea Foam
3: Moonlight
4: Storm

Duration: 19'30"
For large orchestra.
Durations of individual movements: 6', 2'30", 5'30", and 5'30".

Premiere

W160a. September 24, 1912; Queen's Hall Promenade Concert; Sir Henry Wood, conducting. *See*: B342, B344, B351

Other Selected Performances

W160b. September 23, 1913; Queen's Hall Promenade Concert; Frank Bridge, conducting. *See*: B345
W160c. 1919; Queen's Hall Promenade Concert.
W160d. March 22, 1923; Royal Philharmonic Society. *See*: B383
W160e. July 17, 1923; Royal College of Music; Frank Bridge, conducting.
W160f. October 19 and 20, 1923; Cleveland; Cleveland Symphony Orchestra; Frank Bridge, conducting.
W160g. October 26 and 27, 1923; Boston; Boston Symphony Orchestra; Frank Bridge, conducting.
W160h. October 30, 1924; Norwich Triennial Festival; New Queen's Hall Orchestra, Frank Bridge, conducting. *See*: B156, B395, B403
W160i. August 20, 1937; Queen's Hall Promenade Concert.
W160j. August 29, 1938; Queen's Hall Promenade Concert.
W160k. 1971; Aldeburgh Festival.

W161. **Serenade** April 1903 (yr. on printed edition); Reid Bros Ltd. (1906), Chappell, Faber Music

Duration: 2'
For orchestra.
Also in versions for violin or violoncello and piano and for piano. *See*: W49, W134

W162. **Sir Roger de Coverley** Summer 1938; Augener (1939)

Duration: 4'30"
For string orchestra.
Also exists in original version for string quartet and in a version for orchestra. *See*: W50, W163

W163. **Sir Roger de Coverley** October 10, 1922; Stainer & Bell

Duration: 4'30"
For orchestra.

Also exists in original version for string quartet and in version for string orchestra. *See*: W50, W162

Premiere

W163a. October 21, 1922; Queen's Hall Promenade Concert; Frank Bridge, conducting. *See*: B182

Other Selected Performances

W163b. November 1 and 2, 1923; Detroit; Detroit Symphony Orchestra, Frank Bridge, conducting. *See*: B220, B393

W163c. December 26, 1934; BBC Broadcast performance; Frank Bridge, conducting.

W163d. 1968; Aldeburgh Festival.

W164. **Suite** December 1909–January 1910 (yrs. on printed edition); Goodwin Tabb (1920), Curwen (1979)

1: Prelude
2: Intermezzo
3: Nocturne
4: Finale

Duration: 21'
For string orchestra.
Durations of individual movements: 6'45", 3', 7', and 4'1".
Movements dated individually in printed edition: December 26–January 1910, January 1910, December 21, 1909, and December 1909–January 1910.
May have existed in a version for piano duet.
See: B151

Premiere

W164a. 1910?; amateur performance.

Other Selected Performances

W164b. October 7, 1920; Queen's Hall Promenade Concert; Frank Bridge, conducting. *See*: B337

W164c. November 6, 1920; Queen's Hall Promenade Concert; Frank Bridge, conducting. *See*: B246

W164d. January 19, 1921; Jordan Hall, Boston, Boston Musical Association. *See*: B70

W164e. February 21, 1935; Northampton Polytechnic Institute; Frank Bridge, conducting.
W164f. February 26, 1935; Kensington Town Hall; Audrey Melville Orchestra, Frank Bridge, conducting.
W164g. 1979; Aldeburgh Festival.

W165. **Summer** 'sketch written July 1914, score 11th–22nd April 1915' (ms); Augener (1923), Stainer & Bell

Duration: 10'
For orchestra.

Premiere

W165a. March 13, 1916; Royal Philharmonic Society Concert, Queen's Hall; Frank Bridge, conducting. *See*: B252, B299, B379, B381

Other Selected Performances

W165b. November 1 and 2, 1923; Detroit; Detroit Symphony Orchestra, Frank Bridge, conducting. *See*: B220, B393
W165c. 1974; Aldeburgh Festival.

W166. **Symphonic poem** October 18, 1903 (ms); unpublished

Duration: 19'
For orchestra.

Premiere

W166a. May 20, 1904; St. James's Hall – Patron's Fund Concert #1; Frank Bridge, conducting. *See*: B373

W167. **There is a willow grows aslant a brook** January 29, 1927 (ms); Augener (1928) – full score and parts, Augener (1928) – miniature score, Stainer & Bell

Duration: 9'
For small orchestra.

Premiere

W167a. August 20, 1927; Queen's Hall Promenade Concert; Frank Bridge, conducting. *See*: B143, B312, B340

Other Selected Performances

W167b. December 1932; Carmargo Ballet Company.
W167c. March 8, 1941; London Philharmonic Orchestra; Sir Adrian Boult, conducting.
W167d. 1948; Aldeburgh Festival.
W167e. 1964; Aldeburgh Festival.

W168. **Todessehnsucht (Come sweet death)** February 13, 1936; Britten-Pears Library

Duration: 2'
For string orchestra.
Also exists in original version for piano. *See*: W136

W169. **Unfinished symphony** November/December 1940–January (10), 1941 (ms); Faber Music (1979)

Duration: 14'
For string orchestra.
The published edition is the finished first movement as completed by Anthony Pople.
Only fragments exist for possible additional movements.

Premiere

W169a. June 20, 1979; Snape Maltings, Aldeburgh Festival; English Chamber Orchestra, Steuart Bedford, conducting.

W170. **Valse intermezzo à cordes** August 22, 1902 (ms); unpublished

Duration: 7'
For string orchestra.

W171. **Vignettes de danse** Sketched 1925, scored 1938 (ms); Boosey & Hawkes

1: Nicolette
2: Zoraida
3: Carmelita

Duration: 10'30"
For small orchestra.
Durations of individual nos.: 3', 3'30", and 4'.
Dates of scoring of individual nos.: June 1938, July 1938, and July 1938.
Also exists in version for piano with an additional movement, "En Fete," under the title *Vignettes de Marseille*. *See*: W138

Premiere

W171a. May 12, 1941; Broadcast performance from Glasgow; BBC Scottish Orchestra; Guy Warrack, conducting.

SOLO SONGS

W172. **Adoration** November 1905 (ms), revisions – just before publication; revised version – Winthrop Rogers (1918), Boosey & Hawkes

Duration: 4'
For medium voice and piano.
Words by Keats.
Title before publication: *Asleep*.
Also exists in version for medium voice and orchestra. *See*: W173

Premiere

W172a. October 30, 1918; Wigmore Hall. *See*: B215

W173. **Adoration** November 1905 (ms), revisions – prior to 1918; publication revised version - Boosey & Hawkes

Duration: 4'

For medium voice and orchestra.
Words by Keats.
Also exists in version for medium voice and piano. *See*: W172

W174. **All things that we clasp** January 27, 1907 (ms); Winthrop Rogers (1916), Boosey & Hawkes

Duration: 1'40"
For voice and piano.
Words by Heine, translation by Emma Lazarus.

W175. **Berceuse** October 17, 1901 (ms); Thames Publishing (1990)

Duration: 3'
For soprano and orchestra.
Words by Dorothy Wordsworth.

Premiere

W175a. June 20, 1902; Royal College of Music; Delia Mason, vocalist, Frank Bridge, conducting.

W176. **Blow, blow thou winter wind** 1903 (ms); Schirmer (1916), Winthrop Rogers (1916), Boosey & Hawkes

Duration: 1'30"
For medium voice and piano.
Words by Shakespeare.

Premiere

W176a. March 8, 1917; Royal College of Music; Etheldreda Freegarde, vocalist.

W177. **Blow out you bugles** May 1918 (ms); Winthrop Rogers (1919), Boosey & Hawkes

Duration: 7'
For tenor and piano.
Dedicated to Gervase Elwes and his wife.
Words by Rupert Brooke.
Also exists in version for tenor and orchestra. *See*: W177

W178. **Blow out you bugles** (May 1918 (ms); Boosey & Hawkes)

Duration: 7'
For tenor and orchestra.
Dedicated to Gervase Elwes and his wife.
Words by Rupert Brooke.
Also exists in version for tenor and piano. *See*: W176

Premiere

W178a. October 26, 1918; Queen's Hall; Gervase Elwes, vocalist, Frank Bridge, conducting. *See*: B391

Other Selected Performances

W178b. November 30, 1918; New Queen's Hall Orchestra, Gervase Elwes, vocalist, Frank Bridge, conducting. *See*: B285, B349
W178c. July 1, 1919; Royal College of Music Commemoration Concert; Frank Bridge, conducting. *See*: B372
W178d. 1919; Queen's Hall Promenade Concert.
W178e. April 30 and May 1, 1920; Boston; Boston Symphony Orchestra, John McCormack, vocalist. *See*: B224
W178f. August 11, 1932; London; Frank Bridge, conducting.

W179. **Come to me in my dreams** November 1906 (ms); Winthrop Rogers (1918), Boosey & Hawkes

Duration: 3'
For voice and piano.
Slightly revised version was the one published.
Revisions probably date for the time of publication.
Words by Matthew Arnold.

Premiere

W179a. October 30, 1918; Wigmore Hall. *See*: B215

W180. **Cradle song** ca. 1904; unpublished

Duration: 2'
For voice and piano.
Words by Tennyson.

W181. **Dawn and evening** April 1905; *The Vocalist* IV (October 1905), Winthrop Rogers (1916), Boosey & Hawkes

Duration: 2'
For voice and piano.
A revision, set to a different translation, of *Rising when the dawn still faint is*.
Words by Heine, translated by C. A.
Also in a version for voice and orchestra. *See*: W182

W182. **Dawn and evening** April 1905; Winthrop Rogers (1916); Boosey & Hawkes

Duration: 2'
For voice and orchestra.
A revision, set to a different translation, of *Rising when the dawn still faint is*.
Words by Heine, translated by C. A.
Also in a version for voice and piano. *See*: W181

W183. **Day after day** January 1922 (ms); Augener (1925), Galliard (1974), Stainer & Bell

Duration: 4'
For voice and piano.
Words by Rabindranath Tagore.
Also exists in version for voice and orchestra. *See*: W254

Premiere

W183a. April 11, 1970; Royal College of Music.

Other Selected Performances

W183b. 1974; Aldeburgh Festival.

W184. **A Dead violet** March 21, 1904 (ms); Thames Publishing (1982)

Duration: 2'
For medium voice and piano.
Words by Shelley.

Premiere

W184a. December 6, 1904; Aeolian Hall - Patron's Fund Concert #2; F. Aubrey Millward, vocalist. *See*: B326, B329

W185. **Dear, when I look into thine eyes** June 27, 1908 (ms); unpublished

Duration: 2'
For voice and piano.
Words by Heine, translator unknown.

W186. **The Devon maid** July 1903 (yr. on printed edition); *The Vocalist* IV (September 1905), Schirmer (1916), Winthrop Rogers (1916), Boosey & Hawkes (1979)

Duration: 1'30"
For medium voice and piano.
Words by Keats.

W187. **A Dirge** April 7, 1903 (ms); Thames Publishing (1982)

Duration: 45"
For medium voice and piano accompaniment.
Words by Shelley.

Premiere

W187a. December 6, 1904; Aeolian Hall - Patron's Fund Concert #2; F. Aubrey Millward, vocalist. *See*: B326, B329

W188. **Dweller in my deathless dreams** June 1, 1925 (ms); Augener (1926), Galliard (1974), Stainer & Bell

Duration: 4'30"
For voice and piano.
"For John McCormack"
Words by Rabindranath Tagore.
Also exists in version for voice and orchestra. *See*: W255

Premiere

W188a. June 1925; John McCormack, vocalist.

W189. **Easter hymn** ca. 1912 (yr. of publication); Chappell (1912), Thames Publishing (1990)

Duration: 2'30"
For voice and piano.
Arrangement of a 17th century German hymn with English words by Hans Wagemann.
Also exists in versions for SATB and for flute, string quartet, bells, and organ. *See*: W68, W249

Premiere

W189a. February 21, 1918; Royal College of Music; Norah Watson, vocalist.

W190. **E'en as a lovely flower** August 20, 1903 (ms); *The Vocalist* IV (October 1905), Winthrop Rogers (1916), Boosey & Hawkes (1979)

Duration: 3'
For tenor and piano.
Words by Heine, translated by Kate F. Kroeker.
Also in version for tenor and orchestra and for string quartet. *See*: W191, W250

W191. **E'en as a lovely flower** August 20, 1903 (ms); Winthrop Rogers (1916), Boosey & Hawkes

Duration: 3'
For tenor and orchestra.
Words by Heine, translated by Kate F. Kroeker.
Also in versions for tenor and piano and for string quartet. *See*: W190, W250

Premiere

W191a. October 5, 1935; Queen's Hall Promenade Concert; Frank Bridge, conducting.

W192. **Fair daffodils** April 1905 (ms); unpublished

Duration: 2'50"
For voice and piano.
Words by Herrick.
Also exists in a revised, published version. *See*: W193

W193. **Fair daffodils** revised: ca. 1918–1919; Winthrop Rogers (1919), Boosey & Hawkes

Duration: 2'50"
For voice and piano.
Words by Herrick.
Also exists in original, unpublished version. *See*: W192

W194. **Far, far from each other** November 1906; Thames Publishing (1982)

Duration: 3'
For medium voice and piano, with viola obbligato.
Words by Matthew Arnold.

Premiere

W194a. December 9, 1908; Broadwood Concert Rooms; Ivy Sinclair, contralto, Audrey ffolkes, viola, Frank Bridge, piano.

W195. **Fly home my thoughts** Midsummer 1904 (ms); unpublished

Duration: 3'
For voice and orchestra.
Author of words unidentified.

W196. **Go not, happy day** 1903 (yr. on printed edition); *The Vocalist* IV (September 1905), Winthrop Rogers (1916), Boosey & Hawkes

Duration: 1'15"
For voice and piano.
Words by Tennyson.

Also exists in versions for voice and small orchestra and for voice, harp, and strings. *See*: W262, W263

Premiere

W196a. November 25, 1924; Royal College of Music; Ruby MacGilchrist, vocalist.

Other Selected Performances

W196b. 1949; Aldeburgh Festival.
W196c. 1979; Aldeburgh Festival.

W197. **Goldenhair** October 29, 1925 (ms); Chappell (1925), Thames Publishing (1990)

Duration: 1'30"
For voice and piano.
Words by James Joyce.

Selected Performances

W197a. 1979; Aldeburgh Festival.
W197b. 1982; Aldeburgh Festival.

W198. **The Hag** June 18, 1902 (ms); unpublished

Duration: 3'
For baritone and orchestra.
Words by Herrick.

Premiere

W198a. December 9, 1902; Royal College of Music; Albert Garcia, soprano, Frank Bridge, conducting.

Other Selected Performances

W198b. May 20, 1904; St. James's Hall - Patron's Fund Concert #1; Frank Bridge, conducting. *See*: B373
W198c. June 14, 1911; Queen's Hall - Patron's Fund Concert #16; Jamieson Dodds, baritone, London Symphony Orchestra; Frank Bridge, conducting. *See*: B266, B327

W199. **Harebell and pansy** ca. 1904; unpublished

Incomplete.
For voice and orchestra.
Author of words unidentified.

W200. **I praise the tender flower** October 1905, scored January 2, 1906; unpublished

Duration: 2'30"
For high baritone and orchestra.
Words by Robert Bridges.

Premiere

W200a. July 14, 1909; Queen's Hall - Patron's Fund Concert #12; Robert Chignell, baritone, Frank Bridge, conducting. *See*: B328

W201. **If I could choose** Before 1902 (yr. of publication); Keith Prowse (1902), EMI Music

Duration: 1'30"
For voice and piano.
Words by Thomas Ashe.

W202. **Into her keeping** May 4, 1919 (ms); Winthrop Rogers (1919), Boosey & Hawkes

Duration: 2'
For voice and piano.
Words by H. D. Lowry.

W203. **Isobel** September 1912 (ms); Chappell (1913), Thames Publishing (1990)

Duration: 2'30"
For voice and piano.
Words by Digby Goddard-Fenwick.
Also exists in version for strings and piano. *See*: W251

Premiere

W203a. February 27, 1919; Royal College of Music; Ruth Hosken, vocalist.

Other Selected Performances

W203b. June 19, 1919; Aeolian Hall; George Fergusson, vocalist. *See*: B255

W204. **Journey's end** November 21, 1925 - original ms, November 23, 1925 - engraver's ms; Augener (1926), Galliard (1974), Stainer & Bell

Duration: 3'20"
For tenor/high baritone and piano.
Words by Humbert Wolfe.

W205. **Lament** Midsummer 1904 (ms); unpublished

Duration: 2'10"
For voice and orchestra.
Words by Laurence Binyon.

W206. **The Last invocation** September 23, 1918 (ms); Winthrop Rogers (1919), Boosey & Hawkes

Duration: 2'30"
For voice and piano.
Words by Walt Whitman.

W207. **Lean close thy cheek against my cheek** April 10, 1905 (ms); unpublished

Duration: 2'50"
For voice and piano.
Words by Heine, translator unknown.

W208. **Love is a rose** December 31, 1907 (ms); unpublished

Duration: 1'30"

For voice and piano.
Words by Leah Durand.

W209. **Love went a-riding** May 5, 1914 (ms); Schirmer (1916), Winthrop Rogers (1916), Boosey & Hawkes

Duration: 1'30"
For voice and piano.
Words by Mary E. Coleridge.
Also exists in version for voice and orchestra. *See*: W210

Premiere

W209a. March 8, 1917; Royal College of Music; Etheldreda Freegarde, vocalist.

W210. **Love went a-riding** May 5, 1914 (ms); Boosey & Hawkes

Duration: 1'30"
For voice and orchestra.
Words by Mary E. Coleridge.
Also exists in version for voice and piano. *See*: W209

Premiere

W210a. October 5, 1935; Queen's Hall Promenade Concert; Frank Bridge, conducting.

Other Selected Performances

W210b. 1949; Aldeburgh Festival.
W210c. 1950; Aldeburgh Festival.

W211. **Mantle of blue** March 1918 (ms); Winthrop Rogers (1919), Boosey & Hawkes

Duration: 2'30"
For voice and piano.
Words by Padraic Colum.
Also exists in version for voice and orchestra. *See*: W212

Premiere

W211a. October 30, 1918; Wigmore Hall. *See*: B215

W212. **Mantle of blue** March 1918 (ms); Boosey & Hawkes

Duration: 2'30"
For voice and orchestra.
Words by Padraic Colum.
Also exists in version for voice and piano. *See*: W211

W213. **The Mountain voice** July 28, 1903; unpublished

Incomplete.
For voice and piano.
Words by Heine, translator unknown.

W214. **Music when soft voices die** November 11, 1903 (ms); unpublished

Duration: 2'
For high voice and piano.
Words by Shelley.
Also exists in version with viola obbligato. *See*: W215

W215. **Music when soft voices die, with viola** January 11, 1907 (ms); Thames Publishing (1982)

Duration: 2'
For medium voice and piano, with viola obbligato.
Words by Shelley.
Also exists in version without viola obbligato. *See*: W214

Premiere

W215a. December 9, 1908; Broadwood Concert Rooms; Ivy Sinclair, contralto, Audrey ffolkes, viola, Frank Bridge, piano.

W216. **My pent up tears oppress my brain** December 27, 1906 (ms); Thames Publishing (1982)

Duration: 1'30"
For voice and piano.
Author of words unidentified.

W217. **Night lies on the silent highways** January 12, 1904 (ms); Thames Publishing (1982)

Duration: 2'50"
For medium voice and piano.
Words by Heine, translated by Kate F. Kroeker.

Premiere

W217a. December 6, 1904; Aeolian Hall – Patron's Fund Concert #2; F. Aubrey Millward, vocalist. *See*: B326, B329

W218. **O that it were so** ca. 1912; Chappell (1913), Thames Publishing (1990)

Duration: 2'30"
For voice and piano.
Words by Walter Savage Landor.
Also exists in versions for voice and orchestra (two scorings) and in version for voice, piano, and strings. *See*: W219, W264

Premiere

W218a. February 13, 1924; Royal College of Music; Philip B. Warde, vocalist.

Other Selected Performances

W218b. June 24, 1926; Royal College of Music Students' Union "At Home" Concert; Topliss Green, vocalist.
W218c. January 1941; Brighton Art Gallery. *See*: B173

W219. **O that it were so** ca. 1912; Chappell (1913)

Duration: 2'30"

For voice and orchestra in 2 scorings.
Words by Walter Savage Landor.
Also exists in version for voice and piano and in version for voice, piano, and strings. *See*: W218, W264

W220. **The Primrose** Before 1902 (yr. of publication); Keith Prowse (1902), EMI Music

Duration: 2'
For voice and piano.
Words by Herrick.

W221. **Two Recitations** ca. 1903; unpublished

1: The Lovers' quarrel
2: The Maniac

For two speaking voices and piano.
Words for part #1 by Browning, for part #2 by Matthew Gregory "Monk" Lewis.

W222. **Rising when the dawn still faint is** July 28, 1903 (ms); unpublished

Duration: 2'
For voice and piano.
A revision of this work, entitled *Dawn and evening*, was written in April 1905, published in October 1905. The voice and orchestra version of this revision was published in 1916.
Words by Heine, translated by Francis Hueffer.

W223. **So early in the morning, o** February 1918 (ms); Winthrop Rogers (1918), Boosey & Hawkes (slightly revised version)

Duration: 2'30"
For high voice and piano.
Words by James Stephens.

Premiere

W223a. October 30, 1918; Wigmore Hall. *See*: B215

W224. **So perverse** 1905 (yr. on printed edition); *The Vocalist* IV (December 1905), Schirmer (1916), Winthrop Rogers (1916), Boosey & Hawkes

Duration: 1'20"
For medium voice and piano.
Words by Robert Bridges.

Premiere

W224a. October 20, 1931; Grotrian Hall, London; Keith Falkner, vocalist.

Other Selected Performances

W224b. 1950; Aldeburgh Fesitval.

W225. **Song cycle** September 7, 1904 (ms); unpublished

1: Love
2: Life
3: Death

Incomplete.
For voice and piano.
Author of words unidentified.

W226. **Sonnet** April 8, 1901 (ms); unpublished

Duration: 2'30"
For voice and piano.
Words by Shakespeare.

W227. **Speak to me my love** October 8, 1924 (ms); Augener (1925), Galliard (1974), Stainer & Bell

Duration: 4'15"
For voice and piano.
Words by Rabindranath Tagore.
Also exists in version for voice and orchestra. *See*: W265

Selected Performances

W227a. 1974; Aldeburgh Festival.

W228. **Strew no more red roses** April 10, 1913 (ms); Winthrop Rogers (1917), Boosey & Hawkes

Duration: 3'
For voice and piano.
Words by Matthew Arnold.

W229. **Tears, idle tears** 1905 (ms); Thames Publishing (1982)

Duration: 4'30"
For medium voice and piano.
Words by Tennyson.

Premiere

W229a. November 13, 1981; Royal Scottish Academy of Music and Drama (Glasgow); Paul Hindmarsh, tenor, Jack Keaney, piano.

W230. **Thou didst delight my eyes** Scored January 20, 1906; unpublished

Duration: 2'
For high baritone and orchestra.
Words by Robert Bridges.

Premiere

W230a. July 14, 1909; Queen's Hall - Patron's Fund Concert #12; Robert Chignell, baritone, Frank Bridge, conducting. *See*: B328

Other Selected Performances

W230b. June 14, 1911; Queen's Hall - Patron's Fund Concert #16; Jamieson Dodds, baritone, London Symphony Orchestra, Frank Bridge, conducting. *See*: B266, B327

W231. **Thy hand in mine** February 10, 1917 (ms); Winthrop Rogers (1917), Boosey & Hawkes

Duration: 2'10"
For voice and piano or orchestra.
Words by Mary E. Coleridge.

W232. **'Tis but a week** June 1, 1919 (ms); Winthrop Rogers (1919), Boosey & Hawkes

Duration: 2'
For voice and piano.
Words by Gerald Gould.

W233. **To you in France** Probably late October 1917; unpublished

Incomplete.
For voice and piano.
Words by Helen Dircks.

W234. **Variations on Cadet Rousselle** 1918; J. & W. Chester Ltd. (1920)

Duration: 4'
For voice and piano.
Dedicated "to our friend Edwin Evans who suggested this collaboration" - the other portions by Bax, Goossens, and Ireland.
Folk-tune text in French.
Also exists in version for male voices and orchestra and for orchestra. *See*: W252, W261

Premiere

W234a. June 6, 1919; Aeolian Hall; Raimond Collington, soprano, Harriet Cohen, piano.

W235. **The Violets blue** September 5, 1906 (ms); Winthrop Rogers (1916), Boosey & Hawkes

Duration: 1'20"
For voice and piano or string quartet.
Words by Heine, translated by James Thompson.

W236. **What shall I your true love tell** May 31, 1919 (ms); Winthrop Rogers (1919), Boosey & Hawkes

Duration: 4'
For voice and piano.
Words by Francis Thompson.

W237. **When you are old** January 25, 1919 (ms); Chappell (1920), Thames Publishing (1990)

Duration: 3'30"
For high voice and piano.
Words by W. B. Yeats.

Selected Performances

W237a. 1979; Aldeburgh Festival.

W238. **Where e're my bitter teardrops fall** July 30, 1903 (ms); *The Vocalist* (1905), Winthrop Rogers (1916), Boosey & Hawkes (1979)

Duration: 1'30"
For tenor and piano.
Revision is entitled *Three Songs for Tenor Voice.*
Words by Heine, translated by J. E. Wallis.

W239. **Where is it that our soul doth go?** Christmas 1906; Thames Publishing (1982)

Duration: 3'
For medium voice and piano, with viola obbligato.
Words by Heine, translated by Kate F. Kroeker.

Premiere

W239a. December 9, 1908; Broadwood Concert Rooms, Ivy Sinclair, contralto, Audrey ffolkes, viola, Frank Bridge, piano.

W240. **Where she lies asleep** April 1914 (yr. on printed edition); Schirmer (1916), Winthrop Rogers (1916), Boosey & Hawkes

Duration: 2'30"
For voice and piano.
Words by Mary E. Coleridge.
Also exists in version for voice and orchestra. *See*: W241

Premiere

W240a. October 30, 1918; Wigmore Hall. *See*: B215

W241. **Where she lies asleep** April 1914 (yr. on printed edition); Boosey & Hawkes

Duration: 2'30"
For voice and orchestra.
Words by Mary E. Coleridge.
Also exists in version for voice and piano. *See*: W240

THEATER MUSIC

W242. **The Christmas rose** 1919–1929; Augener (1931), Stainer & Bell

Duration: ca. 45'
For soloists, chorus, and orchestra.
An opera in three scenes with a libretto, by Bridge, based on a play for children by Margaret Kemp-Welch and Constance Cotterell.

Premiere

W242a. December 8, 10, and 11, 1931; Parry Opera Theatre, Royal College of Music; Frank Bridge, conducting. *See*: B146, B371, B374, B375

Other Selected Performances

W242b. December 8, 9, 10, and 11, 1965; Parry Opera Theatre, Royal College of Music. *See*: B242
W242c. December 1979; BBC Broadcast; Welsh Symphony Orchestra, Guy Woolfenden, conducting.

W243. **The Two Hunchbacks** Before November 1910; unpublished

1: Allegretto moderato
2: Moderato
3: Andantino
4: Lento
5: Allegretto marziale

Duration: 13'30"
For orchestra.
Durations for individual entr'actes: 3', 3'30", 1'30", 2'45", and 2'45".
Entr'actes to the play *The Two Hunchbacks* by Emile Cammaerts as translated by Tita Brand.

Premiere

W243a. November 15, 1910; Savoy Theatre (Marie Brema's Opera Season); Frank Bridge, conducting. *See*: B291

W244. **In the shop** October–December 1921; Thames Publishing (forthcoming)

1: Introduction
2: Allegro moderato
3: Giant's dance
4: Tempo di minuetto
5: Rent collector's dance
6: Moderato and finale

Duration: 13'40"
For piano duet (4 hands).
Durations of individual movements: 2', 2', 3', 2', 1'45", and 2'25".
A ballet for children of some of Bridge's friends.
Dates of completions for nos. 1, 3, 4, and 6: December 12, 1921, November 12, 1921, October 31, 1921, and December 1921.
Also exists in reduced version for piano solo. *See*: W245

W245. **In the shop** October–December 1921; unpublished

1: Introduction
2: Giant's dance

3: Tempo di minuetto
4: Moderato and finale

Duration: 13'40"
For piano solo.
Durations of individual movements: 2', 2', 3', 2', 1'45", and 2'25".
A ballet for children of some of Bridge's friends.
Dates of completion for no. 1, 3, 4, and 6: December 12, 1921, November 12, 1921, October 31, 1921, and December 1921.
Also exists in expanded version for piano duet (4 hands). *See*: W244

W246. **The Pageant of London** Before May 1911; Thames Publishing (forthcoming)

1: Solemn march (Richard III leaving London)
2: March (Henry VII leaving London)
3: Introduction (Minuet)
4: Pavane
5: La Romanesca (à Gaillard)
6: Lines from Seneca

Duration: 34'
For military band with male voice chorus.
Published edition for concert band.

Premiere

W246a. Second week of June 1911; Crystal Palace (as part of Empire Pageant); W. H. Bell, conducting. *See*: B324

W247. **Threads** July 1921 (ms); Hawkes & Son, Concert Edition (1938)

1: Andante molto moderato
2: Tempo di valse

Duration: 7'30"
For piano.
Durations of individual movements: 3' and 4'30".
Incidental music to the play *Threads* by Frank Stayton.
Also exists in version for small orchestra. *See*: W248

W248. **Threads** July 1921, scored May 1938; Hawkes & Son, Concert Edition (1938), Boosey & Hawkes

1: Andante molto moderato
2: Tempo di Vals

Duration: 7'30"
For small orchestra.
Durations of individual movements: 3' and 4'30".
Incidental music to the play *Threads* by Frank Stayton.
Also exists in version for piano. *See*: W247

Premiere

W248a. August 23–September 17, 1921; St. Jame's Theatre, London (28 performances). *See*: B145, B386

ARRANGEMENTS

CHAMBER MUSIC

W249. **Easter hymn** ca. 1912 (yr. of publication of voice and piano version)

Duration: 2'30"
For flute, string quartet, bells, and organ.
Arrangement found in the estate of composer John Foulds, presumably arranged by him.
Also exists in versions for SATB and for voice and piano. *See*: W68, W189

W250. **E'en as a lovely flower** August 20, 1903 (ms)

Duration: 3'
For string quartet.
String quartet arrangement by A. Fransel.
Also exists in versions for tenor and piano and for tenor and orchestra. *See*: W190, W191

W251. **Isobel** September 1912 (ms); Chappell

Duration: 2'30"
For strings and piano.
Arranged for strings and piano by G. Stacey.
Also exists in versions for voice and piano. *See*: W203

CHORAL MUSIC

W252. **Variations on Cadet Rousselle** 1918; J. & W. Chester Ltd.

Duration: 4'
For solo male voice, men's chorus, and orchestra.
Arranged for male voices and orchestra by Max Saunders.
Text is based on French folk-tune.
Also exists in versions for voice and piano and for orchestra. *See*: W234, W261

ORCHESTRAL MUSIC

W253. **Berceuse** August 18, 1901; Keith Prowse, EMI Music

Duration: 2'30"
For large orchestra.
Arranged for large orchestra by Hubert Bath.
Also exists in versions for violin or violoncello and piano, for piano solo, for small orchestra, and for violin and strings solo. *See*: W4, W96, W140, W141

W254. **Day after day** January 1922 - original version; Stainer & Bell (1982)

Duration: 4'
For voice and orchestra.
Orchestra arrangement by Robert Cornford.
Words by Rabindranath Tagore.
Also exists in original version for voice and piano. *See*: W183

W255. **Dweller in my deathless dreams** June 1, 1925 – original version; Stainer & Bell (1982)

Duration: 4'30"
For voice and orchestra.
Orchestra arrangement by Robert Cornford.
"For John McCormack."
Words by Rabindranath Tagore.
Also exists in original version for voice and piano. *See*: W188

W256. **Elégie** 1904 (yr. on printed edition)

Duration: 4'40"
For violoncello and orchestra.
Orchestrated by Robert Cornford in the late 1970's on commission from the Frank Bridge Trust.
Also exists in original version for violoncello and piano. *See*: W10

W257. **Heart's ease** April 26, 1921

Duration: 2'29"
For orchestra.
Orchestrated by Robert Cornford in the late 1970's.
Also exists in versions for violin and piano and for piano. *See*: W12, W114

W258. **Morning song** April 1918 (yr. on printed edition)

Duration: 4'31"
For violoncello and orchestra.
Orchestrated by Robert Cornford in the late 1970's on commission from the Frank Bridge Trust.
Also exists in original version for violoncello and piano. *See*: W25

W259. **Scherzetto** ca. 1901–1902; Faber Music

Duration: 3'
For violoncello and orchestra.
Orchestration by Robert Cornford.
Also in original version for violoncello and piano. *See*: W46

W260. **The Turtle's retort** ca. 1919

Duration: 4'07"
For orchestra.
Orchestrated by Eric Wetherell in the 1980's.
Also exists in original version for piano. *See*: W137

W261. **Variations on Cadet Rousselle** 1918; J. & W. Chester Ltd. (1931)

Duration: 4'
For orchestra.
Orchestrated by Eugene Goossens, December 1930.
Also exists in versions for voice and piano and for male voices and orchestra. *See*: W234, W252

SOLO SONGS

W262. **Go not, happy day** 1903 (yr. on printed edition); Boosey & Hawkes

Duration: 1'15"
For voice and small orchestra.
Arranged by Wurmser.
Words by Tennyson.
Also exists in versions for voice and piano and for voice, harp, and strings. *See*: W196, W263

W263. **Go not, happy day** 1903 (yr. on printed edition); Boosey & Hawkes

Duration: 1'15"
For voice, harp, and strings.
Arranged by G. Williams.
Words by Tennyson.
Also exists in versions for voice and piano and for voice and small orchestra. *See*: W196, W262

W264. **O that it were so** ca. 1912; Chappell (1913)

Duration: 2'30"
For voice, piano, and strings.

Voice, piano, and strings version arranged by G. Stacey.
Words by Walter Savage Landor.
Also exists in versions for voice and piano and for voice and orchestra in two scorings. *See*: W218, W219

W265. **Speak to me my love** October 8, 1924 - original version; Stainer & Bell (1982)

Duration: 4'15"
For voice and orchestra.
Orchestra arrangement by Robert Cornford.
Words by Rabindranath Tagore.
Also exists in original version for voice and piano. *See*: W227

Discography

This list includes all commercially-produced sound recordings, whether or not currently available. All are 33⅓ rpm unless otherwise noted. "See" references, e.g., *See*: B115, identify citations in the "Bibliography" section.

D1. **Adoration**

D1a. Pearl SHE 577. 1983.
Stephen Varcoe, baritone; Christopher Cox, piano.
In: The Early Bridge
Recorded June 28–29, 1982, Wigmore Hall, London.
"This record has been made with financial assistance from the Frank Bridge Trust."
With his All things that we clasp; Allegretto; Allegro appassionato; Berceuse; Blow, blow thou winter wind; Come to me in my dreams; A Dirge; E'en as a lovely flower; Fair daffodils; Far, far from each other; Music when soft voices die; My pent-up tears oppress my brain; Pensiero; Tears, idle tears; The Violets blue; Where is it that our soul doth go?
See: B325, B420

D2. **All things that we clasp**

D2a. Pearl SHE 577. 1983.
Stephen Varcoe, baritone; Christopher Cox, piano.
In: The Early Bridge

Recorded June 28–29, 1982, Wigmore Hall, London.
"This record has been made with financial assistance from the Frank Bridge Trust."
With his Adoration; Allegretto; Allegro appassionato; Berceuse; Blow, blow thou winter wind; Come to me in my dreams; A Dirge; E'en as lovely flower; Fair daffodils; Far, far from each other; Music when soft voices die; My pent-up tears oppress my brain; Pensiero; Tears, idle tears; The Violets blue; Where is it that our soul doth go?
See: B325, B420

D3. **Allegretto**

D3a. Pearl SHE 577. 1983.
Michael Ponder, viola; John Alley, piano.
In: The Early Bridge
Recorded June 28–29, 1982, Wigmore Hall, London.
"This record has been made with financial assistance from the Frank Bridge Trust."
With his Adoration; All things that we clasp; Allegro appassionato; Berceuse; Blow, blow thou winter wind; Come to me in my dreams; A Dirge; E'en as a lovely flower; Fair daffodils; Far, far from each other; Music when soft voices die; My pent-up tears oppress my brain; Pensiero; Tears, idle tears; The Violets blue; Where is it that our soul doth go?
See: B325, B420

D4. **Allegro appassionato**

D4a. His Master's Voice 7EP 7179. 45 rpm. mono.
Herbert Downes, viola; Gerald Moore, piano.

D4b. Musical Heritage Society MHS 7483 (cass: MHC 9483). 1987.
Previously released by CRD Records in 1985.
Tony Appel, viola; Peter Pettinger, piano.
In: Britten, Bridge and Clarke, music for viola and piano
With his Pensiero and works by Rebecca Clarke and Benjamin Britten.

D4c. Pearl SHE 577. 1983.
Michael Ponder, viola; John Alley, piano.
In: The Early Bridge
Recorded June 28–29, 1982, Wigmore Hall, London.

"This record has been made with financial assistance from the Frank Bridge Trust."
With his Adoration; All things that we clasp; Allegretto; Berceuse; Blow, blow thou winter wind; Come to me in my dreams; A Dirge; E'en as a lovely flower; Fair daffodils; Far, far from each other; Music when soft voices die; My pent-up tears oppress my brain; Pensiero; Tears, idle tears; The Violets blue; Where is it that our soul doth go?
See: B325, B420

D5. **Amaryllis**

D5a. Pearl SHE 586. 1985.
Peter Hanson, violin; Christopher Cox, piano.
Recorded in Wigmore Hall, London.
"Recorded with financial assistance from the Frank Bridge Trust, which acts as a source of information about all aspects of Bridge's music."
With his The Last invocation; Mantle of blue; Miniatures, sets 1-3; Norse legend; Souvenir; Thy hand in mine; 'Tis but a week; What shall I your true love tell?
See: B282, B287

D6. **Arabesque**

D6a. Continuum CCD 1016 (compact disc). 1990.
Peter Jacobs, piano.
In: Frank Bridge: Complete music for piano
"Recorded in association with the Frank Bridge Trust."
With his Capriccio no. 1 in A minor; Capriccio no. 2 in F-sharp minor; A Dedication; A Fairy tale; Gargoyle; Hidden fires; Three Improvisations; In autumn; Miniature pastorals, sets 1–2; A Sea idyll; Winter pastoral.

D7. **Autumn**

D7a. Pearl SHE 551. 1981.
Louis Halsey Singers.
In: A Frank Bridge spicilegium
Recorded in association with the Frank Bridge Trust.

With his The Bee; Divertimenti; Hilli-ho! Hilli-ho!; Love went a-riding; Music when soft voices die; O weary hearts; Two Pieces: Lament; So perverse; Strew no more red roses; Where she lies asleep.

D8. **The Bee**

D8a. Pearl SHE 551. 1981.
Louis Halsey Singers.
In: A Frank Bridge spicilegium
Recorded in association with the Frank Bridge Trust.
With his Autumn; Divertimenti; Hilli-ho! Hilli-ho!; Love went a-riding; Music when soft voices die; O weary hearts; Two Pieces: Lament; So perverse; Strew no more red roses; Where she lies asleep.

D8b. Pearl SHE 593. 1986.
Trinity College Choir; Richard Marlow, director.
Recorded January 10–11, 1986, Trinity College Chapel, Cambridge.
Recorded in association with the Frank Bridge Trust.
With his Evening primrose; Golden slumbers; The Graceful swaying wattle; Hilli-ho! Hilli-ho!; Lay a garland on my hearse; A Litany; O weary heart; Peter Piper; Sister, awake and works by Benjamin Britten.

D9. **Berceuse**

D9a. Pearl SHE 571. 1982.
Moray Welsh, violoncello; Roger Vignoles, piano.
In: British music for cello and piano
Recorded June 4, 1982, EMI Abbey Road Studios, London.
Recorded in association with the Frank Bridge Trust.
With his Cradle song; Elégie; Meditation; Mélodie; Morning song; Scherzo; Serenade and works by Sir Arnold Bax and Percy Grainger.
See: B234, B421

D10. **Berceuse for soprano and orchestra**

D10a. Parnote/Cameo Classics GOCLP 9020. 1929.
Sylvia Eaves, soprano; C. Kenney, piano.

D10b. Pearl SHE 577. 1983.
Patricia Wright, soprano; John Alley, piano.
In: The Early Bridge
Recorded June 28–29, 1982, Wigmore Hall, London.
"This record has been made with financial assistance from the Frank Bridge Trust."
With his Adoration; All things that we clasp; Allegro appassionato; Allegretto; Blow, blow thou winter wind; Come to me in my dreams; A Dirge; E'en as a lovely flower; Fair daffodils; Far, far from each other; Music when soft voices die; My pent-up tears oppress my brain; Pensiero; Tears, idle tears; The Violets blue; Where is it that our soul doth go?
See: B325, B420

D11. **Blow, blow thou winter wind**

D11a. Hyperion A66085. 1985.
Graham Trew, baritone; Roger Vignoles, piano.
In: Songs of England
Recorded June 24-25, 1981.
With his Journey's end; Love went a-riding and works by W. Denis Browne, Frederick Delius, C. Armstrong Gibbs, Patrick Hadley, Michael Head, C. Hubert H. Parry, Roger Quilter, Arthur Somervell, Sir Charles Villiers Stanford and Peter Warlock.
See: B195, B238, B360, B361

D11b. Pearl SHE 577. 1983.
Stephen Varcoe, baritone; Christopher Cox, piano.
In: The Early Bridge
Recorded June 28–29, 1982, Wigmore Hall, London.
"This record has been made with financial assistance from the Frank Bridge Trust."
With his Adoration; All things that we clasp; Allegretto; Allegro appassionato; Berceuse; Come to me in my dreams; A Dirge; E'en as a lovely flower; Fair daffodils; Far, far from each other; Pensiero; Tears, idle tears; Music when soft voices die; My pent-up tears oppress my brain; The Violets blue; Where is it that our soul doth go?
See: B325, B420

D12. **Blow out you bugles**

D12a. Pearl SHE 513–SHE 514. 2 discs. 1974.
David Johnston, tenor; Hank Shaw, trumpet; Jonathan Hinden, piano.
In: Songs and piano music
Recorded April 30, May 1, June 25, and July 25, 1973, Wigmore Hall, London.
Recorded in association with the Frank Bridge Trust.
With his Come to me in my dreams; Day after day; Dweller in my deathless dreams; Go not, happy day; The Hour glass; In autumn: Through the eaves; Journey's end; The Last invocation; Love went a-riding; Mantle of blue; Piano sonata; Three Poems: Solitude; So perverse; Strew no more red roses; 'Tis but a week; What shall I your true love tell?; Where she lies asleep; Winter pastoral.
See: B334

D13. **Canzonetta**

D13a. Pearl SHE 600 (cd: SHECD 9600). 1987.
Chelsea Opera Group Orchestra; Howard Williams, conductor.
In: Frank Bridge: Orchestral works
Recorded September 1986, CBS Studios, London.
"Recordings made with the financial assistance of the Frank Bridge Trust."
With his Elégie, Heart's ease; Morning song; Norse legend; Rosemary; Scherzetto; Threads; The Turtle's retort; Vignettes de danse.

D14. **Capriccio no. 1 in A minor**

D14a. Continuum CCD 1016 (compact disc). 1990.
Peter Jacobs, piano.
In: Frank Bridge: Complete music for piano
"Recorded in association with the Frank Bridge Trust."
With his Arabesque; Capriccio no. 2 in F-sharp minor; A Dedication; A Fairy tale; Gargoyle; Hidden fires; Three Improvisations; In autumn; Miniature pastorals, sets 1–2; A Sea idyll; Winter pastoral.

D15. **Capriccio no. 2 in F-sharp minor**

D15a. Columbia L 1473. acoustic recording. pre-1936.
William Murdoch, piano.

D15b. Continuum CCD 1016 (compact disc). 1990.
Peter Jacobs, piano.
In: Frank Bridge: Complete music for piano
"Recorded in association with the Frank Bridge Trust."
With his Arabesque; Capriccio no. 1 in A minor; Dedication; A Fairy tale; Gargoyle; Hidden fires; Three Improvisations; In autumn; Miniature pastorals, sets 1-2; A Sea idyll; Winter pastoral.

D16. **Four Characteristic pieces**

D16a. Unicorn RHS 359. 1978.
Eric Parkin, piano.
In: Eric Parkin plays piano music by Frank Bridge
Recorded April 5 and August 31, 1978, Bishopsgate Institute, London.
With his Piano sonata; Three Poems; Three Lyrics.
See: B414

D17. **The Christmas rose**

D17a. Pearl SHE 582 (cd: SHE CD 9582). 1983.
Wendy Eathorne, soprano; Eirian James, mezzo-soprano; Maldwyn Davies, tenor; Henry Herford, baritone; David Wilson-Johnson, bass-baritone; Chorus & Orchestra of the Chelsea Opera Group; Howard Williams, conductor.
Recorded September 15-16, 1983, EMI Abbey Road Studios, London.
Recorded in association with the Frank Bridge Trust.
See: B190, B397

D18. **Come to me in my dreams**

D18a. Conifer CFRA 120. 1984.
Elizabeth Harwood, soprano; John Constable, piano.
In: English song recital
Recorded December 6-7, 1983, St. Barnabas Church, North Finchley, London.

With his Goldenhair and works by Frederick Delius, Ralph Vaughan Williams, Sir Arnold Bax, Michael Head, George Lloyd, and Roger Quilter.

D18b. EMI EX290911-3 (cass: EX290911-5). 2 discs.
Kirsten Flagstad, soprano; Edwin McArthur, piano.
With his Love went a-riding; O that it were so.

D18c. Hyperion A66103. 1984.
Anne Dawson, mezzo-soprano; Roderick Barrand, piano.
In: A Recital of English songs
Recorded February 18–19, 1983 in association with the Finzi Trust.
With his Fair daffodils; Go not, happy day; Mantle of blue and works by Howard Ferguson, Gerald Finzi, and E. J. Moeran.
See: B235, B288

D18d. Parlophone RO 20554. 10 in.
Richard Tauber, tenor; Percy Kahn, piano.
With Ronald's Goodnight.

D18e. Pearl SHE 513–SHE 514. 2 discs. 1974.
Valerie Baulard, mezzo-soprano; Roger Vignoles, piano.
In: Songs and piano music
Recorded April 30, May 1, June 15, and July 15, 1973, Wigmore Hall, London.
Recorded in association with the Frank Bridge Trust.
With his Blow out you bugles; Day after day; Dweller in my deathless dreams; Go not, happy day; The Hour glass; In autumn: Through the eaves; Journey's end; The Last invocation; Love went a-riding; Mantle of blue; Piano sonata; Three Poems: Solitude; So perverse; Strew no more red roses; 'Tis but a week; Where she lies asleep; Winter pastoral; What shall I your true love tell?
See: B334

D18f. Pearl SHE 577. 1983.
Stephen Varcoe, baritone; Christopher Cox, piano.
In: The Early Bridge
Recorded June 28–29, 1982, Wigmore Hall, London.
"This record has been made with financial assistance from the Frank Bridge Trust."
With his Adoration; All things that we clasp; Allegretto; Allegro appassionato; Berceuse; Blow, blow thou winter wind; A Dirge;

E'en as a lovely flower; Fair daffodils; Far, far from each other; Music when soft voices die; My pent-up tears oppress my brain; Pensiero; Tears, idle tears; The Violets blue; Where is it that our soul doth go?

See: B325, B420

D18g. Victor 10–1088 (in set: MO–966). 10 in.
Camden CAL 244. mono.
John Charles Thomas, bass; Carol Hollister, piano.
In: Concert favorites
With F. Paolo Tosti's Mattinata.

D19. **Cradle song**

D19a. Parlophone E 11445. 78 rpm. mono.
Henri Temianka, violin; and piano.
With his Three Dances: Moto perpetuo and Bach's Siciliana from Sonata no. 4.

D19b. Pearl SHE 571. 1982.
Moray Welsh, violoncello; Roger Vignoles, piano.
In: British music for cello and piano
Recorded June 4, 1982, EMI Abbey Road Studios, London.
Recorded in association with the Frank Bridge Trust.
With his Berceuse; Elégie; Meditation; Mélodie; Morning song; Scherzo; Serenade and works by Sir Arnold Bax and Percy Grainger.
See: B234, B421

D20. **Dance poem**

D20a. Lyrita SRCS.114. 1979.
London Philharmonic Orchestra; Nicholas Braithwaite, conductor.

Recorded in association with the RVW & Frank Bridge Trusts.
With his Dance rhapsody; Rebus.
See: B335, B411

D21. **Dance rhapsody**

D21a. Lyrita SRCS.114. 1979.
London Philharmonic Orchestra; Nicholas Braithwaite, conductor.
Recorded in association with the RVW & Frank Bridge Trusts.

With his Dance poem; Rebus.
See: B335, B411

D22. **Three Dances - no. 3: Moto perpetuo**

D22a. Parlophone E 11445. 78 rpm. mono.
Henri Temianka, violin; and piano.
With his Cradle song and Bach's Siciliana from Sonata no. 4.

D23. **Day after day**

D23a. Pearl SHE 513–SHE 514. 2 discs. 1974.
Valerie Baulard, mezzo-soprano; Jonathan Hinden, piano.
In: Songs and piano music
Recorded April 30, May 1, June 25, and July 25, 1973, Wigmore Hall, London.
Recorded in association with the Frank Bridge Trust.
With his Blow out you bugles; Come to me in my dreams; Dweller in my deathless dreams; Go not, happy day; The Hour glass; In autumn: Through the eaves; Journey's end; The Last invocation; Love went a-riding; Mantle of blue; Piano sonata; Three Poems: Solitude; So perverse; Strew no more red roses; 'Tis but a week; What shall I your true love tell?; Where she lies asleep; Winter pastoral.
See: B334

D23b. Pearl SHE 568. 1982.
Sarah Walker, mezzo-soprano; Chelsea Opera Group Orchestra; Howard Williams, conductor.
Recorded January 17–18, 1982, EMI Abbey Road Studios, London.
"Recording made with financial assistance from the Frank Bridge Trust."
With his Dweller in my deathless dreams; Isabella; A Prayer; Speak to me my love.
See: B186, B406, B421

D24. **A Dedication**

D24a. Continuum CCD 1016 (compact disc). 1990.
Peter Jacobs, piano.
In: Frank Bridge: Complete music for piano
"Recorded in association with the Frank Bridge Trust."

With his Arabesque; Capriccio no. 1 in A minor; Capriccio no. 2 in F-sharp minor; A Fairy tale; Gargoyle; Hidden fires; Three Improvisations; In autumn; A Sea idyll; Miniature pastorals, sets 1–2; Winter pastoral.

D25. **A Dirge**

D25a. Pearl SHE 577. 1983.
Stephen Varcoe, baritone; Christopher Cox, piano.
In: The Early Bridge
Recorded June 28–29, 1982, Wigmore Hall, London.
"This record has been made with financial assistance from the Frank Bridge Trust."
With his Adoration; All things that we clasp; Allegretto; Allegro appassionato; Berceuse; Blow, blow thou winter wind; Come to me in my dreams; E'en as a lovely flower; Fair daffodils; Far, far from each other; Music when soft voices die; My pent-up tears oppress my brain; Pensiero; Tears, idle tears; The Violets blue; Where is it that our soul doth go?
See: B325, B420

D26. **Divertimenti**

D26a. Pearl SHE 551. 1981.
Phoenix Wind Ensemble.
In: A Frank Bridge spicilegium
Recorded in association with the Frank Bridge Trust.
With his Autumn; The Bee; Hilli-ho! Hilli-ho!; Love went a-riding; Music when soft voices die; O weary hearts; Two Pieces: Lament; So perverse; Strew no more red roses; Where she lies asleep.

D27. **Dweller in my deathless dreams**

D27a. Pearl SHE 513–SHE 514. 2 discs. 1974.
David Johnston, tenor; Jonathan Hinden, piano.
In: Songs and piano music
Recorded April 30, May 1, June 25, and July 25, 1973, Wigmore Hall, London.
Recorded in association with the Frank Bridge Trust.
With his Blow out you bugles; Come to me in my dreams; Day after day; Go not, happy day; The Hour glass; In autumn: Through the eaves; Journey's end; The Last invocation; Love

went a-riding; Mantle of blue; Piano sonata; Three Poems: Solitude; So perverse; Strew no more red roses; 'Tis but a week; What shall I your true love tell?; Where she lies asleep; Winter pastoral.
See: B334

D27b. Pearl SHE 568. 1982.
Sarah Walker, mezzo-soprano; Chelsea Opera Group Orchestra; Howard Williams, conductor.
Recorded January 17–18, 1982, EMI Abbey Road Studios, London.
"Recording made with financial assistance from the Frank Bridge Trust."
With his Day after day; Isabella; A Prayer; Speak to me my love.
See: B186, B406, B421

D28. **E'en as a lovely flower**

D28a. Decca LXT 6126. mono.
London 5889. mono.
Maggie Teyte, soprano; Rita MacKay, piano.
In: Maggie Teyte recital
Side 1: derived from studio recordings of 1932; Side 2: derived from BBC broadcast of 1937.
With works by Johannes Brahms, Charles Cuvillier, Frederick Delius, Anton Dvořák, Gabriel Fauré, Reynaldo Gibson, Hahn, Andre Messager, Jacques Offenbach, Peel, Roger Quilter, Bernhard Romberg, Franz Schumann, and Carl Maria von Weber.
See: B188, B245, B290, B359, B364, B366

D28b. Pearl SHE 577. 1983.
Stephen Varcoe, baritone; Christopher Cox, piano.
In: The Early Bridge
Recorded June 28–29, 1982, Wigmore Hall, London.
"This record has been made with financial assistance from the Frank Bridge Trust."
With his Adoration; All things that we clasp; Allegretto; Allegro appassionato; Berceuse; Blow, blow thou winter wind; Come to me in my dreams; A Dirge; Fair daffodils; Far, far from each other; Music when soft voices die; My pent-up tears oppress my brain; Pensiero; Tears, idle tears; The Violets blue; Where is it that our soul doth go?
See: B325, B420

D29. **Elégie**

D29a. ASV ACA 1001 (cass: ZC ACA 1001). 1981.
Musicmasters MM 20026. 1981.
Julian Lloyd Webber, violoncello; John McCabe, piano.
In: Julian Lloyd Webber plays Britten, Ireland and Bridge
"Recorded by kind permission of the Bridge Trust."
With works by Benjamin Britten and John Ireland.
See: B158, B202, B233

D29b. Pearl SHE 571. 1982.
Moray Welsh, violoncello; Roger Vignoles, piano.
In: British music for cello and piano
Recorded June 4, 1982, EMI Abbey Road Studios, London.
Recorded in association with the Frank Bridge Trust.
With his Berceuse; Cradle song; Meditation; Mélodie; Morning song; Scherzo; Serenade and works by Sir Arnold Bax and Percy Grainger.
See: B234, B421

D29c. Pearl SHE 600 (cd: SHECD 9600). 1987.
Lowri Blake, violoncello; Chelsea Opera Group Orchestra; Howard Williams, conductor.
In: Frank Bridge: Orchestral Works
Recorded September 1986, CBS Studios, London.
"Recordings made with the financial assistance of the Frank Bridge Trust."
With his Canzonetta; Heart's ease; Morning song; Norse legend; Rosemary; Scherzetto; Threads; The Turtle's retort; Vignettes de danse.

D30. **Enter spring**

D30a. EMI/HMV ASD 3190. quad. 1976.
Reissued on EMI/HMV ED290868-1 (cass: ED290868-4). 1986.
Royal Liverpool Philharmonic Orchestra; Sir Charles Groves, conductor.
Recorded in Philharmonic Hall, Liverpool.
With his Lament; Two Old English songs: Cherry ripe; The Sea; Summer.
See: B157, B193, B194, B415

D30b. Pearl SHE 601 (cd: SHECD 9601). 1987.
Cologne Radio Symphony Orchestra; John Carewe, conductor.

Recorded in association with the Frank Bridge Trust.
With his Oration, concerto elegiaco.

D31. **Evening primrose**

D31a. Pearl SHE 593. 1986.
David Mattinson, baritone; Charles Matthews, piano.
Recorded January 10–11, 1986, Trinity College Chapel, Cambridge.
Recorded in association with the Frank Bridge Trust.
With his The Bee; Golden slumbers; The Graceful swaying wattle; Hilli-ho! Hilli-ho!; Lay a garland on my hearse; A Litany; O weary heart; Peter Piper; Sister, awake and works by Benjamin Britten.

D32. **Fair daffodils**

D32a. Hyperion A66103. 1984.
Anne Dawson, mezzo-soprano; Roderick Barrand, piano.
In: A Recital of English songs
Recorded February 18–19, 1983 in association with the Finzi Trust.
With his Come to me in my dreams; Go not, happy day; Mantle of blue and works by Howard Ferguson, Gerald Finzi, and E. J. Moeran.
See: B235, B288

D32b. Pearl SHE 577. 1983.
Stephen Varcoe, baritone; Christopher Cox, piano.
In: The Early Bridge
Recorded June 28–29, 1982, Wigmore Hall, London.
"This record has been made with financial assistance from the Frank Bridge Trust."
With his Adoration; All things that we clasp; Allegretto; Allegro appassionato; Berceuse; Blow, blow thou winter wind; Come to me in my dreams; A Dirge; E'en as a lovely flower; Far, far from each other; Music when soft voices die; My pent-up tears oppress my brain; Pensiero; Tears, idle tears; The Violets blue; Where is it that our soul doth go?
See: B325, B420

D33. **A Fairy tale**

D33a. Continuum CCD 1016 (compact disc). 1990.
Peter Jacobs, piano.
In: Frank Bridge: Complete music for piano
"Recorded in association with the Frank Bridge Trust."
With his Arabesque; Capriccio no. 1 in A minor; Capriccio no. 2 in F-sharp minor; A Dedication; Gargoyle; Hidden fires; Three Improvisations; In autumn; Miniature pastorals, sets 1–2; A Sea idyll; Winter pastoral.

D34. **Far, far from each other**

D34a. Pearl SHE 577. 1983.
Stephen Varcoe, baritone; Christopher Cox, piano.
In: The Early Bridge
Recorded June 28–29, 1982, Wigmore Hall, London.
"This record has been made with financial assistance from the Frank Bridge Trust."
With his Adoration; All things that we clasp; Allegretto; Allegro appassionato; Berceuse; Blow, blow thou winter wind; Come to me in my dreams; A Dirge; E'en as a lovely flower; Fair daffodils; Music when soft voices die; My pent-up tears oppress my brain; Pensiero; Tears, idle tears; The Violets blue; Where is it that our soul doth go?
See: B325, B420

D35. **Gargoyle**

D35a. Continuum CCD 1016 (compact disc). 1990.
Peter Jacobs, piano.
In: Frank Bridge: Complete music for piano
"Recorded in association with the Frank Bridge Trust."
With his Arabesque; Capriccio no. 1 in A minor; Capriccio no. 2 in F-sharp minor; A Dedication; A Fairy tale; Hidden fires; Three Improvisations; In autumn; Miniature pastorals, sets 1–2; A Sea idyll; Winter pastoral.

D36. **Go not, happy day**

D36a. Ace of Clubs ACL 310. mono. 1968.
Richmond R 23187. mono. 1968.
Decca LW 5353. mono. 10 in.

Previously issued on Decca LX 3133, London LS 1032. 1954.
Kathleen Ferrier, contralto; Frederick Stone, piano.
In: Kathleen Ferrier
From a Broadcast performance of June 5, 1952.
With works by George Frideric Handel, Henry Purcell, C. Hubert H. Parry, Sir Charles Villiers Stanford, Ralph Vaughan Williams, Benjamin Britten, Peter Warlock, and Hughes.
See: B228

D36b. Cantilena 6237.
John Stratton, baritone; Avery Byram, piano.

D36c. Columbia D 1431. acoustic recording. 10 in.
Hubert Eisdell, tenor; and piano.

D36d. Decca 'Eclipse' ECS 545. mono. 1970.
London LL 1532. mono. 1970.
London LL 5324. mono. 1970.
Previously issued on Decca LW 5241. mono. 10 in. 1956.
Peter Pears, tenor; Benjamin Britten, piano.
In: An English song recital
With his Love went a-riding and works by Sir Lennox Berkeley, Benjamin Britten, George Butterworth, John Dowland, Ernest Ford, Gustav Holst, John Ireland, E. J. Moeran, Thomas Morley, Arthur Oldham, Philip Rosseter, and Peter Warlock.
See: B168, B171, B177

D36e. Decca LW 5241. mono. 10 in. 1956.
Reissued on Decca 'Eclipse' ECS 545, London LL 1532, and London LL 5324. 1970.
Peter Pears, tenor; Benjamin Britten, piano.
With his Love went a-riding and works by Berkeley, Benjamin Britten, and George Butterworth.
See: B336

D36f. Decca LX 3133. mono. 10 in. 1954.
London LS 1032. 10 in. 1954.
Reissued on Ace of Clubs ACL 310, Richmond R 23187, and Decca LW 5353. mono. 10 in. 1968.
Kathleen Ferrier, contralto; Frederick Stone, piano.
From a broadcast recital from June 5, 1952.
With works by Sir C. Hubert H. Parry, Sir Charles Villiers Stanford, Ralph Vaughan Williams, Peter Warlock, Benjamin Britten and Hughes.
See: B200, B240, B248, B355, B358, B365, B384

D36g. Decca PA 172: AFK 1-7 (cass: KCSP 172). 7 discs. 1963-1971.
Kathleen Ferrier, contralto; Frederick Stone, piano.
In: Kathleen Ferrier
From a collection of performances recorded between 1949 and 1952, including the broadcast performance of June 5, 1952.
With works by Roger Quilter, Sir Charles Villiers Stanford, Peter Warlock, Henry Purcell, George Frideric Handel, Johannes Brahms, Robert Schumann, J. S. Bach, C. Hubert H. Parry, Ralph Vaughan Williams, Hugo Wolf, Ludvig Irgens Jenson, Christoph Willibald Ritter von Gluck, Felix Mendelssohn-Bartholdy, Franz Schubert, and Gustav Mahler.

D36h. His Master's Voice E 234. acoustic recording. 10 in.
Carmen Hill, mezzo-soprano; and piano.

D36i. Hyperion A66103. 1984.
Anne Dawson, mezzo-soprano; Roderick Barrand, piano.
In: A Recital of English songs
Recorded February 18–19, 1983 in association with the Finzi Trust.
With his Come to me in my dreams; Fair daffodils; Mantle of blue and works by Howard Ferguson, Gerald Finzi, and E. J. Moeran.
See: B235, B288

D36j. Pearl SHE 513–SHE 514. 2 discs. 1974.
Valerie Baulard, mezzo-soprano; Roger Vignoles, piano.
In: Songs and piano music
Recorded April 30, May 1, June 25, and July 25, 1973, Wigmore Hall, London.
Recorded in association with the Frank Bridge Trust.
With his Blow out you bugles; Come to me in my dreams; Day after day; Dweller in my deathless dreams; The Hour glass; In autumn: Through the eaves; Journey's end; The Last invocation; Love went a-riding; Mantle of blue; Piano sonata; Three Poems: Solitude; So perverse; Strew no more red roses; 'Tis but a week; What shall I your true love tell?; Where she lies asleep; Winter pastoral.
See: B334

D36k. Vocalion X 9195. acoustic recording. 10 in.
Frank Titterton, tenor; and piano.

D37. **Golden slumbers**

D37a. Pearl SHE 593. 1986.
Trinity College Choir; Richard Marlow, director.
Recorded January 10–11, 1986, Trinity College Chapel, Cambridge.
Recorded in association with the Frank Bridge Trust.
With his The Bee; Evening primrose; The Graceful swaying wattle; Hilli-ho! Hilli-ho!; Lay a garland on my hearse; A Litany; O weary heart; Peter Piper; Sister, awake; and works by Benjamin Britten.

D38. **Goldenhair**

D38a. Argo ZK 28. 2 discs. 1964.
Argo RG 418. mono. 1964.
Argo ZRG 5418. 1964.
Peter Pears, tenor; Benjamin Britten, piano.
In: Twentieth-century English songs
Recorded 1964 in association with the British Council.
With his Journey's end; So perverse; 'Tis but a week; When you are old and works by John Ireland, Richard Rodney Bennett, and Priaulx Rainer.
See: B210, B211, B249, B323, B389, B399

D38b. Conifer CFRA 120. 1984.
Elizabeth Harwood, soprano; John Constable, piano.
In: English song recital
Recorded December 6–7, 1983, St. Barnabas Church, North Finchley, London.
With his Come to me in my dreams and works by Frederick Delius, Ralph Vaughan Williams, Sir Arnold Bax, Michael Head, George Lloyd, and Roger Quilter.

D39. **Gondoliera**

D39a. His Master's Voice C 1057. acoustic recording. pre-1936.
Marjorie Hayward, violin; and piano.

D40. **The Graceful swaying wattle**

D40a. His Master's Voice C 3527.
County Grammar School Choir; and piano.
With works by Peter Warlock and arrangements by Anatol Liadov.

D40b. Pearl SHE 593. 1986.
Trinity College Choir; Charles Matthews, piano; Richard Marlow, director.
Recorded January 10–11, 1986, Trinity College Chapel, Cambridge.
Recorded in association with the Frank Bridge Trust.
With his The Bee; Evening primrose; Golden slumbers; Hilli-ho! Hilli-ho!; Lay a garland on my hearse; A Litany; O weary heart; Peter Piper; Sister, awake.

D41. **Heart's ease**

D41a. Pearl SHE 600 (cd: SHECD 9600). 1987.
Chelsea Opera Group Orchestra; Howard Williams, conductor.
In: Frank Bridge: Orchestral works
Recorded September 1986, CBS Studios, London.
"Recordings made with the financial assistance of the Frank Bridge Trust."
With his Canzonetta; Elégie; Morning song; Norse legend; Rosemary; Scherzetto; Threads; The Turtle's retort; Vignettes de danse.

D42. **Hidden fires**

D42a. Continuum CCD 1016 (compact disc). 1990.
Peter Jacobs, piano.
In: Frank Bridge: Complete music for piano
"Recorded in association with the Frank Bridge Trust."
With his Arabesque; Capriccio no. 1 in A minor; Capriccio no. 2 in F-sharp minor; A Dedication; A Fairy tale; Gargoyle; Three Improvisations; In autumn; Miniature pastorals, sets 1–2; A Sea idyll; Winter pastoral.

D43. **Hilli-ho! Hilli-ho!**

D43a. Pearl SHE 551. 1981.
Louis Halsey Singers.

In: A Frank Bridge spicilegium
Recorded in association with the Frank Bridge Trust.
With his Autumn; The Bee; Divertimenti; Love went a-riding; Music when soft voices die; O weary hearts; Two Pieces: Lament; So perverse; Strew no more red roses; Where she lies asleep.

D43b. Pearl SHE 593. 1986.
Trinity College Choir; Richard Marlow, director.
Recorded January 10–11, 1986, Trinity College Chapel, Cambridge.
Recorded in association with the Frank Bridge Trust.
With his The Bee; Evening primrose; Golden slumbers; The Graceful swaying wattle; Lay a garland on my hearse; A Litany; O weary heart; Peter Piper; Sister, awake; and works by Benjamin Britten.

D44. **The Hour glass**

D44a. Pearl SHE 513–SHE 514. 2 discs. 1974.
Peter Wallfisch, piano.
In: Songs and piano music
Recorded April 30, May 1, June 25, and July 25, 1973, Wigmore Hall, London.
Recorded in association with the Frank Bridge Trust.
With his Blow out you bugles; Come to me in my dreams; Day after day; Dweller in my deathless dreams; Go not, happy day; In autumn: Through the eaves; Journey's end; The Last invocation; Love went a-riding; Mantle of blue; Piano sonata; Three Poems: Solitude; So perverse; Strew no more red roses; 'Tis but a week; What shall I your true love tell?; Where she lies asleep; Winter pastoral.
See: B334

D45. **The Hour glass – no. 2: The Dew fairy**

D45a. Alpha DB 148 C. 197-?
John Clegg, piano.
In: John Clegg interprete au piano
With works by John Ireland, Sir Arnold Bax, E. J. Moeran, Sir Lennox Berkeley, and Alan Rawsthorne.

D46. **Three Idylls**

D46a. Columbia L 1704–L 1705. 78 rpm. mono. pre–1931.
American Columbia 50217 D–50218 D. 78 rpm. mono. pre–1931.
London Quartet.
Recorded October–November 1925.

D46b. Decca SDD 497. 1977.
London STS 15439. 1977.
Gabrieli String Quartet.
In: Music of Britten and Bridge
Recorded February 1976 at the Snape Maltings.
With his Novelletten and works by Benjamin Britten.
See: B174, B216, B225, B333, B407

D46c. His Master's Voice D 915–D 916. acoustic recording.
Virtuoso Quartet.

D47. **Three Idylls - movements 1 and 3**

D47a. His Master's Voice D 479. acoustic recording.
Philharmonic Quartet.

D48. **Three Idylls - movements 2 and 3**

D48a. Vocalion R 6110. acoustic recording. 10 in.
London Quartet.

D49. **Three Improvisations**

D49a. Continuum CCD 1016 (compact disc). 1990.
Peter Jacobs, piano.
In: Frank Bridge: Complete music for piano
"Recorded in association with the Frank Bridge Trust."
With his Arabesque; Capriccio no. 1 in A minor; Capriccio no. 2 in F-sharp minor; A Dedication; A Fairy tale; Gargoyle; Hidden fires; In autumn; Miniature pastorals, sets 1–2; A Sea idyll; Winter pastoral.

D50. **In autumn**

D50a. Continuum CCD 1016 (compact disc). 1990.
Peter Jacobs, piano.
In: Frank Bridge: Complete music for piano
"Recorded in association with the Frank Bridge Trust."
With his Arabesque; Capriccio no. 1 in A minor; Capriccio no. 2 in F-sharp minor; A Dedication; A Fairy tale; Gargoyle; Hidden fires; Three Improvisations; Miniature pastorals, sets 1–2; A Sea idyll; Winter pastoral.

D51. **In autumn - no. 2: Through the eaves**

D51a. Pearl SHE 513–SHE 514. 2 discs. 1974.
Peter Wallfisch, piano.
In: Songs and piano music
Recorded April 30, May 1, June 25, and July 25, 1973, Wigmore Hall, London.
Recorded in association with the Frank Bridge Trust.
With his Blow out you bugles; Come to me in my dreams; Day after day; Dweller in my deathless dreams; Go not, happy day; The Hour glass; Journey's end; The Last invocation; Love went a-riding; Mantle of blue; Piano sonata; Three Poems: Solitude; So perverse; Strew no more red roses; 'Tis but a week; What shall I your true love tell?; Where she lies asleep; Winter pastoral.
See: B334

D52. **An Irish melody**

D52a. Chandos ABRD 1073 (cass: ABTD 1073; cd: CHAN 8426). 1983.
Also issued on Chandos DBRD 4001 (cass: DBTD 4001). 4 discs. 1983.
Delmé String Quartet.
In: Music for string quartet
Recorded March 26 and 27, 1982, Church of St. George the Martyr, Bloomsbury, London.
"Recorded with financial assistance from the Frank Bridge Trust."
With his Two Old English songs; Sir Roger de Coverley; String quartet no. 2 in G minor.
See: B230, B420

D52b. Chandos DBRD 4001 (cass: DBTD 4001). 4 discs. 1983.
Also issued on Chandos ABRD 1073 (cass: ABTD 1073; cd: CHAN 8426). 1983.
Delmé String Quartet.
In: Music for a summer's day
Recorded March and June 1982, Church of St. George the Martyr, Bloomsbury, London.
With his Two Old English songs; Sir Roger de Coverley; String quartet no. 2 in G minor and works by Sir Arnold Bax, Ralph Vaughan Williams, Arthur Bliss, John Ireland, Geoffrey Bush, Eugene Goossens, E. J. Moeran, Cyril Scott, Alan Bush, Benjamin Britten, and Alan Rawsthorne.

D52c. Columbia L 1019. acoustic recording.
London Quartet.

D52d. Columbia L 1716. 78 rpm. mono.
London Quartet.
Recorded October–November 1925.

D52e. His Master's Voice C 1470. 78 rpm. mono.
Virtuoso Quartet.
With works by Joseph Haydn.

D52f. Victor/Bluebird LBC 1086. mono.
American Art Quartet.
With works by Percy Grainger, Peter Ilich Tchaikovsky, and Felix Mendelssohn-Bartoldy.

D53. **Isabella**

D53a. Pearl SHE 568. 1982.
Prospect Music Group; Howard Williams, conductor.
Recorded January 17–18, 1982, EMI Abbey Road Studios, London.
"Recording made with financial assistance from the Frank Bridge Trust."
With his Day after day; Dweller in my deathless dreams; A Prayer; Speak to me my love.
See: B186, B406, B421

D54. **Isobel**

D54a. His Master's Voice E 361. acoustic recording. 10 in.
Leila Megane, mezzo-soprano; and piano.

D54b. Parlophone R 2015. 78 rpm. mono. 10 in.
Vladimir Rosing, tenor; Myers Foggin, piano.
With Peter Ilich Tchaikovsky's Don Juan's serenade.

D55. **Journey's end**

D55a. Argo ZK 28. 2 discs. 1964.
Argo RG 418. mono. 1964.
Argo ZRG 5418. 1964.
Peter Pears, tenor; Benjamin Britten, piano.
In: Twentieth-century English songs
Recorded 1964 in association with the British Council.
With his Goldenhair; So perverse; 'Tis but a week; When you are old and works by John Ireland, Richard Rodney Bennett, and Priaulx Rainer.
See: B210, B211, B249, B323, B389, B399

D55b. Hyperion A66085. 1984.
Graham Trew, baritone; Roger Vignoles, piano.
In: Songs of England
Recorded June 24–25, 1981.
With his Blow, blow thou winter wind; Love went a-riding and songs by W. Denis Browne, Frederick Delius, C. Armstrong Gibbs, Patrick Hadley, Michael Head, C. Hubert H. Parry, Roger Quilter, Arthur Somervell, Sir Charles Villiers Stanford, and Peter Warlock.
See: B195, B238, B360, B361

D55c. Pearl SHE 513–SHE 514. 2 discs. 1974.
Valerie Baulard, mezzo-soprano; Roger Vignoles, piano.
In: Songs and piano music
Recorded April 30, May 1, June 25, and July 25, 1973, Wigmore Hall, London.
Recorded in association with the Frank Bridge Trust.
With his Blow out you bugles; Come to me in my dreams; Day after day; Dweller in my deathless dreams; Go not, happy day; The Hour glass; In autumn: Through the eaves; The Last invocation; Love went a-riding; Mantle of blue; Piano sonata; Three Poems: Solitude; So perverse; Strew no more red roses;

'Tis but a week; What shall I your true love tell?; Where she lies asleep; Winter pastoral.
See: B334

D56. **Lament**

D56a. EMI/HMV ASD 3190. quad. 1976.
Reissued on EMI/HMV ED290868-1 (cass: ED290868-4). 1986.
Royal Liverpool Philharmonic Orchestra; Sir Charles Groves, conductor.
Recorded in Philharmonic Hall, Liverpool.
With his Enter Spring; Two Old English songs: Cherry Ripe; The Sea; Summer.
See: B157, B193, B194, B415

D56b. Lyrita SRCS.73. 1978.
HNH Records HNH 4078. 1978.
London Philharmonic Orchestra; Sir Adrian Boult, conductor.
With his Two Old English songs; Rosemary; Sir Roger de Coverley; Suite.
See: B170, B214, B243, B410

D57. **The Last invocation**

D57a. Pearl SHE 513–SHE 514. 2 discs. 1974.
Valerie Baulard, mezzo-soprano; Jonathan Hinden, piano.
In: Songs and piano music
Recorded April 30, May 1, June 25, and July 25, 1973, Wigmore Hall, London.
Recorded in association with the Frank Bridge Trust.
With his Blow out you bugles; Day after day; Dweller in my deathless dreams; Go not, happy day; The Hour glass; In autumn: Through the eaves; Journey's end; Love went a-riding; Mantle of blue; Piano sonata; Three Poems: Solitude; So perverse; Strew no more red roses; 'Tis but a week; What shall I your true love tell?; Where she lies asleep; Winter pastoral.
See: B334

D57b. Pearl SHE 586. 1985.
Patricia Wright, soprano; Christopher Cox, piano.
Recorded in Wigmore Hall, London.
"Recorded with financial assistance from the Frank Bridge Trust, which acts as a source of information about all aspects of Bridge's music."

With his Amaryllis; Mantle of blue; Miniatures, sets 1-3; Norse legend; Souvenir; Thy hand in mine; 'Tis but a week; What shall I your true love tell?
See: B282, B287

D58. **Lay a garland on my hearse**

D58a. Pearl SHE 593. 1986.
Trinity College Choir; Charles Matthews, piano; Richard Marlow, director.
Recorded January 10–11, 1986, Trinity College Chapel, Cambridge.
Recorded in association with the Frank Bridge Trust.
With his The Bee; Evening primrose; Golden slumbers; The Graceful swaying wattle; Hilli-ho! Hilli-ho!; A Litany; O weary heart; Peter Piper; Sister, awake and works by Benjamin Britten.

D59. **Lento (In memoriam C.H.H.P.)**

D59a. Pearl SHE 545. 1980.
Stuart Campbell, organ.
In: The Organ music of Frank Bridge
Recorded in Memorial Chapel, University of Glasgow.
Recorded in association with the Frank Bridge Trust.
With his Organ pieces, bks. 1–2; Three Pieces; Three Pieces (1939).
See: B201

D60. **A Litany**

D60a. Pearl SHE 593. 1986.
Trinity College Choir; Richard Marlow, director.
Recorded January 10–11, 1986, Trinity College Chapel, Cambridge.
Recorded in association with the Frank Bridge Trust.
With his The Bee; Evening primrose; Golden slumbers; The Graceful swaying wattle; Hilli-ho! Hilli-ho!; Lay a garland on my hearse; O weary heart; Peter Piper; Sister, awake and works by Benjamin Britten.

D61. **Love went a-riding**

D61a. Beltona 787. 78 rpm. mono. 10 in. pre-1927.
Ethel Kemish, soprano; and piano.

D61b. Columbia 17242 D. 78 rpm. mono. 10 in.
Charles Kullman, tenor; Fritz Kitzinger, piano.
With Sergei Rachmaninoff's In the silence of the secret night.

D61c. Columbia 3660. acoustic recording. 10 in.
William Heseltine, tenor; and piano.

D61d. Columbia DB 2083. 78 rpm. mono. 10 in.
Henry Wendon, tenor; Gerald Moore, piano.
With Samuel Coleridge-Taylor's Elinore.

D61e. Decca F 1648 (in set: M 77). 78 rpm. mono. 10 in.
Frank Titterton, tenor; and piano.
With O'Hara's There is no death.

D61f. Decca LW 5241. mono. 10 in. 1956.
Reissued on Decca 'Eclipse' ECS 545. mono., London LL 1532, and London LL 5324. 1970.
Peter Pears, tenor; Benjamin Britten, piano.
With his Go not, happy day and works by Sir Lennox Berkeley, Benjamin Britten, and George Butterworth.
See: B336

D61g. Decca 'Eclipse' ECS 545. mono. 1970.
London LL 1532. mono.
London LL 5324. mono.
Previously issued on Decca LW 5241. mono. 10 in. 1956.
Peter Pears, tenor; Benjamin Britten, piano.
In: An English song recital
With his Go not, happy day and works by Sir Lennox Berkeley, Benjamin Britten, George Butterworth, John Dowland, Ernest Ford, Gustav Holst, John Ireland, E. J. Moeran, Thomas Morley, Arthur Oldham, Philip Rosseter, and Peter Warlock.
See: B168, B171, B177

D61h. Delos D/CD 3029 (compact disc). 1988.
Arleen Auger, soprano; Dalton Baldwin, piano.
In: Love songs
Recorded March 7–8, 1988, First Congregational Church, Los Angeles, California.

With works by Aaron Copland, Jayme Ovalle, Richard Strauss, Joseph Marx, Francis Poulenc, Pietro Cimara, Roger Quilter, Oscar Straus, Robert Schumann, Gustav Mahler, Joaquin Turina, Edouard Lippe, Noel Coward, Charles Gounod, Franz Schubert, Stephen Foster, Stefano Donaudy, Benjamin Britten, and Frederick Loewe.

D61i. EMI EX290911-3 (cass: EX290911-5). 2 discs.
Kirsten Flagstad, mezzo-soprano; Edwin McArthur, piano.
Recorded in 1917.
With his Come to me in my dreams; O that it were so.

D61j. Golden Age of Opera EJS 338. mono. 1955.
Kirsten Flagstad, soprano; and piano.

D61k. Golden Age of Opera EJS 402. 78 rpm. mono. 10 in.
Kirsten Flagstad, soprano; and piano.

D61l. His Master's Voice ALP 2068. mono.
His Master's Voice ASD 616.
Joan Hammond, soprano; Ivor Newton, piano.

D61m. His Master's Voice B 2756. acoustic recording. 10 in.
Browning Mummery, bass; and piano.

D61n. His Master's Voice DA 1588. 78 rpm. mono. 10 in.
Kirsten Flagstad, soprano; Edwin McArthur, piano.
With James H. Rogers' At parting.

D61o. His Master's Voice E 251. acoustic recording. 10 in.
Olga Haley, mezzo-soprano; and piano.

D61p. His Master's Voice E 414. 78 rpm. mono. 10 in.
Tudor Davies, tenor; and piano.

D61q. His Master's Voice HQM 1114. acoustic recording.
Columbia L 1325. acoustic recording. 10 in.
Gervase Elwes, tenor; and piano.

D61r. Hyperion A66085. 1984.
Graham Trew, baritone, Roger Vignoles, piano.
In: Songs of England
Recorded June 24-25, 1981.
With his Blow, blow thou winter wind; Journey's end and works by W. Denis Browne, Frederic Delius, C. Armstrong Gibbs,

Patrick Hadley, Michael Head, C. Hubert H. Parry, Roger Quilter, Arthur Somervell, Sir Charles Villiers Stanford, and Peter Warlock.
See: B195, B238, B360, B361

D61s. Parnote/Sunday Opera SY03. mono.
Browning Mummery, bass; and piano.
With works by Michael W. Balfe, Keel, Ernest Ford, Franz Schumann, F. Paolo Tosti, and Sanderson.

D61t. Pearl SHE 513–SHE 514. 2 discs. 1974.
David Johnston, tenor; Jonathan Hinden, piano.
In: Songs and piano music
Recorded April 30, May 1, June 25, and July 25, 1973, Wigmore Hall, London.
Recorded in association with the Frank Bridge Trust.
With his Blow out you bugles; Come to me in my dreams; Day after day; Dweller in my deathless dreams; Go not, happy day; The Hour glass; In autumn: Through the eaves; Journey's end; The Last invocation; Mantle of blue; Piano sonata; Three Poems: Solitude; So perverse; Strew no more red roses; 'Tis but a week; What shall I your true love tell?; Where she lies asleep; Winter pastoral.
See: B334

D61u. Pearl SHE 551. 1981.
David Johnston, tenor; Jonathan Hinden, piano.
In: A Frank Bridge spicilegium
Recorded in association with the Frank Bridge Trust.
With his Autumn; The Bee; Divertimenti; Hilli-ho! Hilli-ho!; Music when soft voices die; O weary hearts; Two Pieces: Lament; So perverse; Strew no more red roses; Where she lies asleep.

D61v. United Artists UAL 3477. mono. 1966.
United Artists UAS 6477. 1966.
Jan Peerce, tenor; and piano.
In: Concert in Paris
With works by Alessandro Stradella, Francesco Durante, Sir Henry R. Bishop, Emile Paladilhe, Felix Fourdrain, Samuel Barber, Franz Schubert, J. Osma, and Guiseppe Verdi.

D61w. Victor 2009. 78 rpm. mono. 10 in.
Kirsten Flagstad, soprano; Edwin McArthur, piano.
With Anton Dvořák's Songs my mother taught me.

D61x. Zonophone Z 2346. acoustic recording. 10 in.
Frank Webster, tenor; and orchestra.

D62. **Three Lyrics**

D62a. Unicorn RHS 359. 1979.
Eric Parkin, piano.
In: Eric Parkin plays piano music by Frank Bridge
Recorded April 5 and August 31, 1978, Bishopsgate Institute, London.
With his Four Characteristic pieces; Piano sonata; Three Poems.
See: B414

D63. **Mantle of blue**

D63a. Hyperion A66103. 1984.
Anne Dawson, mezzo-soprano; Roderick Barrand, piano.
In: A Recital of English songs
Recorded February 18-19, 1983 in association with the Finzi Trust.
With his Come to me in my dreams; Fair daffodils; Go not, happy day; and works by Howard Ferguson, Gerald Finzi, and E. J. Moeran.
See: B235, B288

D63b. Pearl SHE 513–SHE 514. 2 discs. 1974.
Valerie Baulard, mezzo-soprano; Jonathan Hinden, piano.
In: Songs and piano music
Recorded April 30, May 1, June 25, and July 25, 1973, Wigmore Hall, London.
Recorded in association with the Frank Bridge Trust.
With his Blow out you bugles; Come to me in my dreams; Day after day; Dweller in my deathless dreams; Go not, happy day; The Hour glass; In autumn: Through the eaves; Journey's end; The Last invocation; Love went a-riding; Piano sonata; Three Poems: Solitude; So perverse; Strew no more red roses; 'Tis but a week; What shall I your true love tell?; Where she lies asleep; Winter pastoral.
See: B334

D63c. Pearl SHE 586. 1985.
Patricia Wright, soprano; Christopher Cox, piano.
Recorded in Wigmore Hall, London.

"Recorded with financial assistance from the Frank Bridge Trust, which acts as a source of information about all aspects of Bridge's music."
With his Amaryllis; The Last invocation; Miniatures, sets 1–3; Norse legend; Souvenir; Thy hand in mine; 'Tis but a week; What shall I your true love tell?
See: B282, B287

D64. **Meditation**

D64a. Pearl SHE 571. 1982.
Moray Welsh, violoncello; Roger Vignoles, piano.
In: British music for cello and piano
Recorded June 4, 1982, EMI Abbey Road Studios, London.
Recorded in association with the Frank Bridge Trust.
With his Cradle song; Elégie; Mélodie; Morning song; Scherzo; Serenade; Berceuse and works by Sir Arnold Bax and Percy Grainger.
See: B234, B421

D65. **Mélodie**

D65a. Columbia SW 95.
Felix Salmond, violoncello; and piano.

D65b. Pearl SHE 571. 1982.
Moray Welsh, violoncello; Roger Vignoles, piano.
In: British music for cello and piano
Recorded June 4, 1982, EMI Abbey Road Studios, London.
Recorded in association with the Frank Bridge Trust.
With his Cradle song; Elégie; Meditation; Morning song; Scherzo; Serenade; Berceuse and works by Sir Arnold Bax and Percy Grainger.
See: B234, B421

D66. **Miniature pastorals, set 1**

D66a. Continuum CCD 1016 (compact disc). 1990.
Peter Jacobs, piano.
In: Frank Bridge: Complete music for piano
"Recorded in association with the Frank Bridge Trust."

With his Arabesque; Capriccio no. 1 in A minor; Capriccio no. 2 in F-sharp minor; A Dedication; A Fairy tale; Gargoyle; Hidden fires; Three Improvisations; In autumn; Miniature pastorals, set 2; A Sea idyll; Winter pastoral.

D67. **Miniature pastorals, set 2**

D67a. Continuum CCD 1016 (compact disc). 1990.
Peter Jacobs, piano.
In: Frank Bridge: Complete music for piano
"Recorded in association with the Frank Bridge Trust."
With his Arabesque; Capriccio no. 1 in A minor; Capriccio no. 2 in F-sharp minor; A Dedication; A Fairy tale; Gargoyle; Hidden fires; Three Improvisations; In autumn; Miniature pastorals, set 1; A Sea idyll; Winter pastoral.

D68. **Miniatures, set 1**

D68a. Milan Yancich HR-111-112–HR-113-114 (cassettes). 1986.
Milan Yancich, horn.
In: Trios with horns galore!
With his Miniatures, sets 2–3 and works by Franz Schubert, Carl Reinecke, Heinrich von Herzogenberg, Leo Sowerby, Heinrich Molbe, A. Russell, Gabriel Marie, Peter Tschaikowsky, Claude Debussy, Richard Strauss, and Gabriel Pierne.

D68b. Pearl SHE 586. 1985.
Hanson Trio.
Recorded in Wigmore Hall, London.
"Recorded with financial assistance from the Frank Bridge Trust, which acts as a source of information about all aspects of Bridge's music."
With his Amaryllis; The Last invocation; Mantle of blue; Miniatures, sets 2–3; Norse legend; Souvenir; Thy hand in mine; 'Tis but a week; What shall I your true love tell?
See: B282, B287

D69. **Miniatures, set 1 – no. 1: Minuet**

D69a. Columbia L 1198. acoustic recording. pre–1936.
Arthur Catterall, violin; W. H. Squire, violoncello; William Murdoch, piano.
With his Miniatures, set 3: Hornpipe.

D70. **Miniatures, set 2**

D70a. Milan Yancich HR-111-112–HR-113-114 (cassettes). 1986.
Milan Yancich, horn.
In: Trios with horns galore!
With his Miniatures, sets 1 and 3 and works by Franz Schubert, Carl Reinecke, Heinrich von Herzogenberg, Leo Sowerby, Heinrich Molbe, A. Russell, Gabriel Marie, Peter Tschaikowsky, Claude Debussy, Richard Strauss, and Gabriel Pierne.

D70b. Pearl SHE 586. 1985.
Hanson Trio.
Recorded in Wigmore Hall, London.
"Recorded with financial assistance from the Frank Bridge Trust, which acts as a source of information about all aspects of Bridge's music."
With his Amaryllis; The Last invocation; Mantle of blue; Miniatures, sets 1 and 3; Norse legend; Souvenir; Thy hand in mine; 'Tis but a week; What shall I your true love tell?
See: B282, B287

D71. **Miniatures, set 3**

D71a. Argo ZK 40. 1978.
Argo ZRG 850. 1978.
Tunnell Trio.
Recorded December 1976, Christ Church, Flood Street, London.
With his Phantasy in F-sharp minor; Piano trio (1929).
See: B226, B416

D71b. Milan Yancich HR-111-112–HR-113-114 (cassettes). 1986.
Milan Yancich, horn.
In: Trios with horns galore!
With his Miniatures, sets 1–2 and works by Franz Schubert, Carl Reinecke, Heinrich von Herzogenberg, Leo Sowerby, Heinrich Molbe, A. Russell, Gabriel Marie, Peter Tschaikowsky, Claude Debussy, Richard Strauss, and Gabriel Pierne.

D71c. Pearl SHE 586. 1985.
Hanson Trio.
Recorded in Wigmore Hall, London.
"Recorded with financial assistance from the Frank Bridge Trust, which acts as a source of information about all aspects of Bridge's music."

With his Amaryllis; The Last invocation; Mantle of blue; Miniatures, sets 1–2; Norse legend; Souvenir; Thy hand in mine; 'Tis but a week; What shall I your true love tell?
See: B282, B287

D72. **Miniatures, set 3 – no. 2: Hornpipe**

D72a. Columbia L 1198. acoustic recording. pre–1936.
Arthur Catterall, violin; W. H. Squire, violoncello; William Murdoch, piano.
With his Miniatures, set 1: Minuet.

D73. **Morning song**

D73a. Pearl SHE 571. 1982.
Moray Welsh, violoncello; Roger Vignoles, piano.
In: British music for cello and piano
Recorded June 4, 1982, EMI Abbey Road Studios, London.
Recorded in association with the Frank Bridge Trust.
With his Cradle song; Elégie; Meditation; Mélodie; Scherzo; Serenade; Berceuse and works by Sir Arnold Bax and Percy Grainger.
See: B234, B421

D73b. Pearl SHE 600 (cd: SHECD 9600). 1987.
Lowri Blake, violoncello; Chelsea Opera Group Orchestra; Howard Williams, conductor.
In: Frank Bridge: Orchestral works
Recorded September 1986, CBS Studios, London.
"Recordings made with the financial assistance of the Frank Bridge Trust."
With his Canzonetta; Elégie; Heart's ease; Norse legend; Rosemary; Scherzetto; Threads; The Turtle's retort; Vignettes de danse.

D74. **Music when soft voices die**

D74a. Pearl SHE 551. 1981.
Louis Halsey Singers.
In: A Frank Bridge spicilegium
With his Autumn; The Bee; Divertimenti; Hilli-ho! Hilli-ho!; Love went a-riding; O weary hearts; Two Pieces: Lament; So perverse; Strew no more red roses; Where she lies asleep.

D75. **Music when soft voices die, with viola**

D75a. Pearl SHE 577. 1983.
Patricia Wright, soprano; Michael Ponder, viola; John Alley, piano.
In: The Early Bridge
Recorded June 28–29, 1982, Wigmore Hall, London.
"Made with financial assistance from the Frank Bridge Trust."
With his Adoration; All things that we clasp; Allegretto; Allegro appassionato; Berceuse; Blow, blow thou winter wind; Come to me in my dreams; A Dirge; E'en as a lovely flower; Fair daffodils; Far, far from each other; My pent-up tears oppress my brain; Pensiero; Tears, idle tears; The Violets blue; Where is it that our soul doth go?
See: B325, B420

D76. **My pent-up tears oppress my brain**

D76a. Pearl SHE 577. 1983.
Stephen Varcoe, baritone; Christopher Cox, piano.
In: The Early Bridge
Recorded June 28-29, 1982, Wigmore Hall, London.
"Made with financial assistance from the Frank Bridge Trust."
With his Adoration; All things that we clasp; Allegretto; Allegro appassionato; Berceuse; Blow, blow thou winter wind; Come to me in my dreams; A Dirge; E'en as a lovely flower; Fair daffodils; Far, far from each other; Music when soft voices die; Pensiero; Tears, idle tears; The Violets blue; Where is it that our soul doth go?
See: B325, B420

D77. **Norse legend**

D77a. Pearl SHE 586. 1985.
Peter Hanson, violin; Christopher Cox, piano.
Recorded in Wigmore Hall, London.
"Recorded with financial assistance from the Frank Bridge Trust, which acts as a source of information about all aspects of Bridge's music."
With his Amaryllis; The Last invocation; Mantle of blue; Miniatures, sets 1–3; Souvenir; 'Tis but a week; Thy hand in mine; What shall I your true love tell?
See: B282, B287

D77b. Pearl SHE 600 (cd: SHECD 9600). 1987.
Chelsea Opera Group Orchestra; Howard Williams, conductor.
In: Frank Bridge: Orchestral works
Recorded September 1986, CBS Studios, London.
"Recordings made with the financial assistance of the Frank Bridge Trust."
With his Canzonetta; Elégie; Heart's ease; Morning song; Rosemary; Scherzetto; Threads; The Turtle's retort; Vignettes de danse.

D78. **Novelletten**

D78a. Decca SDD 497. 1977.
London STS 15439. 1977.
Gabrieli String Quartet.
In: Music of Britten and Bridge
Recorded February 1976 at the Snape Maltings.
With his Three Idylls and works by Benjamin Britten.
See: B174, B216, B225, B333, B407

D79. **Novelletten – movements 1 and 3**

D79a. Vocalion D 02155. 78 rpm. mono.
Spencer Dyke Quartet.

D80. **Novelletten – movement 3**

D80a. His Master's Voice C 1663. 78 rpm. mono.
Victor 9739. 78 rpm. mono.
Virtuoso Quartet.

D81. **O that it were so**

D81a. Columbia 5318. acoustic recording. 10 in.
A. Robert Poole, bass; and piano.

D81b. EMI EX290911-3 (cass: EX290911-5). 2 discs.
Kristen Flagstad, soprano; Edwin McArthur, piano.
Recorded in 1918.
With his Come to me in my dreams; Love went a-riding.

D81c. His Master's Voice 2–3326. acoustic recording. 10 in.
Olga Haley, mezzo-soprano; Mrs. Edward Haley, piano.

D81d. His Master's Voice CLP 3587. mono. ca. 1966.
His Master's Voice CSD 3587. ca. 1966.
Frederick Harvey, bass; Gerald Moore, piano.

D81e. His Master's Voice E 370. acoustic recording. 10 in.
Carmen Hill, mezzo-soprano; and piano.

D81f. Victor LM 2266. mono. 1958.
(Australian) Victor L 16201. 78 rpm. mono.
Leonard Warren, baritone; Willard Sektberg, piano.
In: Leonard Warren on tour in Russia
Recorded May 1958, Leningrad and Kiev.
With works by J. S. Bach, Ludwig van Beethoven, George Bizet, Guilio Caccini, Gabriel Fauré, Vittorio Giannini, Charles T. Griffes, Vincent D'Indy, Ruggerio Leoncavallo, Maurice Ravel, F. Paolo Tost, and Giuseppi Verdi.
See: B286, B289, B322, B362

D81g. Vocalion K 05081. acoustic recording. 10 in.
Marie Cartwright, alto; and piano.

D82. **O weary hearts**

D82a. Pearl SHE 551. 1981.
Louis Halsey Singers.
In: A Frank Bridge spicilegium
Recorded in association with the Frank Bridge Trust.
With his Autumn; The Bee; Divertimenti; Hilli-ho! Hilli-ho!; Love went a-riding; Music when soft voices die; Two Pieces: Lament; So perverse; Strew no more red roses; Where she lies asleep.

D82b. Pearl SHE 593. 1986.
Trinity College Choir; Richard Marlow, director.
Recorded January 10–11, 1986, Trinity College Chapel, Cambridge.
Recorded in association with the Frank Bridge Trust.
With his The Bee; Evening primrose; Golden slumbers; The Graceful swaying wattle; Hilli-ho! Hilli-ho!; Lay a garland on my hearse; A Litany; Peter Piper; Sister, awake and works by Benjamin Britten.

D83. **Two Old English songs**

D83a. American Decca set A 270. 78 rpm. mono.
Gordon Quartet.

D83b. Boosey & Hawkes S 2249. 78 rpm. mono. 10 in.
New Concert Orchestra; Nay Nyll, conductor.

D83c. Chandos ABRD 1073 (cass: ABTD 1073; cd: CHAN 8426). 1983.
Also issued on Chandos DBRD 4001 (cass: DBTD 4001). 4 discs. 1983.
Delmé String Quartet.
In: Music for string quartet
Recorded March 26 and 27, 1982, Church of St. George the Martyr, Bloomsbury, London.
"Recorded with financial assistance from the Frank Bridge Trust."
With his An Irish Melody; Sir Roger de Coverley; String quartet no. 2 in G minor.
See: B230, B420

D83d. Chandos DBRD 4001 (cass: DBTD 4001). 4 discs. 1983.
Also issued on Chandos ABRD 1073 (cass: ABTD 1073; cd: CHAN 8426). 1983.
Delmé String Quartet.
In: Music for a summer's day
Recorded March and June 1982, Church of St. George the Martyr, Bloomsbury, London.
With his An Irish Melody; Sir Roger de Coverley; String quartet no. 2 in G minor and works by Sir Arnold Bax, Ralph Vaughan Williams, Arthur Bliss, John Ireland, Geoffrey Bush, Eugene Goossens, E. J. Moeran, Cyril Scott, Alan Bush, Benjamin Britten, and Alan Rawsthorne.

D83e. Columbia 9178. 78 rpm. mono.
Catterall Quartet.

D83f. Decca 20173. 78 rpm. mono. 10 in.
Decca F 2388.
London Chamber Orchestra; Anthony Bernard, conductor.

D83g. Decca 71071. 45 rpm. mono. ca. 1955.
New Symphony Orchestra; Eugene Goossens, conductor.

D83h. His Master's Voice D 14. 10 in. acoustic recording.
His Master's Voice E 1. acoustic recording.
London Quartet.

D83i. Lyrita SRCS.73. 1978.
HNH Records HNH 4078. 1978.
London Philharmonic Orchestra; Sir Adrian Boult, conductor.
With his Lament; Rosemary; Sir Roger de Coverley; Suite.
See: B170, B214, B243, B410

D84. **Two Old English songs – no. 1: Sally in our alley**

D84a. TOL/Schwann VMS 2075.
Berlin RIAS Sinfonietta; David Atherton, conductor.
With works by Benjamin Britten, Gustav Holst, Sir C. Hubert H. Parry, and Peter Warlock.

D84b. Victor 4569. 10 in.
Boston "Pops" Orchestra; Arthur Fiedler, conductor.
With Stephen Foster's Oh, Susannah!

D85. **Two Old English songs – no. 2: Cherry ripe**

D85a. EMI/HMV ASD 3190. quad. 1976.
Reissued on EMI/HMV ED290868-1 (cass: ED290868-4). 1986.
Royal Liverpool Philharmonic Orchestra; Sir Charles Groves, conductor.
Recorded in Philharmonic Hall, Liverpool.
With his Enter spring; Lament; The Sea; Summer.
See: B157, B193, B194, B415

D85b. Octacross 303. 78 rpm. mono. 10 cm.
Stratton Quartet.

D85c. Polydor 10541. 78 rpm. mono. 10 in.
Prisca Quartet.
With Percy Grainger's Molly on the shore.

D86. **Oration, concerto elegiaco**

D86a. EMI EL749716–1 (cass: EL749716–4; cd: CDC 7 49716–2). 1988.
Steven Isserlis, violoncello; City of London Sinfonia; Richard Hickox, conductor.
Recorded March 12 and 14, 1987 in EMI Abbey Road Studios, London.
With Benjamin Britten's Violoncello symphony, op. 68.

D86b. Lyrita SRCS.104. 1979.
Julian Lloyd Webber, violoncello; London Philharmonic Orchestra; Nicholas Braithwaite, conductor.
"Recorded in association with the RVW & Bridge Trusts."
With his Two Poems; Unfinished symphony.
See: B189, B335, B412

D86c. Pearl SHE 601 (cd: SHECD 9601). 1987.
Alexander Baillie, violoncello; Cologne Radio Symphony Orchestra; John Carewe, conductor.
Recorded in association with the Frank Bridge Trust.
With his Enter spring.

D87. **Organ pieces, book 1**

D87a. Pearl SHE 545. 1980.
Stuart Campbell, organ.
In: The Organ music of Frank Bridge
Recorded in Memorial Chapel, University of Glasgow.
Recorded in association with the Frank Bridge Trust.
With his Lento (In memoriam C.H.H.P.); Organ pieces, bk. 2; Three Pieces; Three Pieces (1939).
See: B201

D87b. Vista VPS 1051. 1977.
Geoffrey Tristram, organ.
Recorded in Christchurch Priory, Dorset.
With works by Sir C. Hubert H. Parry, Charles Villiers Stanford, Louis Vierne, and Percy Whitlock.
See: B385, B418

D88. **Organ pieces, book 1 – no. 1: Allegretto grazioso**

D88a. Apollo Sound AS 1004. mono.
Stanley Curtis, organ.
Recorded in Westminster Chapel.
With his Organ pieces, bk. 1 – no. 3: Allegro marziale.

D88b. EMI/HMV CSD 3678. 1970.
Philip Marshall, organ.
In: Lincoln Minster
With his Organ pieces, bk. 2 – no. 2: Andantino and works by Felix Mendelssohn-Bartholdy, Johannes Brahms, Charles Wood, and C. Hubert H. Parry.

D88c. Priory PRCD 270 (compact disc). 1988.
Paul Trepte, organ.
In: English music from St. Edmundsbury Cathedral
Recorded July 11–13, 1988 in St. Edmundsbury Cathedral, Suffolk.
With his Three Pieces for organ: Adagio in E major and works by Harold Darke, Edward Bairstow, Ralph Vaughan Williams, John Ireland, William Harris, and Herbert Howells.

D89. **Organ pieces, book 1 – no. 3: Allegro marziale**

D89a. Apollo Sound AS 1004. mono.
Stanley Curtis, organ.
Recorded in Westminster Chapel.
With his Organ pieces, bk. 1 – no. 1: Allegretto grazioso.

D89b. EMI/HMV CSD 3677. 1970.
Odeon CSD 3677. 1970.
Christopher Dearnley, organ.
In: St. Paul's Cathedral
Recorded in St. Paul's Cathedral, London.
With works by Henry Purcell, Felix Mendelssohn-Bartholdy, Camille Saint-Säens, Sir Arthur Bliss, Herbert Howells, and Charles Ives.

D90. **Organ pieces, book 2**

D90a. Pearl SHE 545. 1980.
Stuart Campbell, organ.
In: The Organ music of Frank Bridge

Recorded in Memorial Chapel, University of Glasgow.
Recorded in association with the Frank Bridge Trust.
With his Lento (In memoriam C.H.H.P.); Organ pieces, bk. 1; Three Pieces; Three Pieces (1939).
See: B201

D91. **Organ pieces, book 2 – no. 2: Andantino**

D91a. EMI/HMV CSD 3678. 1970.
Philip Marshall, organ.
In: Lincoln Minster
With his Organ pieces, bk. 1 – no. 1: Allegretto grazioso and works by Felix Mendelssohn-Bartholdy, Johannes Brahms, Charles Wood, and C. Hubert H. Parry.

D92. **Pensiero**

D92a. Musical Heritage Society MHC 7483 (cass: MHC 9483). 1987.
Previously released by CRD Records in 1985.
Tony Appel, viola; Peter Pettinger, piano.
In: Britten, Bridge and Clarke, music for viola and piano
With his Allegro appassionato and works by Rebecca Clarke and Benjamin Britten.

D92b. Pearl SHE 577. 1983.
Patricia Wright, soprano; John Alley, piano.
In: The Early Bridge
Recorded June 28–29, 1982, Wigmore Hall, London.
"This record has been made with financial assistance from the Frank Bridge Trust."
With his Adoration; All things that we clasp; Allegretto; Allegro appassionato; Berceuse; Blow, blow thou winter wind; Come to me in my dreams; A Dirge; E'en as a lovely flower; Fair daffodils; Far, far from each other; Tears, idle tears; Music when soft voices die; My pent-up tears oppress my brain; The Violets blue; Where is it that our soul doth go?
See: B325, B420

D93. **Peter Piper**

D93a. Pearl SHE 593. 1986.
Trinity College Choir; Richard Marlow, director.

Recorded January 10–11, 1986, Trinity College Chapel, Cambridge.
Recorded in association with the Frank Bridge Trust.
With his The Bee; Evening primrose; Golden slumbers; The Graceful swaying wattle; Hilli-ho! Hilli-ho!; Lay a garland on my hearse; A Litany; O weary heart; Sister, awake and works by Benjamin Britten.

D94. **Phantasm**

D94a. Conifer CDCF 175 (compact disc) (cass: MCFC 175). 1990.
Kathryn Sturrock, piano.
With works by John Ireland and William Walton.

D94b. Lyrita SRCS.91. 1977.
HNH Records HNH 4042. 1977.
Peter Wallfisch, piano; London Philharmonic Orchestra; Nicholas Braithwaite, conductor.
"Recorded in association with the Frank Bridge Trust."
With E. J. Moeran's Rhapsody.
See: B218, B330, B333, B353, B400, B409

D95. **Phantasy in C minor**

D95a. Decca K 945–K 946. 2 discs. 78 rpm. mono.
Grinke Trio.

D95b. Enigma Classics K.53578. 1979.
Reissued on Nonesuch 71405 (cass: 71405–4) and Musical Heritage Society MHS 4691. 1982.
Music Group of London.
"An original Academy Sound & Vision recording."
With his Piano quintet (1912).
See: B196, B206, B253, B413, B421

D95c. Hyperion CDA66279 (compact disc) (cass: KA66279). 1988.
Dartington Piano Trio.
Recorded July 10–11, 1987.
With his Phantasy in F-sharp minor; Piano trio (1929).

D96. **Phantasy in F-sharp minor**

D96a. Argo ZK 40. 1978.
Argo ZRG 850. 1978.
Tunnell Trio with Brian Hawkins, violin.
Recorded December 1976, Christ Church, Flood Street, London.
With his Miniatures, set 3; Piano trio (1929).
See: B226, B416

D96b. Columbia 946. acoustic recording.
English String Quartet.
Recorded May 24, 1923.

D96c. Hyperion CDA66279 (compact disc) (cass: KA66279). 1988.
Dartington Piano Trio with Patrick Ireland, viola.
Recorded July 10–11, 1987.
With his Phantasy in C minor; Piano trio (1929).

D96d. Pearl SHE 570. 1982.
Hanson String Quartet.
Recorded March 6–7, 1982, St. Peter's Church, Notting Hill, London.
Recorded in association with the Frank Bridge Trust.
With his String sextet in E-flat major.
See: B408, B421

D96e. Phoenix DGS 1047 (cass: DGSC 1047). 1985.
Dorian Ensemble.
Recorded at the Guild Church of St. Katharine Cree, London.
With Sir William Walton's Piano Quartet.

D97. **Piano quintet (1912)**

D97a. ASV CD DCA 678 (compact disc) (cass: ZC DCA 678). 1989.
Coull String Quartet with Allan Schiller, piano.
Recorded August 1988, Adrian Boult Hall, Birmingham.
With Edward Elgar's Piano quintet, op. 84.
See: B402

D97b. Enigma Classics K.53578. 1979.
Reissued on Nonesuch 71405 (cass: 71405–4) and Musical Heritage Society MHS 4691. 1982.
Music Group of London.
"An original Academy Sound & Vision recording."

With his Phantasy in F-sharp minor.
See: B196, B206, B253, B413, B421

D98. **Piano sonata**

D98a. Conifer (forthcoming)
Kathyrn Sturrock, piano.

D98b. Finnadar SR 9031. 1981.
Meral Güneyman, piano.
In: Meral Güneyman: the piano music of Bridge, Decaux & Webern
Recorded November 26 and December 5, 1980, RCA Recording Studios, New York, New York.
With works by Anton Webern and Abel Decaux.
See: B352, B398

D98c. Pearl SHE 513–SHE 514. 2 discs. 1974.
Peter Wallfisch, piano.
In: Songs and piano music
Recorded April 30, May 1, June 25, and July 25, 1973, Wigmore Hall, London.
Recorded in association with the Frank Bridge Trust.
With his Blow out you bugles; Come to me in my dreams; Day after day; Dweller in my deathless dreams; Go not, happy day; The Hour glass; In autumn: Through the eaves; Journey's end; The Last invocation; Love went a-riding; Mantle of blue; Three Poems: Solitude; So perverse; Strew no more red roses; 'Tis but a week; What shall I your true love tell?; Where she lies asleep; Winter Pastoral.
See: B334

D98d. Unicorn RHS 359. 1979.
Eric Parkin, piano.
In: Eric Parkin plays piano music by Frank Bridge
Recorded April 5 and August 31, 1978, Bishopsgate Institute, London.
With his Four Characteristic Pieces; Three Lyrics; Three Poems.
See: B414

D99. **Piano trio (1929)**

D99a. Argo ZK 40. 1978.
Argo ZRG 850. 1978.

Tunnell Trio.
Recorded December 1976, Christ Church, Flood Street, London.
With his Miniatures, set 3; Phantasy in F-sharp minor.
See: B226, B416

D99b. Chandos ABRD 1205 (cass: ABTD 1205; cd: CHAN 8495). 1987.
Borodin Trio.
Recorded July 11–12, 1986, Layer Marney Parish Church, Essex.
With Sir Arnold Bax's Piano Trio in B-flat.

D99c. Hyperion CDA66279 (compact disc) (cass: KA66279). 1988.
Dartington Piano Trio.
Recorded July 10–11, 1987.
With his Phantasy in C minor; Phantasy in F-sharp minor.

D99d. Pearl SHECD 9610 (compact disc). 1989.
Hiroko Yajima, violin; Lowri Blake, violoncello; Stephen Prutsman, piano.
Recorded in association with the Frank Bridge Trust.
With his Violoncello sonata in D minor; Spring song.

D100. **Two Pieces – no. 2: Lament**

D100a. Pearl SHE 551. 1981.
Michael Ponder and Tomas Tichauer, violas.
In: A Frank Bridge spicilegium
Recorded in association with the Frank Bridge Trust.
With his Autumn; The Bee; Divertimenti; Hilli-ho! Hilli-ho!; Love went a-riding; Music when soft voices die; O weary hearts; So perverse; Strew no more red roses; Where she lies asleep.

D101. **Three Pieces for organ**

D101a. Pearl SHE 545. 1980.
Stuart Campbell, organ.
In: The Organ music of Frank Bridge
Recorded in Memorial Chapel, University of Glasgow.
Recorded in association with the Frank Bridge Trust.
With his Lento (In memoriam C.H.H.P.); Organ pieces, bks. 1–2; Three Pieces (1939).

D102. **Three Pieces for organ – no. 2: Adagio in E major**

D102a. Abbey E 7613. 45 rpm. mono.
Christopher Dearnley, organ.
Recorded in Salisbury Cathedral.

D102b. Argo 414 647–1ZW (cass: 414 647–4GW).
Simon Preston, organ.

D102c. Argo ZRG 528.
Simon Preston, organ.
Recorded in Colston Hall, Bristol.

D102d. Conifer/Caprice CAP 1002.
Adrian Partington, organ.

D102e. Hyperion A66018. 1981.
Stephen Darlington, organ.
In: English music of the 20th century
Recorded October 15–17, 1980, Cathedral and Abbey Church of St. Alban, St. Albans.
With works by Sir Edward Elgar, Kenneth Leighton, Bryan Kelly, Sir Edward Bairstow, Herbert Howells, and Sir Charles Villiers Stanford.

D102f. MCPS MW 934. 2 discs. 1983.
Gillian Weir, organ.
In: Gillian Weir plays the 1861 William Hill Mulholland Grand Organ in the Ulster Hall, Belfast.
Recorded May 4–5, 1983, Ulster Hall, Belfast.
With works by Giacomo Meyerbeer, Felix Mendelssohn, Petr Eben, Antonio Valente, Girolamo Frescobaldi, Domenico Zipoli, John Stanley, J. S. Bach, Olivier Messiaen, Cesar Franck, Henri Mulet, Francois Couperin, and Marcel Dupre.

D102g. Priory PRCD 270 (compact disc). 1988.
Paul Trepte, organ.
In: English music from St. Edmundsbury Cathedral.
Recorded July 11–13, 1988 in St. Edmundsbury Cathedral, Suffolk.
With his Allegretto grazioso and works by Harold Darke, Edward Bairstow, Ralph Vaughan Williams, John Ireland, William Harris, and Herbert Howells.

D102h. Saville 853S–2000. 1968.
Frederick Swann, organ.

In: Sounds of Saville
Recorded in Cathedral Church of St. Paul, Boston, Massachusetts.
With works by J. S. Bach, Gerre Hancock, and Zoltan Kodaly.

D102i. Vista VPS 1001. 1969.
Christopher Herrick, organ.
In: Organ music from St. Paul's Cathedral, London
Recorded in St. Paul's Cathedral, London.
With works by Arthur Wills, Max Reger, Franz Liszt, Jehan Alain, and Olivier Messian.
See: B417

D102j. Wealdon WS 149.
Eric Suddrick, organ.
Recorded at Cheltenham College.
With his Three Pieces for organ: Allegro con spirito in B-flat major and works by Sir Lennox Berkeley, Alberto Ginastera, Henri Mulet, C. Hubert H. Parry, and Camille Saint-Säens.

D103. **Three Pieces for organ – no. 3: Allegro con spirito in B-flat major**

D103a. Wealdon WS 149.
Eric Suddrick, organ.
Recorded at Cheltenham College.
With his Three Pieces for organ: Adagio in E major and works by Sir Lennox Berkeley, Alberto Ginastera, Henri Mulet, C. Hubert H. Parry, and Camille Saint-Säens.

D104. **Three Pieces for organ (1939)**

D104a. Pearl SHE 545. 1980.
Stuart Campbell, organ.
In: The Organ music of Frank Bridge
Recorded in Memorial Chapel, University of Glasgow.
Recorded in association with the Frank Bridge Trust.
With his Lento (In memoriam C.H.H.P.); Organ pieces, bks. 1–2; Three Pieces.

D104b. Wealdon WS 151.
Raymond Humphrey, organ (no. 1–2); Michael Fleming, organ (no. 3).
Recorded in Winchester College Chapel.

D105. **Two Poems**

D105a. Lyrita SRCS.104. 1979.
London Philharmonic Orchestra; Nicholas Braithwaite, conductor.
"Recorded in association with the RVW & Bridge Trusts."
With his Oration, concerto elegiaco; Unfinished symphony.
See: B189, B335, B412

D106. **Two Poems - no. 2: Allegro con brio**

D106a. Columbia L 1678. 78 rpm. mono. 10 in.
New Queen's Hall Orchestra; Frank Bridge, conductor.
Recorded February 12, 1925.
With his Sir Roger de Coverley.

D107. **Three Poems**

D107a. Unicorn RHS 359. 1978.
Eric Parkin, piano.
In: Eric Parkin plays piano music by Frank Bridge
Recorded April 5 and August 31, 1978, Bishopsgate Institute, London.
With his Four Characteristic pieces; Three Lyrics; Piano sonata
See: B414

D108. **Three Poems - no. 1: Solitude**

D108a. Pearl SHE 513-SHE 514. 2 discs. 1974.
Peter Wallfisch, piano.
In: Songs and piano music
Recorded April 30, May 1, June 25, and July 25, 1973, Wigmore Hall, London.
Recorded in association with the Frank Bridge Trust.
With his Blow out you bugles; Come to me in my dreams; Day after day; Dweller in my deathless dreams; Go not, happy day; The Hour glass; In autumn: Through the leaves; Journey's end; The Last invocation; Love went a-riding; Mantle of blue; Piano sonata; So perverse; Strew no more red roses; 'Tis but a week; What shall I your true love tell?; Where she lies asleep; Winter pastoral.
See: B334

D109. **A Prayer**

D109a. Pearl SHE 568. 1982.
Chelsea Opera Group Orchestra and Chorus; Howard Williams, conductor.
Recorded January 17–18, 1982, EMI Abbey Road Studios, London.
"Recording made with financial assistance from the Frank Bridge Trust."
With his Day after day; Dweller in my deathless dreams; Isabella; Speak to me my love.
See: B186, B406, B421

D110. **Rebus**

D110a. Lyrita SRCS.114. 1979.
London Philharmonic Orchestra; Nicholas Braithwaite, conductor.
Recorded in association with the RVW & Bridge Trusts.
With his Dance poem; Dance rhapsody.
See: B335, B411

D111. **Rhapsody**

D111a. Pearl SHE 547. 1978.
John Georgiadis and Neil Watson, violins; Brian Hawkins, viola.
Recorded at St. Peter's Church, Bayswater, London.
Recorded in association with the Frank Bridge Trust.
With works by Sir Arnold Bax and Sir Lennox Berkeley.
See: B213, B231

D112. **Rosemary**

D112a. Boosey & Hawkes OT 2190.
New Concert Orchestra; Jack Leon, conductor.

D112b. Lyrita SRCS.73. 1978.
HNH Records HNH 4078. 1978.
London Philharmonic Orchestra; Sir Adrian Boult, conductor.
With his Lament; Two Old English Songs; Sir Roger de Coverley; Suite.
See: B170, B214, B243, B410

D112c. Pearl SHE 600 (cd: SHECD 9600). 1987.
Chelsea Opera Group Orchestra; Howard Williams, conductor.
In: Frank Bridge: Orchestral works
Recorded September 1986, CBS Studios, London.
"Recordings made with the financial assistance of the Frank Bridge Trust."
With his Canzonetta; Elégie; Heart's ease; Morning song; Norse legend; Scherzetto; Threads; The Turtle's retort; Vignettes de danse.

D113. **Scherzetto**

D113a. RCA Red Seal RL 25383 (cass: RK 25383). 1981.
RCA GL 70797 (cass: GK 70797).
Julian Lloyd Webber, violoncello; National Philharmonic Orchestra; Charles Gerhardt, conductor.
In: Cello man
Recorded September 1981, Walthamstow Town Hall.
With works by Joseph Canteloube, Manuel De Falla, Camille Saint-Säens, Gabriel Fauré, J. S. Bach, David Popper, Frederick Delius, and Max Bruch.

D113b. Pearl SHE 600 (cd: SHECD 9600). 1987.
Lowri Blake, violoncello; Chelsea Opera Group Orchestra; Howard Williams, conductor.
In: Frank Bridge: Orchestral works
Recorded September 1986, CBS Studios, London.
"Recordings made with the financial assistance of the Frank Bridge Trust."
With his Canzonetta; Elégie; Heart's ease; Morning song; Norse legend; Rosemary; Threads; The Turtle's retort; Vignettes de danse.

D114. **Scherzo**

D114a. Pearl SHE 571. 1982.
Moray Welsh, violoncello; Roger Vignoles, piano.
In: British music for cello and piano
Recorded June 4, 1982, EMI Abbey Road Studios, London.
Recorded in association with the Frank Bridge Trust.

With his Berceuse; Cradle song; Elégie; Meditation; Mélodie; Morning song; Serenade and works by Sir Arnold Bax and Percy Grainger.
See: B234, B421

D115. **The Sea**

D115a. Chandos ABRD 1184 (cass: ABTD 1184; cd: CHAN 8474). 1986.
Ulster Orchestra; Vernon Handley, conductor.
In: Music for the sea
Recorded March 25–27, 1986, Ulster Hall, Belfast.
With works by Sir Arnold Bax and Benjamin Britten.

D115b. Columbia L 1500–L 1501. acoustic recording.
Reissued on Opal OPAL 801. mono. 1982.
London Symphony Orchestra; Frank Bridge, conductor.
Recorded July 26, 1923.

D115c. EMI/HMV ASD 3190. quad. 1976.
Reissued on EMI/HMV ED290868-1 (cass: ED290868-4). 1986.
Royal Liverpool Philharmonic Orchestra; Sir Charles Groves, conductor.
Recorded in Philharmonic Hall, Liverpool.
With his Enter Spring; Lament; Two Old English songs: Cherry Ripe; Summer.
See: B157, B193, B194, B415

D115d. Opal OPAL 801. mono. 1982.
Previously issued on Columbia L 1500–L 1501, 935, L 1388–L 1389, and L 1822–L 1823.
London Symphony Orchestra; Frank Bridge, conductor.
In: The Composers conduct
Recorded 1920–1926.
With works by Rutland Boughton, Julius Harrison, and Sir Hamilton Harty.

D116. **A Sea idyll**

D116a. Continuum CCD 1016 (compact disc). 1990.
Peter Jacobs, piano.
In: Frank Bridge: Complete music for piano
"Recorded in association with the Frank Bridge Trust."

With his Arabesque; Capriccio no. 1 in A minor; Capriccio no. 2 in F-sharp minor; A Dedication; A Fairy tale; Gargoyle; Hidden fires; Three Improvisations; In autumn; Miniature pastorals, sets 1–2; Winter pastoral.

D117. **Serenade**

D117a. His Master's Voice B 1871. 10 in. acoustic recording.
Marjorie Hayward, violin; and piano.

D117b. Pearl SHE 571. 1982.
Moray Welsh, violoncello; Roger Vignoles, piano.
In: British music for cello and piano
Recorded June 4, 1982, EMI Abbey Road Studios, London.
Recorded in association with the Frank Bridge Trust.
With his Berceuse; Cradle song; Elégie; Meditation; Mélodie; Morning song; Scherzo; and works by Sir Arnold Bax and Percy Grainger.
See: B234, B421

D117c. Vocalion R 6018. acoustic recording. 10 in.
Felix Salmond, violoncello; and piano.

D118. **Sir Roger de Coverley**

D118a. Bond Street Music/Supraphon 411 639-1.
English Chamber Orchestra; Benjamin Britten, conductor.

D118b. Chandos ABRD 1073 (cass: ABTD 1073; cd: CHAN 8426). 1983.
Also issued on Chandos DBRD 4001 (cass: DBTD 4001). 4 discs. 1983.
Delmé String Quartet.
In: Music for string quartet
Recorded March 26 and 27, 1982, Church of St. George the Martyr, Bloomsbury, London.
"Recorded with financial assistance from the Frank Bridge Trust."
With his An Irish melody; Two Old English songs; String quartet no. 2 in G minor.
See: B230, B420

D118c. Chandos DBRD 4001 (cass: DBTD 4001). 4 discs. 1983.
Also issued on Chandos ABRD 1073 (cass: ABTD 1073; cd: CHAN 8426). 1983.
Delmé String Quartet.
In: Music for a summer's day
Recorded March and June 1982, Church of St. George the Martyr, Bloomsbury, London.
With his An Irish melody; Two Old English songs; String quartet no. 2 in G minor and works by Sir Arnold Bax, Ralph Vaughan Williams, Arthur Bliss, John Ireland, Geoffrey Bush, Eugene Goossens, E. J. Moeran, Cyril Scott, Alan Bush, Benjamin Britten, and Alan Rawsthorne.

D118d. Columbia L 1678. 78 rpm. mono. 10 in.
New Queen's Hall Orchestra; Frank Bridge, conductor.
Recorded February 12, 1925.
With his Two Poems: Allegro con brio.

D118e. Decca SXL 6405 (cass: KSXC 6405). 1969.
London CS 6618. 1969.
Reissued on London 425 160–4LM. 1989.
English Chamber Orchestra; Benjamin Britten, conductor.
In: Britten conducts English music for strings
With works by Henry Purcell, Edward Elgar, Benjamin Britten, and Frederick Delius.
See: B227, B236, B401

D118f. KMC2 9003.
English Chamber Orchestra; Benjamin Britten, conductor.

D118g. Lyrita SRCS.73. 1978.
HNH Records HNH 4078. 1978.
London Philharmonic Orchestra; Sir Adrian Boult, conductor.
With his Lament; Two Old English Songs; Rosemary; Suite.
See: B170, B214, B243, B410

D119. **Sister, awake**

D119a. Pearl SHE 593. 1986.
Trinity College Choir; Charles Matthews, piano; Richard Marlow, director.
Recorded January 10–11, 1986, Trinity College Chapel, Cambridge.
Recorded in association with the Frank Bridge Trust.

With his The Bee; Evening primrose; Golden slumbers; The Graceful swaying wattle; Hilli-ho! Hilli-ho!; Lay a garland on my hearse; A Litany; O weary heart; Peter Piper and works by Benjamin Britten.

D120. **Three Sketches**

D120a. Saga 5445. 1977.
Richard Deering, piano.
In: English piano music
With works by Eugene Goossens, Cyril Scott, John Ireland, York Bowen, and Sir Arnold Bax.
See: B229, B333

D121. **Three Sketches - no. 2: Rosemary**

D121a. Fidelity Sound 633F-2015. 1964.
Gerson Yessin, piano.
In: Junior festival list, 1962-64
With works by I. Brussels, Joan Last, J. Raymond, Claude Debussy, Samuel Dolin, Rudolf Ganz, Colin Taylor, Hazel Cobb, Hutchens, Béla Bartók, Gilbert Allen, P. Cook, Marvin Kahn, Joaquin Turina, I. Mason, Heitor Villa-Lobos, Claude Pascal, Oscar Lorenzo Fernandez, and Alberto Ginastera.

D121b. Saga 5400.
Edward Moore, piano.

D122. **So perverse**

D122a. Argo ZK 28. 2 discs. 1964.
Argo RG 418. mono. 1964.
Argo ZRG 5418. 1964.
Peter Pears, tenor; Benjamin Britten, piano.
In: Twentieth-century English songs
Recorded 1964 in association with the British Council.
With his Goldenhair; Journey's end; 'Tis but a week; When you are old and works by John Ireland, Richard Rodney Bennett, and Priaulx Rainer.
See: B210, B211, B249, B323, B389, B399

D122b. Pearl SHE 513-SHE 514. 2 discs. 1974.
David Johnston, tenor; Jonathan Hinden, piano.

In: Songs and piano music
Recorded April 30, May 1, June 25, and July 25, 1973, Wigmore Hall, London.
Recorded in association with the Frank Bridge Trust.
With his Blow out you bugles; Come to me in my dreams; Day after day; Dweller in my deathless dreams; Go not, happy day; The Hour glass; In autumn: Through the eaves; Journey's end; The Last invocation; Love went a-riding; Mantle of blue; Piano sonata; Three Poems: Solitude; Strew no more red roses; 'Tis but a week; What shall I your true love tell?; Where she lies asleep; Winter pastoral.
See: B334

D122c. Pearl SHE 551. 1981.
David Johnston, tenor; Jonathan Hinden, piano.
In: A Frank Bridge spicilegium
Recorded in association with the Frank Bridge Trust.
With his The Bee; Divertimenti; Hilli-ho! Hilli-ho!; Love went a-riding; Music when soft voices die; O weary hearts; Two Pieces: Lament; Strew no more red roses; Where she lies asleep.

D123. **Souvenir**

D123a. Pearl SHE 586. 1985.
Peter Hanson, violin; Christopher Cox, piano.
Recorded in Wigmore Hall, London.
"Recorded with financial assistance from the Frank Bridge Trust, which acts as a source of information about all aspects of Bridge's music."
With his Amaryllis; The Last invocation; Mantle of blue; Miniatures, sets 1-3; Norse legend; Thy hand in mine; 'Tis but a week; What shall I your true love tell?
See: B282, B287

D124. **Speak to me my love**

D124a. Pearl SHE 568. 1982.
Sarah Walker, mezzo-soprano; Chelsea Opera Group Orchestra; Howard Williams, conductor.
Recorded January 17–18, 1982, EMI Abbey Road Studios, London.
"Recording made with financial assistance from the Frank Bridge Trust."

With his Day after day, Dweller in my deathless dreams; Isabella; A Prayer.
See: B186, B406, B421

D125. **Spring song**

D125a. Pearl SHECD 9610 (compact disc). 1989.
Lowri Blake, violoncello; Caroline Palmer, piano.
Recorded in association with the Frank Bridge Trust.
With his Piano trio (1929); Violoncello sonata in D minor.

D126. **Strew no more red roses**

D126a. Pearl SHE 513–SHE 514. 2 discs. 1974.
David Johnston, tenor; Jonathan Hinden, piano.
In: Songs and piano music
Recorded April 30, May 1, June 25, and July 25, 1973, Wigmore Hall, London.
Recorded in association with the Frank Bridge Trust.
With his Blow out you bugles; Come to me in my dreams; Day after day; Dweller in my deathless dreams; Go not, happy day; The Hour glass; In autumn: Through the eaves; Journey's end; The Last invocation; Love went a-riding; Mantle of blue; Piano sonata; Three Poems: Solitude; So perverse; 'Tis but a week; What shall I your true love tell?; Where she lies asleep; Winter pastoral.
See: B334

D126b. Pearl SHE 551. 1981.
David Johnston, tenor; Jonathan Hinden, piano.
In: A Frank Bridge spicilegium
Recorded in association with the Frank Bridge Trust.
With his Autumn; The Bee; Divertimenti; Hilli-ho! Hilli-ho!; Love went a-riding; Music when soft voices die; O weary hearts; Two Pieces: Lament; So perverse; Where she lies asleep.

D127. **String quartet no. 1 in E minor**

D127a. Pearl SHE 563. 1980.
Hanson String Quartet.
Recorded February 23–24, 1980, St. Peter's Church, Notting Hill, London.

"Recording made with the financial assistance of the Frank Bridge Trust."
With E. J. Moeran's String trio in G.
See: B232, B422

D128. **String quartet no. 2 in G minor**

D128a. Chandos ABRD 1073 (cass: ARTD 1073; cd: CHAN 8426). 1983.
Also issued on Chandos DBRD 4001 (cass: DBTD 4001). 4 discs. 1983.
Delmé String Quartet.
In: Music for string quartet
Recorded March 26 and 27, 1982, Church of St. George the Martyr, Bloomsbury, London.
"Recorded with financial assistance from the Frank Bridge Trust."
With his An Irish melody; Two Old English songs; Sir Roger de Coverley.
See: B230, B420

D128b. Chandos DBRD 4001 (cass: DBTD 4001). 4 discs. 1983.
Also issued on Chandos ABRD 1073 (cass: ABTD 1073; cd: CHAN 8426). 1983.
Delmé String Quartet.
In: Music for a summer's day
Recorded March and June 1982, Church of St. George the Martyr, Bloomsbury, London.
With his An Irish melody; Two Old English songs; Sir Roger de Coverley and works by Sir Arnold Bax, Ralph Vaughan Williams, Arthur Bliss, John Ireland, Geoffrey Bush, Eugene Goossens, E. J. Moeran, Cyril Scott, Alan Bush, Benjamin Britten, and Alan Rawsthorne.

D129. **String quartet no. 3**

D129a. Argo ZRG 714. 1973.
Allegri String Quartet.
"Recorded in association with the British Council."
With his String quartet no. 4.
See: B169, B217, B294, B405

D130. **String quartet no. 4**

D130a. Argo ZRG 714. 1973.
Allegri String Quartet.
"Recorded in association with the British Council."
With his String quartet no. 3.
See: B169, B217, B294, B405

D131. **String sextet in E-flat major**

D131a. Pearl SHE 570. 1982.
Hanson String Quartet; Stephen Tess, viola; Lionel Handy, violoncello.
Recorded March 6–7, 1982, St. Peter's Church, Notting Hill, London.
Recorded in association with the Frank Bridge Trust.
With his Phantasy in F-sharp minor.
See: B408, B421

D132. **Suite**

D132a. Chandos ABRD 1112 (cass: ABTD 1112; cd: CHAN 8390). 1984.
English Chamber Orchestra; David Garforth, conductor.
In: Music of John Ireland & Frank Bridge
Recorded December 1983, Church of St. Barnabas, Finchley, London.
"This record has been made with financial support from The Frank Bridge Trust and The John Ireland Trust."
With works by John Ireland.
See: B191, B281, B357

D132b. Chandos CBR 1018 (cass: CBT 1018; cd: CHAN 8373). 1985.
Musical Heritage Society MHS 7203. 1985.
Previously issued on RCA Red Seal RL 25184 (cass: RK 25184). 1979.
Bournemouth Sinfonietta; Norman Del Mar, conductor.
In: Bridge, Bantock & Butterworth
Recorded January 1978, Guildhall, Southampton.
With his There is a willow grows aslant a brook; Summer and works by Granville Bantock and George Butterworth.

D132c. Decca X 250–X 252. mono. 78 rpm. 3 discs.
Boyd Neel String Orchestra; Boyd Neel, conductor.
Recorded in 1939.

D132d. Lyrita SRCS.73. 1978.
HNH Records HNH 4078. 1978.
London Philharmonic Orchestra; Sir Adrian Boult, conductor.
With his Lament; Two Old English songs; Rosemary; Sir Roger de Coverley.
See: B170, B214, B243, B410

D132e. Nimbus NI 5068 (compact disc). 1987.
English String Orchestra; William Boughton, conductor.
Recorded June 27–29, 1986, Great Hall, University of Birmingham.
With works by George Butterworth and Sir C. Hubert H. Parry.

D132f. Nimbus NI 5210/12 (compact disc). 1989.
English String Orchestra; William Boughton, conductor.
In: The Spirit of England
With works by Benjamin Britten, Frederick Delius, Edward Elgar, Gerald Finzi, Gustav Holst, Sir C. Hubert H. Parry, Ralph Vaughan Williams, and Peter Warlock.

D132g. RCA Red Seal RL 25184 (cass: RK 25184). 1979.
Reissued on Chandos CBR 1018 (cass: CBT 1018; cd: CHAN 8373) and Musical Heritage Society MHS 7203. 1985.
Bournemouth Sinfonietta; Norman Del Mar, conductor.
In: Butterworth, Bridge & Bantock
Recorded January 1978, Guildhall, Southampton.
With his There is a willow grows aslant a brook; Summer and works by Granville Bantock and George Butterworth.

D133. **Summer**

D133a. Chandos CBR 1018 (cass: CBT 1018; cd: CHAN 8373). 1985.
Musical Heritage Society MHS 7203. 1985.
Previously issued on RCA Red Seal RL 25184 (cass: RK 25184). 1979.
Bournemouth Sinfonietta; Norman Del Mar, conductor.
In: Bridge, Bantock & Butterworth
Recorded January 1978, Guildhall, Southampton.
With his Suite; There is a willow grows aslant a brook and works by Granville Bantock and George Butterworth.

D133b. EMI/HMV ASD 3190. quad. 1976.
Reissued on EMI/HMV ED290868-1 (cass: ED290868-4). 1986.
Royal Liverpool Philharmonic Orchestra; Sir Charles Groves, conductor.
Recorded in Philharmonic Hall, Liverpool.
With his Enter Spring; Lament; Two Old English songs: Cherry Ripe; The Sea.
See: B157, B193, B194, B415

D133c. RCA Red Seal RL 25184 (cass: RK 25184). 1979.
Reissued on Chandos CBR 1018 (cass: CBT 1018; cd: CHAN 8373) and Musical Heritage Society MHS 7203. 1985.
Bournemouth Sinfonietta; Norman Del Mar, conductor.
In: Butterworth, Bridge & Bantock
Recorded January 1978, Guildhall, Southampton.
With his Suite; There is a willow grows aslant a brook and works by Granville Bantock and George Butterworth.

D134. **Tears, idle tears**

D134a. Pearl SHE 577. 1983.
Stephen Varcoe, baritone; Christopher Cox, piano.
In: The Early Bridge
Recorded June 28-29, 1982, Wigmore Hall, London.
"This record has been made with financial assistance from the Frank Bridge Trust."
With his Adoration; All things that we clasp; Allegretto; Allegro appassionato; Berceuse; Blow, blow thou winter wind; Come to me in my dreams; A Dirge; E'en as a lovely flower; Fair daffodils; Far, far from each other; Music when soft voices die; My pent-up tears oppress my brain; Pensiero; The Violets blue; Where is it that our soul doth go?
See: B325, B420

D135. **There is a willow grows aslant a brook**

D135a. Chandos CBR 1018 (cass: CBT 1018; cd: CHAN 8373). 1985.
Musical Heritage Society MHS 7203. 1985.
Previously issued on RCA Red Seal RL 25184 (cass: RK 25184). 1979.
Bournemouth Sinfonietta; Norman Del Mar, conductor.
In: Bridge, Bantock & Butterworth
Recorded January 1978, Guildhall, Southampton.

With his Suite; Summer and works by Granville Bantock and George Butterworth.

D135b. EMI EL749765-1 (cass: EL749756–4; cd: CDC 7 49756–2). 1987.
English Chamber Orchestra; Jeffrey Tate, conductor.
With works by George Butterworth, E. J. Moeran, and Sir Arnold Bax.

D135c. EMI/HMV CSD 3696. 1971.
Odeon CSD 3696. 1971.
EMI/HMV ESD 7100 (cass: TC–ESD 7100). 1971.
English Sinfonia; Neville Dilkes, conductor.
With works by Sir Hamilton Harty, Sir Arnold Bax, and George Butterworth.
See: B192, B237

D135d. RCA Red Seal RL 25184 (cass: RK 25184). 1979.
Reissued on Chandos CBR 1018 (cass: CBT 1018; cd: CHAN 8373) and Musical Heritage Society MHS 7203. 1985.
Bournemouth Sinfonietta; Norman Del Mar, conductor.
In: Butterworth, Bridge & Bantock
Recorded January 1978, Guildhall, Southampton.
With his Suite, Summer and works by Granville Bantock and George Butterworth.

D136. **Threads**

D136a. Pearl SHE 600 (cd: SHECD 9600). 1987.
Chelsea Opera Group Orchestra; Howard Williams, conductor.
In: Frank Bridge: Orchestral Works
Recorded September 1986, CBS Studios, London.
"Recordings made with the financial assistance of the Frank Bridge Trust."
With his Canzonetta; Elégie; Heart's ease; Morning song; Norse legend; Rosemary; Scherzetto; The Turtle's retort; Vignettes de danse.

D137. **Thy hand in mine**

D137a. Pearl SHE 586. 1985.
Patricia Wright, soprano; Christopher Cox, piano.
Recorded in Wigmore Hall, London.

"Recorded with financial assistance from the Frank Bridge Trust, which acts as a source of information about all aspects of Bridge's music."
With his Amaryllis; The Last invocation; Mantle of blue; Miniatures, sets 1-3; Norse legend; Souvenir; 'Tis but a week; What shall I your true love tell?
See: B282, B287

D138. **'Tis but a week**

D138a. Argo ZK 28. 2 discs. 1964.
Argo RG 418. mono. 1964.
Argo ZRG 5418. 1964.
Peter Pears, tenor; Benjamin Britten, piano.
In: Twentieth-century English songs
Recorded 1964 in association with the British Council.
With his Goldenhair; Journey's end; So perverse; When you are old and works by John Ireland, Richard Rodney Bennett, and Priaulx Rainer.
See: B210, B211, B249, B323, B389, B399

D138b. Pearl SHE 513–SHE 514. 2 discs. 1974.
Valerie Baulard, mezzo-soprano; Jonathan Hinden, piano.
In: Songs and piano music
Recorded April 30, May 1, June 25, and July 25, 1973, Wigmore Hall, London.
Recorded in association with the Frank Bridge Trust.
With his Blow out you bugles; Day after day; Dweller in my deathless dreams; Go not, happy day; The Hour glass; In autumn: Through the eaves; Journey's end; The Last invocation; Love went a-riding; Mantle of blue; Piano sonata; Three Poems: Solitude; So perverse; Strew no more red roses; What shall I your true love tell?; Where she lies asleep; Winter pastoral.
See: B334

D138c. Pearl SHE 586. 1985.
Patricia Wright, soprano; Christopher Cox, piano.
Recorded in Wigmore Hall, London.
"Recorded with financial assistance from the Frank Bridge Trust, which acts as a source of information about all aspects of Bridge's music."

With his Amaryllis; The Last invocation; Mantle of blue; Miniatures, sets 1-3; Norse legend; Souvenir; Thy hand in mine; What shall I your true love tell?
See: B282, B287

D139. **The Turtle's retort**

D139a. Pearl SHE 600 (cd: SHECD 9600). 1987.
Chelsea Opera Group Orchestra; Howard Williams, conductor.
In: Frank Bridge: Orchestral works
Recorded September 1986, CBS Studios, London.
"Recordings made with the financial assistance of the Frank Bridge Trust."
With his Canzonetta; Elégie; Heart's ease; Morning song; Norse legend; Rosemary; Scherzetto; Threads; Vignettes de danse.

D140. **Unfinished symphony**

D140a. Lyrita SRCS.104. 1979.
London Philharmonic Orchestra; Nicholas Braithwaite, conductor.
"Recorded in association with the RVW & Bridge Trusts."
With his Oration, concerto elegiaco; Two Poems.
See: B189, B335, B412

D141. **Vignettes de danse**

D141a. Pearl SHE 600 (cd: SHECD 9600). 1987.
Chelsea Opera Group Orchestra; Howard Williams, conductor.
In: Frank Bridge: Orchestral works
Recorded September 1986, CBS Studios, London.
"Recordings made with the financial assistance of the Frank Bridge Trust."
With his Norse legend; Rosemary; Canzonetta; Morning song; Elégie; Scherzetto; Threads; Heart's ease; The Turtle's retort.

D142. **The Violets blue**

D142a. Pearl SHE 577. 1983.
Stephen Varcoe, baritone; Christopher Cox, piano.
In: The Early Bridge
Recorded June 28–29, 1982, Wigmore Hall, London.

"This record has been made with financial assistance from the Frank Bridge Trust."
With his Adoration; All things that we clasp; Allegretto; Allegro appassionato; Berceuse; Blow, blow thou winter wind; Come to me in my dreams; A Dirge; E'en as a lovely flower; Fair daffodils; Far, far from each other; Music when soft voices die; My pent-up tears oppress my brain; Pensiero; Tears, idle tears; Where is it that our soul doth go?
See: B325, B420

D143. **Violin sonata (1932)**

D143a. Pearl SHE 541. 1977.
Levon Chilingirian, violin; Clifford Benson, piano.
Recorded 1976–1977, Wigmore Hall, London.
Recorded in association with the Frank Bridge Trust.
With his Violoncello sonata in D minor.

D143b. Terpsichore 1982 022. 1983.
Hans Mannes, violoncello; Dominque Cornil, piano.
With his Violoncello sonata in D minor.

D144. **Violoncello sonata in D minor**

D144a. Chandos ABRD 1209 (cass: ABTD 1209; cd: CHAN 8499). 1987.
Raphael Wallfisch, violoncello; Peter Wallfisch, piano.
With works by Frederick Delius, Sir Arnold Bax, and Sir William Walton.

D144b. Decca 591.293 (cass: 4–591.293). 1970.
Decca SXL 6426. 1970.
Decca SXL 7074. 1970.
London CS 6649. 1970.
London CS 8649. 1970.
Mstislav Rostropovich, violoncello; Benjamin Britten, piano.
With Franz Schubert's Sonata arpeggione.
See: B175, B212, B244, B250

D144c. Magnum Force/Prelude PRS 2505.
Norman Procter, violoncello; Paul Hamburger, piano.

D144d. Maxsound MSCC 20–MSCC 21; MSCB 20–MSCB 21 (cassettes)
Caroline Dale, violoncello; K. Swallow, piano.

D144e. Nimbus 2117. quad. 1978.
Christian Hocks, violoncello; Martin Jones, piano.
Recorded May 16–17, Wyastone Leys.
With Zoltan Kodaly's Cello sonata, op. 8.

D144f. Pearl SHE 541. 1977.
Rohan de Sarum, violoncello; Druvi de Sarum, piano.
Recorded 1976–1977, Wigmore Hall, London.
Recorded in association with the Frank Bridge Trust.
With his Violin sonata (1932).

D144g. Pearl SHECD 9610 (compact disc). 1989.
Lowri Blake, violoncello; Caroline Palmer, piano.
Recorded in association with the Frank Bridge Trust.
With his: Piano trio (1929); Spring song.

D144h. Terpsichore 1982 022. 1983.
Hans Mannes, violoncello; Dominque Cornil, piano.
With his Violin sonata (1932), arr.

D145. **What shall I your true love tell?**

D145a. Pearl SHE 513–SHE 514. 2 discs. 1974.
Valerie Baulard, mezzo-soprano; Roger Vignoles, piano.
In: Songs and piano music
Recorded April 30, May 1, June 25, and July 25, 1973, Wigmore Hall, London.
Recorded in association with the Frank Bridge Trust.
With his Blow out you bugles; Come to me in my dreams; Day after day; Dweller in my deathless dreams; Go not, happy day; The Hour glass; In autumn: Through the eaves; Journey's end; The Last invocation; Love went a-riding; Mantle of blue; Piano sonata; Three Poems: Solitude; So perverse; Strew no more red roses; 'Tis but a week; Where she lies asleep; Winter pastoral.
See: B334

D145b. Pearl SHE 586. 1985.
Patricia Wright, soprano; Christopher Cox, piano.
"Recorded with financial assistance from the Frank Bridge Trust, which acts as a source of information about all aspects of Bridge's music."

With his Amaryllis; The Last invocation; Mantle of blue; Miniatures, sets 1-3; Souvenir; Thy hand in mine; 'Tis but a week; Norse legend.
See: B282, B287

D146. **When you are old**

D146a. Argo ZK 28. 2 discs. 1964.
Argo RG 418. mono. 1964.
Argo ZRG 5418. 1964.
Peter Pears, tenor; Benjamin Britten, piano.
In: Twentieth-century English songs
Recorded 1964 in association with the British Council.
With his Goldenhair; Journey's end; So perverse; 'Tis but a week and works by John Ireland, Richard Rodney Bennett, and Priaulx Rainer.
See: B210, B211, B249, B323, B389, B399

D147. **Where is it that our soul doth go?**

D147a. Pearl SHE 577. 1983.
Patricia Wright, soprano; Michael Ponder, viola; John Alley, piano.
In: The Early Bridge
Recorded June 28–29, 1982, Wigmore Hall, London.
"This record has been made with financial assistance from the Frank Bridge Trust."
With his Adoration; All things that we clasp; Allegretto; Allegro appassionato; Berceuse; Blow, blow thou winter wind; Come to me in my dreams; A Dirge; E'en as a lovely flower; Fair daffodils; Far, far from each other; Music when soft voices die; My pent-up tears oppress my brain; Pensiero; Tears, idle tears; The Violets blue.
See: B325, B420

D148. **Where she lies asleep**

D148a. Pearl SHE 513–SHE 514. 2 discs. 1974.
David Johnston, tenor; Jonathan Hinden, piano.
In: Songs and piano music
Recorded April 30, May 1, June 25, and July 25, 1973, Wigmore Hall, London.
Recorded in association with the Frank Bridge Trust.

With his Blow out you bugles; Come to me in my dreams; Day after day; Dweller in my deathless dreams; Go not, happy day; The Hour glass; In Autumn: Through the eaves; Journey's end; The Last invocation; Love went a-riding; Mantle of blue; Piano sonata; Three Poems: Solitude; So perverse; Strew no more red roses; 'Tis but a week; What shall I your true love tell?; Winter pastoral.

See: B334

D148b. Pearl SHE 551. 1981.

David Johnston, tenor; Jonathan Hinden, piano.

In: A Frank Bridge spicilegium

Recorded in association with the Frank Bridge Trust.

With his Autumn; The Bee; Divertimenti; Hilli-ho! Hilli-ho!; Love went a-riding; Music when soft voices die; O weary hearts; Two Pieces: Lament; So perverse; Strew no more red roses.

D149. **Winter pastoral**

D149a. Continuum CCD 1016 (compact disc). 1990.

Peter Jacobs, piano.

In: Frank Bridge: Complete music for piano

"Recorded in association with the Frank Bridge Trust."

With his Arabesque; Capriccio no. 1 in A minor; Capriccio no. 2 in F-sharp minor; A Dedication; A Fairy tale; Gargoyle; Hidden fires; Three Improvisations; In autumn; Miniature pastorals, sets 1 2; A Sea idyll.

D149b. Pearl SHE 513–SHE 514. 2 discs. 1974.

Peter Wallfisch, piano.

In: Songs and piano music

Recorded April 30, May 1, June 25, and July 25, 1973, Wigmore Hall, London.

Recorded in association with the Frank Bridge Trust.

With his Blow out you bugles; Come to me in my dreams; Day after day; Dweller in my deathless dreams; Go not, happy day; The Hour glass; In autumn: Through the eaves; Journey's end; The Last invocation; Love went a-riding; Mantle of blue; Piano sonata; Three Poems: Solitude; So perverse; Strew no more red roses; 'Tis but a week; What shall I your true love tell?; Where she lies asleep

See: B334

Bibliography

"See" references, e.g., *See*: W61d, refer to individual works and particular performances of those works as described in the "Works and Performances" section and "See" references, e.g., *See*: D7, refer to recordings described in the "Discography" section.

BOOKS AND ARTICLES

B1. Antcliffe, Herbert. "Frank Bridge." *Sackbut* 5 (May 1925): 286–88.

A description of Bridge's musical activities up to 1925, including conducting and performing engagements. The author encourages Bridge to compose for the stage. He feels that Bridge's talent lies there.

B2. Banfield, Stephen David. "British Chamber Music at the Turn of the Century: Parry, Stanford, Mackenzie." *The Musical Times* 115 (March 1974): 211–13.

An article which, in discussing Stanford as a teacher of chamber music, places Bridge in the category of those students who rebelled against Stanford's "perfect models."

B3. ———. *Sensibility and English Song: Critical Studies of the Early 20th Century*. 2 vols. Cambridge: Cambridge University Press, 1985.

An in-depth discussion of song composition in the early 20th century. Song lists are included for fifty-four composers, including Bridge. Bridge's "60-odd solo songs" are discussed in six pages of narrative.

The author concludes that Bridge "can hardly be considered a song composer of major importance."

B4. ———. "'Too much of Albion'? Mrs. Coolidge and her British Connections." *American Music* 4 (1986): 59–88.
An excellent, detailed description of Elizabeth Sprague Coolidge's work with British musicians, this article discusses at length her relationship with Frank Bridge.

B5. Bishop, John. "Frank Bridge." *Composer* (London) 57 (Spring 1976): 23–26.
After presenting a short biography, the author describes, in brief, the neglect of Bridge's music after his death and the revival beginning to take place in the 1970's.

B6. ———, ed. *Frank Bridge: Centenary Festival.* N.p., 1979.
This is a thirty-two page program book outlining the activities of Bridge's centenary festival held in Eastbourne June 15–17, 1979. Included is an introduction by Sir Peter Pears and analytic descriptions of the works performed during the festival as well as articles on Bridge by Peter Pirie, Benjamin Britten (from a talk on BBC in 1947), and John Bishop.

B7. Bliss, Sir Arthur. *As I Remember*. London: Faber and Faber, 1970.
This work contains six lines of text describing Bridge's approach to judging composition contests—that of checking the ending of the work to learn of the composer's individuality.

B8. Bray, Trevor. "Bridge's Novelletten and Idylls." *The Musical Times* 117 (November 1976): 905–6.
Provides a discussion and brief analysis of the works. Compares compositional techniques used in the two pieces, placing them in their historical context.

B9. ———. "Frank Bridge and His 'Quasi-Adopted Son.'" *Music Review* 45 (May 1984): 135–38.
In this article, the author suggests discarding the standard explanation that Bridge's seemingly radical stylistic change was due to the war's effect on him. In its place, he suggests that the change is made gradually and the major refocusing was a result of Bridge's sorrow over his childlessness.

B10. ———. "Frank Bridge and Mrs. Coolidge." *Music and Musicians* 26 (October 1977): 28–30.
After an introduction to the relationship that Bridge and Elizabeth Sprague Coolidge shared, the author presents an analysis and description of his *Phantasm*, one of several works dedicated to Mrs. Coolidge.

B11. ———. "Music Reviews: Bridge." *The Musical Times* 124 (December 1983): 756.

A review of a cross-section of music in print by Bridge. Examples are provided that demonstrate his inclination to compose salon music as well as examples of music that demonstrate "considerable distinction."

B12. Bridge, Frank. "Sir Charles Stanford and his Pupils." *RCM Magazine* 20, no. 2 (1924): 55–61.

This article is a series of brief, untitled essays by students of Sir Charles Stanford written on the occasion of his death. Bridge's essay praises Stanford as a "master-mind at work." Other essays are by persons such as Rebecca Clarke, James Friskin, and Vaughan-Williams.

B13. "British Piano Music." *Times – Literary Supplement* (London), 10 August 1916, p. 380.

Bridge's *Three Poems* and *Arabesque* are discussed in this article, along with works by Edgar Bainton, Ernest Austin, and Eugene Goossens. The author notes that these composers have come to realize that "the piano offers a ready means of communication between the artist and his public and [they] have set to themselves to explore its possibilities."

B14. Britten, Benjamin. "Britten Looking Back." *Musical America* 84 (February 1964): 4–5.

In this article, Britten describes his experiences with Bridge from their first meeting through his college days. He also discusses influences Bridge had on him outside that of structured composition lessons.

B15. ———. "Early Influences: A Tribute to Frank Bridge (1879–1941)." *Composer* (London) 19 (Spring 1966): 2–3.

In this article, Britten describes his experiences with Bridge, from their first meeting through his college days. He also mentions influences Bridge had on him outside that of structured composition lessons.

B16. ———. "Trio (Rhapsody)." Program notes for performance at Eighth Aldeburgh Festival, Jubilee Hall, Aldeburgh, 24 June 1965.

In this article about Bridge's *Rhapsody*, Britten describes his recollection of discussions about the work he had with Bridge when he was a boy. He describes the work as having a "strong fantastic character, very personal themes, and wonderfully resourceful writing for the instruments."

B17. Bye, Frederick. "Frank Bridge's Sonata for 'Cello and Piano." *Strad* (July 1930): 136–37.

An analytic discussion of Bridge's Violoncello sonata in D minor. The author encourages more frequent performances of the work.

B18. C. "Mr. Frank Bridge and the Philharmonic." *The Musical Times* 63 (April 1922): 251.

This is a review of the February 23, 1922 concert by the Royal Philharmonic Society at which Bridge conducted, replacing both Sir Landon Ronald and Mr. Eugene Goossens because of illness. The concert is described as one which "was not to be denied real brilliance," one for which Bridge "deserves to be held in remembrance."

B19. "Carnegie United Kingdom Trust: The Music-Publication Scheme." *The Musical Times* 58 (May 1917): 218.

An announcement of the seven works selected for publication with funding from the Carnegie Trust. Bridge's *The Sea* is one of the seven, selected from a group of 136 entries.

B20. "Carnegie United Kingdom Trust: Scheme of Musical Composition Prizes." *The Musical Times* 57 (December 1916): 552–53.

An announcement and description of the plan devised by the Carnegie Trustees to fund the publication of original British works. Bridge's *The Sea* was published under this arrangement.

B21. "Chamber Music." *Times - Literary Supplement* (London), 10 March 1921, p. 158.

This article presents a lengthy discussion of Bridge's chamber music, in particular his String quintet in E minor and String sextet in E-flat major published just prior to the writing of this article. The author mentions the increasing frequency in which Bridge's chamber music is receiving publication. He speaks of the music's attractiveness, especially to the players. Also discussed is Bridge's freedom from mannerisms which is viewed as refreshing at first but later confusing.

B22. "Charles Villiers Stanford—By Some of His Pupils." *Music and Letters* 5 (July 1924): 193–207.

This article consists of short essays by sixteen Stanford students on his influence and/or their experiences under his tutelage. Frank Bridge contributes one of the sixteen essays.

B23. Cohen, Harriet. *A Bundle of Time*. London: Faber and Faber, 1969.

Short excerpts describe Cohen's impression of Frank Bridge as a "very fine viola player of the English Quartet." Mention is made of rehearsing the "extremely difficult Frank Bridge trio" and of its first few performances, with Cohen as pianist. A brief discussion is given on the commissioning of *A Bach Book for Harriet Cohen* for which Bridge wrote *Todessehnsucht*.

B24. Cole, Hugo. "Composer without Problems." *Country Life* (February 10, 1979): 388.

This article, the title of which is taken from a quote about Bridge in an article by Herbert Howells, briefly sketches Bridge's life and then discusses Bridge's works and differing styles as they were viewed by Bridge's contemporaries and as they were viewed by the author and his contemporaries.

B25. Colles, Henry Cope. *The Royal College of Music: A Jubilee Record, 1883–1933*. London: Macmillan, 1933.

Later incorporated into Colles and Cruft's *The Royal College of Music: A Centenary Record, 1883–1983*, this history mentions the founding of The English String Quartet in 1909 and the first performance of *The Christmas rose* in 1931.

B26. Colles, Henry Cope, and Cruft, John. *The Royal College of Music: A Centenary Record, 1883–1983*. London: Royal College of Music, 1982.

This work is an expansion by Cruft of Colles' history from 1883–1933. In it is mentioned the founding of the English String Quartet in 1909, consisting of Tom Morris, Herbert Kinsey, Frank Bridge, and Ivor James. Appendices list Bridge's election as a Fellow of the Royal College of Music in 1924 and as a winner of the Tagore Medal in 1903, and give 1931 as the first performance of *The Christmas rose* at the Royal College of Music's Parry Theatre.

B27. Cox, David. *The Henry Wood Proms*. London: British Broadcasting Corp., 1980.

This book traces the history of London's promenade concerts from their beginnings in 1895 to 1979. Appendices list premieres performed as part of the concerts, including five premieres of Bridge works.

B28. Dale, S. S. "Contemporary Cello Concerti LXIII: Bridge." *Strad* 88 (April 1978): 1151–61.

The opening of this article laments the lack of notice Bridge's music had received in the past. The author then turns to a biographical description of Bridge, focusing particular emphasis on his technique and skill as a conductor. The closing section is an analytical discussion of his *Oration*.

B29. Davies, Oliver, and Hayle, Kenneth. "Catalogue of a Collection of the Musical Manuscripts of Frank Bridge (1879–1941)." London, 1962.

This work is a catalog of Bridge's manuscripts held in the Royal College of Music Library. It has been superseded by a newer catalog which references the collection by "H." numbers as used in the thematic catalog compiled by Paul Hindmarsh.

B30. Dickinson, Peter. "Lord Berners, 1883–1950: A British Avant-Gardist at the Time of World War I." *The Musical Times* 124 (November 1983): 669–72.

In an attempt to place Lord Berners and his music in the British music scene of the early 1900's, the author compares his works to works of other contemporary composers. Bridge's *Three Poems* is analyzed and compared with Berner's *Fragments psychologiques*.

B31. Domville, Eric. "A Time there was...: The Conclusion of our Survey of English National Music." *Fugue* 3 (July–August 1979): 45–49.

A survey of English nationals, this article contains one paragraph on Bridge. He is described as writing in a more sophisticated manner than the other nationalists and in a way that, while English, is decidedly different than the others.

B32. Douglas, D. "Frank Bridge: A Great Sussex Musician." *Sussex County Magazine* (March 1941): 99–100.

This article presents a brief biography of Frank Bridge. In doing so, great praise is given first for his contributions as a composer, then as a conductor, and finally as a violist. The tone of the article is clearly demonstrated in its final sentence: "Any period of his life, therefore, that he has been in a position to write music, has been spent towards uplift in the thoughts of mankind."

B33. Dunhill, Thomas F. *Chamber Music: A Treatise for Students*. London: Macmillan, 1913; reprint ed., London: Macmillan, 1925.

In the chapter entitled "Strings with Pianoforte" the author discusses Bridge's Phantasy in F-sharp minor. He describes it as a "recent example, typifying some quite modern trends of thought."

B34. Elkin, Robert. *Queen's Hall, 1893–1941*. London: Rider, 1944.

Brief mention is made of Bridge's role as conductor or composer in the BBC Symphony Concerts in 1934, the 1915 concerts organized by Isidore de Lara, and the Chappell Popular Concerts of the 1920's. This book provides substantial background on the musical life of this hall during Bridge's career.

B35. ———. *Royal Philharmonic: The Annals of the Royal Philharmonic Society*. London: Rider, 1947.

Contains an account of Bridge playing the role of "ambulance conductor" in February 1922, a name received because of his frequent calls to fill in for ill conductors. An appendix lists the Society's programs from 1912 to 1945. According to this list, three of Bridge's works were performed and he conducted two concerts during this time.

B36. "English Music: Treasures of our Native Art." *Times* (London), 19 June 1915, p. 11d.

This article discusses several concerts at which works by Bridge were performed. The author hopes that through this discussion, a new appreciation of English music will be fostered.

B37. Evans, Edwin. "Frank Bridge: 1879–1941." *The Listener* (March 6, 1941): 353.

In this article, the author describes Bridge's compositional output. He divides the sketch into four genres: orchestral music, chamber music, piano music, and songs. The reader is also informed of an upcoming memorial concert of Bridge songs and orchestral works to be broadcast on March 12, 1941.

B38. ———. "In Memoriam: Frank Bridge and Sir Hamilton Harty." *Music Review* 2 (1941): 159–66.

Bridge's major works are discussed in the first section of this article, Harty's in the second section.

B39. ———. "Modern British Composers: I - Frank Bridge." *The Musical Times* 60 (February 1919): 55–61.

A descriptive analysis of Bridge's early compositional style. Several works are presented as illustrative. The article ends with a list of works and their publisher.

B40. Evans, Peter. *The Music of Benjamin Britten*. Minneapolis: University of Minnesota Press, 1979.

Mention is made of Bridge as Britten's teacher but most of the half dozen references to Bridge in this work are made about Bridge's musical influences as actually seen in Britten's music.

B41. "Foreign Notes: Bologna." *The Musical Times* 47 (June 1906): 417.

An announcement of a competition offered by the Royal Philharmonic Academy for the best string quartet. Bridge submitted his String quartet no. 1 in E minor before the closing date of October 31, 1906.

B42. Foreman, Lewis. *From Parry to Britten: British Music in Letters, 1900–1945*. Portland, Oregon: Amadeus Press, 1987.

This work contains 248 letters, two from Bridge to Benjamin Britten and one from Bridge to Elizabeth Sprague Coolidge. Reference is made to Bridge and/or his compositions in several letters by others. An interesting overview of music life in Great Britain during Bridge's life.

B43. ________. "Reputation...Bought or Made?" *The Musical Times* 121 (January 1980): 27.

This article discusses the reason behind "the upsurge of interest in recordings of music by such composers as Frank Bridge and Gerald Finzi." This new interest is explained as the result of a planned investment of royalties in order to enable financial support of record production.

B44. Foreman, Lewis; Hughes, Eric; and Walker, Malcolm. "Frank Bridge (1879–1941): A Discography." *Recorded Sound* 66–67 (April–July 1977): 669–73.

A thorough, but now dated discography containing an alphabetical listing of recorded works, including material on BBC Transcription disks, material in the British Institute of Recorded Sound, and the Library of Congress private disks. A second section lists Bridge's recordings of his own music and a third lists Bridge's recordings of works by other composers.

B45. "Frank Bridge." *New York Times*, 12 January 1941, p. 46.

A five sentence obituary notice announcing Bridge's death at the age of 61 of a heart attack.

B46. *Frank Bridge: Chamber & Orchestral Works*. London: Augener, [1930].

This is Augener's listing of Bridge works which they had available for purchase. Seventeen such works are advertised, each with a two to three line musical incipit.

B47. "Funerals: Mr. F. Bridge." *Times* (London), 17 January 1941, p. 7.

A short account of Bridge's funeral, which took place on Wednesday, January 15, 1941.

B48. Galant, Jed Adie. "The Solo Piano Works of Frank Bridge." D.M.A. dissertation, Peabody Institute of John Hopkins University, 1987.

Following an extensive biography, the author analyzes Bridge's piano music. Each work is described as to form and harmonic treatment. In most cases, quotes by contemporaries, some from reviews of first performances and others by those who have studied the works, are included.

B49. Glock, William. "Music and Musicians: Frank Bridge." *Observer* (London), 19 January 1941, p. 3.

An obituary, thirty-one lines in length, in which Bridge is described as "one of our finest musicians." His wide-ranging musical skills and his generosity, particularly in regard to his students, are mentioned.

B50. Goddard, Scott. "Frank Bridge." *Monthly Musical Record* 71 (April 1941): 59–63.

This survey of Bridge works, written on his death, is the author's attempt to show "what one listener heard in a certain composer's music during 1941." Bridge is described, in conclusion, as "a fine and complete artist and musician."

B51. Goodfriend, James. "Going on Record: Centen- and other -aries." *Stereo Review* 42 (February 1979): 70.

This article is a brief discussion of centenaries of five composers, of which Bridge is one. Very briefly mentioned are his two styles and works which typify each of them.

B52. Goossens, Eugene. *Overtures and Beginners: A Musical Autobiography.* London: Methuen, 1951; reprint ed., Westport, Conn.: Greenwood Press, 1972.

Very brief mention of Bridge is made in this work, the primary comment being Goossens regard of him as "the best string writer of his generation."

B53. Hindmarsh, Paul. "Allegro moderato." Program notes for performance at Aldeburgh Festival, Snape Maltings, 20 June 1979.

These notes inform the reader that at the time of his death, Bridge had orchestrated all but the last twenty-one bars of the first movement of the *Unfinished symphony*. For this performance the last section was orchestrated and prepared for performance by Anthony Pople.

B54. ———. *Frank Bridge: A Thematic Catalogue, 1900-1941*. London: Faber Music, Ltd., 1983.

A major publication on Frank Bridge, this work provides information such as incipits, manuscript locations, composition and publication dates, and descriptions of varying lengths, on the circumstances surrounding the composition and/or performance of the majority of the Bridge's works.

B55. ———. "Frank Bridge - Centenary Survey." *Music Teacher* 58 (July 1979): 15-18; 58 (August 1979): 11–13.

In this two part article, the author describes Bridge's life and works, broken down into five clearly-defined periods: 1. 1900–1903: Nursery years, 2. 1904–1912: Edwardian phase, 3. 1913–1924: Transitional period, 4. 1924–1932: Progressive years, and 5. 1936–1941: Classical phase.

B56. Holbrooke, Joseph. *Contemporary British Composers*. London: Palmer, 1925.

This biographical dictionary presents a ten page sketch of Bridge and his works. Written before his change in style, the comments are all glowing, the author calling Bridge "the figure of happiness in British music."

B57. Holst, Imogen. *Britten*. London: Faber and Faber, 1966.

Contains quotes by Britten on the influence of Bridge's teaching on his works and on his life.

B58. Howells, Herbert. "Frank Bridge." *Music and Letters* 22 (July 1941): 208–15.

In this article, the author describes Bridge as "the composer without problems." The basic characteristics of the music of Bridge's two stylistic periods are outlined, stressing Bridge's competence and knowledge of his actions and their consequences.

B59. Howes, Frank. *The English Musical Renaissance*. New York: Stein and Day, 1966.

This work contains slightly over two pages of praise of Bridge's early works and criticism of his later writings in which he began to "uglify his music to keep it up to date." An interesting account of the author's perception of Bridge's significance as viewed in the 1960's.

B60. Hull, A. Eaglefield. "The Neo-British School." *Monthly Musical Record* 51 (March 1921): 52–53; 52 (April 1921): 76–77; 53 (May 1921): 100–101; 54 (June 1921): 124–25.

The author presents short sketches of the major musical output of composers he feels belong to the Neo-British School. By the final installment he has described the music of composers such as John Ireland, Arnold Bax, Cyril Scott, and Frank Bridge and has changed the composers' collective name to Neo-British Composers.

B61. Hurd, Michael. *Benjamin Britten*. London: Novello, 1966.

This short twenty page biography contains a three paragraph description of Frank Bridge and his influence on Britten.

B62. "Invalids." *Times* (London), 27 October 1936, p. 14.

A one sentence statement that Bridge had been ill with bronchitis but was feeling better.

B63. James, Ivor. "The Good Old Days." *RCM Magazine* 50, no. 3 (1954): 99–102.

This article is a description of the author's experiences at the Royal College of Music. Admitted in 1899, James was a contemporary of

Bridge and recounts many experiences they shared as members of the English String Quartet.

B64. ———. "Obituary: Frank Bridge." *RCM Magazine* 37, no. 1 (1941): 22–24.
An obituary in praise of Bridge by a friend. Ivor James also mentions his bluntness, which sometimes handicapped him as a conductor.

B65. Johnson, Stephen. "Pupil and mentor." *Gramophone* 65 (May 1988): 1555.
In this article the author interviews Steven Isserlis, the cellist performing Bridge's *Oration* for EMI on EL749716-1. The cellist shares his view of Bridge's musical imagery as "never crude" but instead very poignant. Isserlis describes the work as one in which Bridge did not have the audience in mind but was definitely considering the players - it "stretches you - [the players] technically as well as emotionally."

B66. Keating, Roderick Maurice. "The Songs of Frank Bridge." D.M.A. dissertation, University of Texas at Austin, 1970.
This work is divided into five parts. Part I is a brief biography. Part II is entitled "The English Musical Renaissance." Contemporaries of Bridge and the musical environment in which Bridge composed are discussed. Part III is a chronological list of songs by Bridge. The music itself is discussed in Part IV while the texts to the songs are discussed in Part V which is entitled "Bridge and English Poetry."

B67. Kendall, Alan. *Benjamin Britten*. Introduction by Yehudi Menuhin. London: Macmillan, 1973; reprint ed., London: Macmillan, 1974.
This work presents a solid discussion of Frank Bridge's influence, both musically and personally, on Benjamin Britten.

B68. Kennedy, Michael. *The Works of Vaughan Williams*. London: Oxford University Press, 1964.
In this work, brief mention is made of Bridge, in one instance in a quote by Vaughan Williams. In this quote, he laments the results of Bridge's writing music "effectively."

B69. Kinsey, Herbert. "The Chips." *RCM Magazine* 52, no. 2 (1956): 47–48.
In this article, the author describes his memories of the "Chips Quartet" which consisted of the author, Tom Morris, Frank Bridge, and Ivor James. The description is of a lively group who frequently performed at the Royal College of Music Union "At Homes."

B70. Lahee, Henry C. *Annals of Music in America*. Boston: Marshall Jones, 1922.
This work attempts a complete recording of music in the United States from 1640 to 1921. First performances of significant works are

chronicled. Listed is a performance of Bridge's Suite on January 19, 1921, at a concert given by the Boston Musical Association.

B71. "The Late Frank Bridge." *New York Times*, 23 February 1941, p. 6X, col. e.
An obituary notice consisting primarily of quotes of William Glock, music critic of the *London Observer*.

B72. "Latest Wills." *Times* (London), 30 January 1961, p. 12.
A listing of Bridge's wife's, Mrs. Ethel Elmore Bridge, estate and to whom it was to be left. A portion was to go to the Royal College of Music in hopes that they would be able to arrange for an annual performance or two of Bridge's major works.

B73. Longmire, John. *John Ireland: Portrait of a Friend.* London: John Baker, 1969.
This work is a sketch of the life and works of John Ireland in which a quote from one of his letters describes his feeling that composers, such as Frank Bridge, have been totally neglected and that this should not be.

B74. "Miscellaneous." *The Musical Times* 56 (July 1915): 433–34.
An announcement of the choosing of Bridge's String quartet no. 2 in G minor as the winner in the 1915 Cobbett Competition.

B75. Mitchell, Donald. *Britten and Auden in the Thirties - The Year 1936.* Seattle: University of Washington Press, 1981.
This book describes, through the use of Britten's diary, Britten's relationship with Auden. In doing so, scattered references are made to Britten's activities with and his respect for Frank Bridge.

B76. Mitchell, Donald, and Keller, Hans, eds. *Benjamin Britten: A Commentary on his Works from a Group of Specialists*. London: Barrie and Rockliff, 1952; reprint ed., Westport, Conn.: Greenwood Press, 1972.
A collection of essays on various aspects of Britten's life and works, this book contains a brief description of Britten's first encounter with Bridge and the resultant teacher/pupil relationship.

B77. "New Music: Full Scores." *The Musical Times* 70 (January 1929): 45–46.
An announcement that Bridge's String quartet no. 3 had been published by Augener.

B78. "New Music: Pianoforte Music." *The Musical Times* 66 (August 1925): 704–6.

A review of the newly printed music for Bridge's *Three Lyrics* and *In autumn*. The pieces are described as being "more persistently dissonant than is usual" but "contain much that is harmonically striking."

B79. Nolan, P. J. "American Methods will Create Ideal Audiences." *Musical America* 39 (November 17, 1923): 3.

This article is an interview with Bridge, conducted while he was in the United States. During the interview, Bridge praises American orchestras and discusses the need to wait for accurate appraisals of the musical "Renaissance" in Great Britain.

B80. "Noted Musician Began Career at Brighton." *The Brighton and Hove Herald*, 18 January 1941, p. 5e.

This obituary outlines Bridge's early life as a student at the Brighton School of Music and a performer with the orchestra in Brighton conducted by his father. The Whinyates Quartet performed music by Haydn and Beethoven at his funeral. He was cremated on the Wednesday following his death on a Friday.

B81. "Notes of Musicians Here and Afield." *New York Times*, 6 November 1938, p. 8X, col. d.

A report of the awarding of Elizabeth Sprague Coolidge medals to Hugo Kortschak, Jacques Gordon, and Frank Bridge.

B82. "Obituary." *The Musical Times* 82 (February 1941): 79–80.

A biographical sketch of Bridge's life with reference to his cultivation of a "harmonic system for which he had less natural gift" than the system he applied in earlier works. This is given as the reason his works "did not stand well with the concert-going public."

B83. "Obituary: Mr. Frank Bridge." *Daily Telegraph* (London), 13 January 1941, p. 3.

An obituary, polite but not glowing.

B84. "Obituary: Mr. Frank Bridge." *Times* (London), 13 January 1941, p. 4b.

An announcement of Bridge's death, describing him as "composer, conductor, and viola master."

B85. "Obituary: Mr. Frank Bridge - Composer, Conductor, and Viola Player." *Times* (London), 13 January 1941, p. 7d.

An announcement of Bridge's death followed by a brief biographical sketch.

B86. "Occasional Notes." *The Musical Times* 46 (June 1905): 384.
An announcement of a prize awarded Bridge by Mr. Mark Hambourg for his Capriccio no. 1 in A minor. The prize of ten guineas was given to the composer of "the best short pianoforte solo, prelude, nocturne, barcarolle, romance, or scherzino." The capriccio was chosen from 96 compositions composed by those aging from 10 to 26 years.

B87. "Occasional Notes." *The Musical Times* 46 (July 1905): 455.
An announcement of the Worshipful Company of Musicians' The Cobbett Prize. The prizes were to be awarded to a "composition of a short piece of music for stringed instruments." Bridge was subsequently awarded second prize for his Phantasie in F minor.

B88. "Occasional Notes." *The Musical Times* 46 (December 1905): 791.
An announcement of the Cobbett Musical Competition outlining the subject of the competition as "a short 'Phantasy' in the form of a String Quartet for two violins, viola and violoncello. The parts must be of equal importance, and the duration of the piece should not exceed twelve minutes. Though the Phantasy is to be performed without a break, it may consist of different sections varying in *tempi* and rhythms." Bridge was subsequently awarded second prize for his Phantasie in F minor.

B89. "Occasional Notes." *The Musical Times* 48 (June 1907): 379–81.
An announcement of the "Cobbett Musical Competition No. 2" offered by the Worshipful Company of Musicians for a string trio Phantasie.

B90. "Occasional Notes." *The Musical Times* 55 (May 1914): 304–5.
An announcement of the offer, by W. W. Cobbett of Ł50 for an original string quartet. The closing date of the competition is listed as December 31, 1914. Bridge submitted his String quartet no. 2 in G minor.

B91. Oliver, Michael. "After the Renaissance: A Survey of British Music from 1920 to 1945." *Gramophone* 61 (August 1983): 219–24.
Describing the years 1920–1945 as a "waiting period," the author highlights the efforts of six composers during this time, one of whom was Bridge.

B92. "Orchestras in Profusion." *New York Times*, 11 November 1923, p. 6X, col. g.
An announcement of an upcoming performance of Bridge's *Two Poems* in New York's Aeolian Hall. A sketch of Bridge also appears on this page with the caption announcing this upcoming performance.

B93. Ottaway, Hugh. "Twentieth-Century English Music." In *Guide to Modern Music on Records*, 8-36. Edited by Robert Simpson and Oliver Prenn. London: Anthony Blond, 1958.

In this essay, the author describes English twentieth-century music as having a "curiously odd complexion." In speaking of Bridge's music specifically, he describes his "total eclipse" as partly attributable to his "failure to grasp the nature of the English musical crisis." The author feels, however, that Bridge's chamber works, in particular, are worthy of greater recognition.

B94. Payne, Anthony. "After a Century of Neglect." *Daily Telegraph* (London), 2 December 1972, p. 13.

In this article, the author laments the past neglect of Frank Bridge's music and calls for a wider dissemination of his work.

B95. ———. "Britten and the String Quartet." *Tempo* 163 (December 1987): 2–6.

This article examines Benjamin Britten's string quartets, particularly the early works. The examination focuses on the changing influences that Bridge, as Britten's teacher, had on Britten. This influence is reflected in these early chamber works.

B96. ———. "Englands zweite Renaissance in der Musik." *Oesterreichische Musikzeitschrift* 41 (March–April 1986): 149–54.

This article presents a brief discussion on British music from 1900 to 1930, touching on composers such as Elgar, Delius, Vaughan Williams, Holst, and Bridge. The author considers this period England's second Renaissance.

B97. ———. *Frank Bridge: Radical and Conservative*. London: Thames Publishing, 1984.

An analytic discussion of Bridge's musical output, divided into six groups: 1. Early chamber music, 2. First orchestral works, 3. Middle period, 4. Years of transition, 5. Final harvest, and 6. Final orchestral works.

B98. ———. "Introduction to Frank Bridge." In *Building a Library: A Listener's Guide to Record Collecting*, pp. 152–57. Edited by John Lade. Oxford: Oxford University, 1979.

This essay outlines and critiques recordings of Bridge's works available at that time. A total of eleven recordings are discussed.

B99. ———. "The Music of Frank Bridge." *Tempo* 106 (September 1973): 18–25; 107 (December 1973): 11–18.

The two articles, "The Early Years" and "The Last Years," present analytical discussions of Bridge's major works. These articles are an earlier, abbreviated form of the main body of *The Music of Frank Bridge* published by Thames in 1976.

B100. ———. "Seeing Frank Bridge Whole." *Daily Telegraph* (London), 8 December 1973, p. 11c.
This article describes the events in 1973 which promoted the music of Bridge. These included an Argo recording of String quartet no. 3 and no. 4 and a series of programs by the BBC in the autumn of 1973.

B101. Payne, Anthony; Foreman, Lewis; and Bishop, John. *The Music of Frank Bridge*. London: Thames Publishing, 1976.
An analytic discussion of Bridge's works follows a brief introduction. The work closes with a bibliography and selected discography.

B102. Pears, Sir Peter. "Frank Bridge (1879–1941)." *Recorded Sound* 66–67 (April–July 1977): 666–68.
A transcript of a lecture given in March 1971 by the author. Bridge's life and musical output are briefly outlined by Pears, who knew Bridge well from 1937 to 1939. The transcript closes with a talk by Benjamin Britten on Bridge that was broadcast by the BBC.

B103. Pirie, Peter J. "Bantock and his Generation." *The Musical Times* 109 (August 1968): 715–17.
This article discusses the careers and music of composers who studied with Frederick Corder at the Royal Academy of Music. Pupils of Stanford at the Royal College of Music are also discussed. The differences between the two teachers and their effects on their pupils are outlined.

B104. ———. "Debussy and English Music." *The Musical Times* 108 (July 1967): 599–601.
In this article Debussy is viewed through an examination of English composers of his time—both their influence on him and his on them. Bridge is mentioned as exhibiting Debussian characteristics in his later music.

B105. ———. *The English Musical Renaissance*. New York: St. Martin's Press, 1979.
A chronological narrative describing English music of the twentieth century. Bridge is prominently discussed in a positive light.

B106. ———. *Frank Bridge*. London: Triad Press, 1971.
Beginning and ending with great lamentations on the lack of recognition of Bridge during his life up to 1971, this work is essentially a descriptive analysis of his major works.

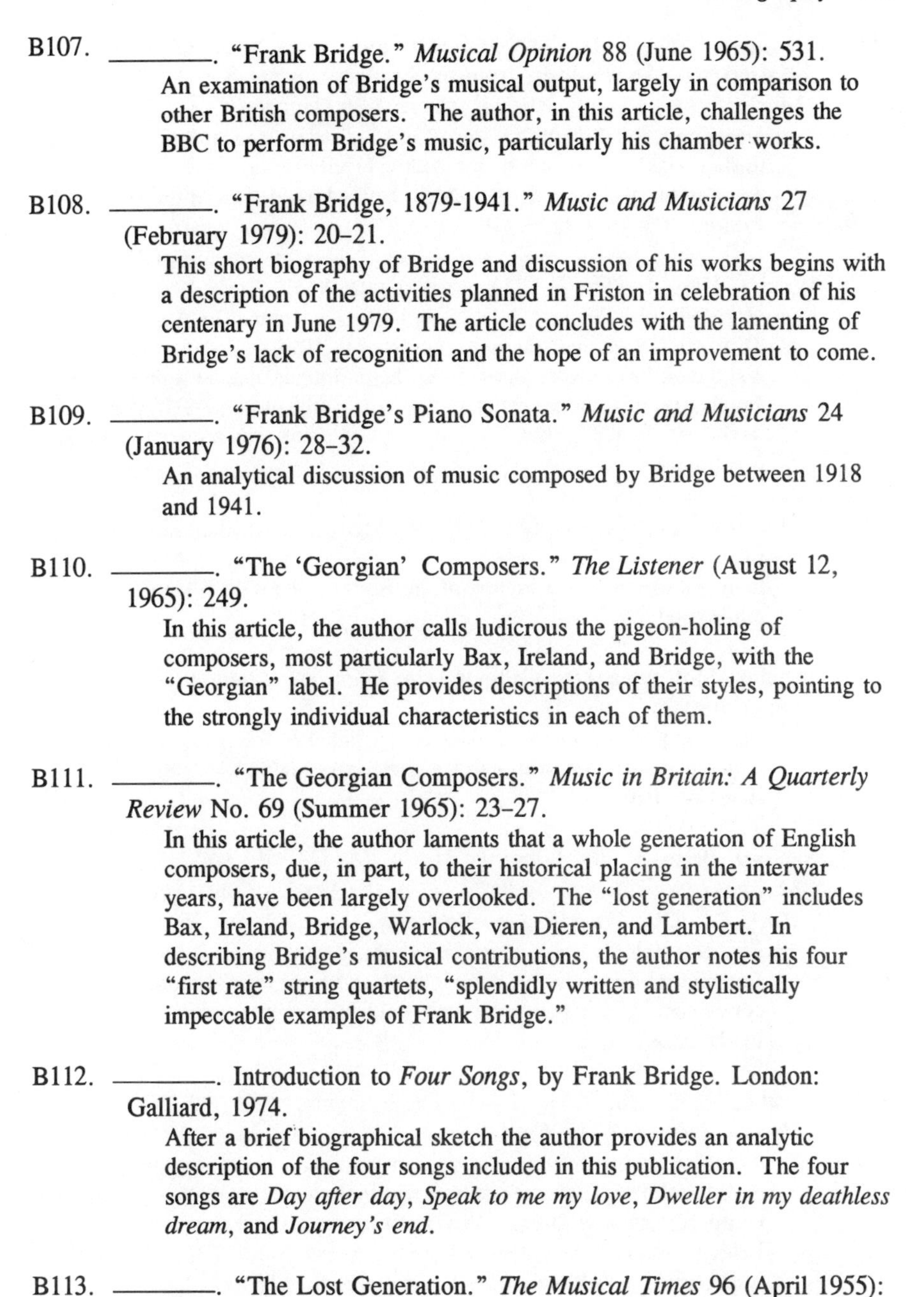

B107. ———. "Frank Bridge." *Musical Opinion* 88 (June 1965): 531.

An examination of Bridge's musical output, largely in comparison to other British composers. The author, in this article, challenges the BBC to perform Bridge's music, particularly his chamber works.

B108. ———. "Frank Bridge, 1879-1941." *Music and Musicians* 27 (February 1979): 20–21.

This short biography of Bridge and discussion of his works begins with a description of the activities planned in Friston in celebration of his centenary in June 1979. The article concludes with the lamenting of Bridge's lack of recognition and the hope of an improvement to come.

B109. ———. "Frank Bridge's Piano Sonata." *Music and Musicians* 24 (January 1976): 28–32.

An analytical discussion of music composed by Bridge between 1918 and 1941.

B110. ———. "The 'Georgian' Composers." *The Listener* (August 12, 1965): 249.

In this article, the author calls ludicrous the pigeon-holing of composers, most particularly Bax, Ireland, and Bridge, with the "Georgian" label. He provides descriptions of their styles, pointing to the strongly individual characteristics in each of them.

B111. ———. "The Georgian Composers." *Music in Britain: A Quarterly Review* No. 69 (Summer 1965): 23–27.

In this article, the author laments that a whole generation of English composers, due, in part, to their historical placing in the interwar years, have been largely overlooked. The "lost generation" includes Bax, Ireland, Bridge, Warlock, van Dieren, and Lambert. In describing Bridge's musical contributions, the author notes his four "first rate" string quartets, "splendidly written and stylistically impeccable examples of Frank Bridge."

B112. ———. Introduction to *Four Songs*, by Frank Bridge. London: Galliard, 1974.

After a brief biographical sketch the author provides an analytic description of the four songs included in this publication. The four songs are *Day after day*, *Speak to me my love*, *Dweller in my deathless dream*, and *Journey's end*.

B113. ———. "The Lost Generation." *The Musical Times* 96 (April 1955): 194–95.

Bridge, Bax, van Dieren, and Ireland, among others, are discussed as the author laments the decline of English composers active between the wars, due in large part, he feels, to their "unfortunate placing in time."

B114. ________. "The Unfashionable Generation: Notes on Some Minor Masters who Swam Apart from the Mainstream of Twentieth-Century Music." *High Fidelity/Musical America* 16 (January 1966): 59–62.

Described as belonging to "the forgotten" as well as to "the unfashionable" generation, the author briefly describes and pleas for recognition of the music of John Ireland, Arnold Bax, and Frank Bridge.

B115. Rhodes, Harold. "The R.C.M. of 50 Years Ago." *RCM Magazine* 50, no. 3 (1954): 98–99.

This article describes the atmosphere of the Royal College of Music and the author's experiences there, beginning as a student in 1904. Frank Bridge is mentioned as being constantly present. Although having graduated earlier, Bridge's viola playing was apparently still in great demand.

B116. "The Royal Collegian Abroad." *RCM Magazine* 20, no. 2 (1924): 66–68.

Bridge's election as a Fellow of the Royal College of Music is announced.

B117. Schafer, Murray. *British Composers in Interview*. London: Faber and Faber, 1963.

Interviews of sixteen composers are included in this work. Brief mention is made of Bridge in the interviews of John Ireland and Benjamin Britten.

B118. Scholes, Percy A. *The Mirror of Music, 1844–1944: A Century of Musical Life in Britain as Reflected in the Pages of the "Musical Times."* 2 vols. London: Novello, 1947.

This two volume work contains a single paragraph on Bridge, describing him as "a fine viola player and a very good orchestral conductor." Of his compositions, only instrumental works are mentioned.

B119. Sorabji, Kaikhosru. "The Modern Piano Sonata." *Musical News and Herald* (January 2, 1926): 4–7.

An essay on the then current state of piano sonata composing. The author defines the modern sonata and then describes modern sonatas by composers such as Dukas, d'Indy, Szymanowski, and Scriabin. Bridge's Piano sonata, touched upon last, is described as "of very little importance" whose best parts are derived directly from Ireland.

B120. Souster, Tim. "Frank Bridge's Cello Sonata." *The Listener* (December 23, 1965): 1048.

In this article, the author discusses Bridge as a composer of "consummate technique and a strong personality." In doing so he centers his discussion on Bridge's Violoncello sonata in D minor. Aspects of the sonata are compared with techniques used by other composers. Concluding, the author cites Bridge as one who was "able to steer a clear course at this time through the debris of war and the entanglements of fashion."

B121. Speyer, Edward. *My Life and Friends*. London: Cobden-Sanderson, 1937.

In his autobiography, Speyer gives an account of his chairmanship of the Classical Concert Society and the participation of the English String Quartet, to which Bridge belonged. Also included is a letter by F. S. Kelly to the Speyers which mentions the "very clever and gifted composer Frank Bridge." A more thorough discussion of the Speyers' relationship with Bridge details his membership in the Ridgehurst Quartet, so named after the Speyers' home.

B122. Stanford, P. "Notes: Bridge Centenary." *Composer* (London) 65 (Winter 1978-1979): 8.

A paragraph-long announcement of the activities of the Frank Bridge Trust in commemoration of the centenary of Bridge's birth.

B123. Strode, Rosamund, comp. *Music of Forty Festivals: A List of Works Performed at Aldeburgh Festivals from 1948 to 1987.* Aldeburgh, Suffolk: Britten-Pears Foundation, 1987.

This source lists, alphabetically by composer, major works performed at Aldeburgh Festivals from 1948 to 1987. Two Bridge works were given their premiere performances there. They were *Rhapsody* and the *Unfinished symphony*.

B124. Stulken, Marilyn Kay. "AGO Milwaukee's English Romantic Organ Music Festival: An Introduction." *American Organist* 22 (April 1988): 58–63.

This article briefly describes English Romantic organ music. In an effort to introduce twelve composers whose music exemplifies this style, brief biographies are included. Bridge's biography appears as well as those of C. Hubert H. Parry, Charles Stanford, and John Ireland, among others.

B125. Tertis, Lionel. *My Viola and I: A Complete Autobiography*. London: Elek, 1974.

This work includes a list of works "written for the author" which includes Bridge's *Allegro appassionato*, *Pensiero*, and *Two Pieces*.

B126. "To Honor Mrs. E. Coolidge." *New York Times*, 13 October 1930, p. 21c.

A description of the festivities planned for the Coolidge Festival of Music to be held in Chicago, beginning that evening, at which Bridge's Piano trio (1929) will be performed.

B127. Walton, William. "Modern Movement in Music." *School Music Review* 39 (January 15, 1929): 258–59; 39 (March 15, 1929): 326–27; 39 (April 15, 1929): 366–68.

This is a twelve-part essay on problems in aesthetics. In part eleven Walton describes Bridge as a "modernist in the making." To illustrate this, he gives short excerpts from piano sketches from 1914, 1920, and 1924 and traces what he sees as the development of a modern idiom in the works.

B128. Warrack, Guy. "Royal College of Music: The First Eighty-Five Years 1883–1968 and Beyond." (Typewritten)

This unpublished manuscript traces the history of the Royal College of Music's first eighty-five years, much as the Colles and the Cruft trace the first fifty and one hundred years respectively. An interesting fact included on Bridge's role in the life of the school is his election in 1899 as a Royal College of Music Composition Scholar. He is described by the author as a brilliant student who "achieved distinction in later life."

B129. Warrack, John. "A Note on Frank Bridge." *Tempo* 66-67 (1963): 27–32.

This article presents a sketch of Bridge through a discussion of his chamber music.

B130. Webber, Julian Lloyd. "The Cello Music of Frank Bridge." *The Strad* 86 (April 1976): 905–7.

In this article, Bridge's early works for cello are mentioned but the focus lies in the discussion of the Violoncello sonata in D minor and *Oration*.

B131. Westrup, Sir Jack A. "Frank Bridge." In *British Music of our Time*, pp. 75–82. Edited by Alfred Louis Bacharach. Harmondsworth, Middlesex, England: Pelican, 1946.

A brief discussion of Bridge's major compositions and their stylistic relationships to one another.

B132. White, Eric Walter. *Benjamin Britten: His Life and Operas*. 2nd ed. Edited by John Evans. Berkeley: University of California Press, 1983.

A biographical sketch of Britten's life with an emphasis on his operas. Brief, one page mention is made of Britten's first encounter with Bridge's music and their ensuing relationship as pupil and teacher.

B133. Wimbush, Roger. "Here and There." *Gramophone* 49 (November 1971): 812–17.

An announcement and short review of Peter Pirie's work on Frank Bridge. Published by Triad in 1971, the reviewer praises the timeliness of the work while lamenting the author's attacks on other composers.

B134. Wood, Hugh. "Frank Bridge and the Land without Music." *Tempo* 121 (June 1977): 7–11.

The author hails the "rediscovery of a major Unjustly Neglected Composer," namely Bridge. In the article Wood explains that the Englishman's feelings of musical inferiority may, in part, be responsible for the original neglect and the subsequent need to rediscover.

B135. Wood, Sir Henry Joseph. *My Life of Music*. With an introduction by Sir Hugh Allen. London: Gollancz, 1938.

In his autobiography, Wood describes his exposure and work with pieces such as *Isobel*, *Love went a-riding*, *O that it were so*, *The Sea*, and *Easter hymn*. He praises all works, calling them splendid, great, and beautifully written.

B136. Zeyringer, Franz. *Literatur für Viola*. Hartberg: Julius Schonwetter, 1963; revised ed., Hartberg: Julius Schonwetter, 1976.

This work lists Bridge compositions under categories Two Violins, Viola and Piano, and Two Violins and Viola. Information provided includes title, date of composition and/or publishing, and publisher and date when available.

REVIEWS

B137. A., T. "New Music: Pianoforte." *The Musical Times* 67 (April 1926): 331–33.

This article presents a review of Augener's printing of Bridge's Piano sonata. It is described as "a big work, uncompromising in its demands both on the performer and on the listener." *See*: W127

B138. "Aeolian Hall." *Daily Telegraph* (London), 5 November 1915, p. 11c.

Review of the first performance of String quartet no. 2 in G minor performed by the London String Quartet in Aeolian Hall. The first and the last movement were described as less pleasing than the second which "completely won the hearts of the audience." *See*: W56a

B139. "Aeolian Hall." *Daily Telegraph* (London), 19 June 1916, p. 11c.
A review of the first performance of *Two Old English songs*. Called "two Quartets for Strings" by the reviewer, they are described separately, the first which Bridge "nobly refrained from disguising" the "old song" and the second which "the audience so greatly enjoyed that they insisted on its repetition." *See*: W28a

B140. Aldrich, Richard. "Chamber Music Festival Opens." *New York Times*, 28 September 1923, p. 10a.
A review of a performance on September 27, 1923 of Bridge's String sextet in E-flat major. The work, receiving this, its United States premiere, was performed at the Berkshire Festival of Chamber Music by the London String Quartet, Edward Kreiner, viola and, Willem Willeke, violoncello. Bridge is described as "by no means one of the extreme moderns." His sextet was much applauded and Bridge was called to the platform. *See*: W60d

B141. Arpeggio. "The Norwich Musical Festival - Mr. Frank Bridge's New Rhapsody." *East Anglian Daily Times* (Ipswich), 29 October 1927, p. 7e.
A review of the performances at the Norwich Musical Festival. The reviewer describes Bridge's *Enter spring* a "riotous piece of harsh-sounding noise." *See*: W148a

B142. B., E. "London Promenade Concerts: New Work by Frank Bridge." *Manchester Guardian*, 26 September 1930, p. 16d.
A review of the first London performance of Bridge's *Enter spring* at Queen's Hall on September 25, 1930. The author praises the performance, which is conducted by Bridge, but laments the work as being too lengthy and lacking "sufficiency of striking ideas to hold attention throughout." *See*: W148b

B143. ————. "The Promenade Concerts: Season's First Novelty." *Manchester Guardian*, 22 August 1927, p. 8d.
A review of the first performance of Bridge's *There is a willow grows aslant a brook*. The reviewer felt this work to not be a "tremendously important contribution to modern British music." *See*: W167a

B144. ————. "Two English Piano Sonatas." *Manchester Guardian*, 2 December 1927, p. 17f.
A review of a performance of Bridge's Piano sonata in London on December 1, 1927. Alan Bush performed and was severely criticized for his program choices. With regard to Bridge's Piano sonata, the reviewer compares it favorably with Ireland's Piano sonata, also on the program, leaving differences in preference between the two works as "largely one of personal attitude." *See*: W127c

B145. B., E. A. "Mr. Lyn Harding as Actor Manager – Success of *Threads* at the St. James Theatre." *The Evening News*, 24 August 1921, p. 3c.
This review of *Threads*, which does not specifically mention Bridge's role in its production, describes the audience's favorable reaction to the theater work as a whole. Even though the plot and its characters are described as somewhat lacking, the reviewer expects the play to be popular. *See*: W248a

B146. B., F. "*The Christmas Rose*: A New English Opera." *Daily Telegraph* (London), 9 December 1931, p. 8d.
A review of the first performance of *The Christmas rose* by students at the Royal College of Music. The music in the first scene is criticized for its rich texture and color, a contradiction to its simple text. The music of the second and third scenes are described as more appropriately matched to the action. *See*: W242a

B147. ———. "A Frank Bridge Overture: First Performance." *Daily Telegraph* (London), 24 February 1941, p. 3c.
A review of the first performance of Bridge's *Rebus*. Performed "in memory of the composer," the work is described as full of "vitality" and "charming ideas." Although perhaps difficult to grasp, the work made a "favourable impression." *See*: W158a

B148. ———. "New Music: Chamber Music." *The Musical Times* 71 (May 1930): 422.
A review of three newly published chamber music works including Bridge's Piano trio in D minor. The reviewer finds the work "profoundly disappointing" and writes that he feel Bridge has "put technical interest before aesthetic pleasure." *See*: W38

B149. ———. "New Music: Chamber Music – Augener." *The Musical Times* 75 (January 1934): 43.
A review of an Augener printing of Bridge's Violin sonata. While reading the work with "considerable pleasure," the reviewer questions Bridge's skill with "modern harmonies." *See*: W64

B150. ———. "New Music: Full Scores." *The Musical Times* 81 (January 1940): 20–21.
A review of an Augener printing, in miniature score, of Bridge's String quartet no. 4. The work is described as "rich in ideas and admirable in texture" as well as "more consistently dissonant" than his earlier works. *See*: W58

B151. ———. "New Music: Music for Strings." *The Musical Times* 62 (March 1921): 177.

A review of the Goodwin Tabb printing of Bridge's Suite. It is discussed only briefly in light of the work's recent performances at the Queen's Hall Promenade Concerts. *See*: W164

B152. ———. "New Music: String and Chamber Music." *The Musical Times* 62 (September 1921): 628–29.

This article presents review of newly published music. The reviewer reports that Bridge's String sextet in E-flat major, published by Augener, demonstrates his perfect and easy command of the chamber music medium. *See*: W60

B153. ———. "Promenade Concert: Bax's Third Symphony." *Daily Telegraph* (London), 26 September 1930, p. 8c.

A review of a performance of Bridge's *Enter spring*. While "very brilliant" and "technically admirable," the reviewer felt the work was not "conceived as a whole." *See*: W148b

B154. B., J. E. H. "Evening Concert, Suggia and Frank Bridge's New Work." *Eastern Daily Press* (Norwich), 28 October 1927, p. 7c.

In this review of the first performance of Bridge's *Enter spring*, the reviewer notes that Bridge, like Stravinsky, "relies on colour for bizarre, brilliant and startling effects." The work is described as difficult, particularly on one hearing. This renders it "practically impossible to form any judgment of this intriguing work at the moment," according to the reviewer. *See*: W148a

B155. Barrett, Francis E. "Grand Opera in English." *The Musical Times* 54 (December 1913): 806–7.

A review of a short season of grand opera during which Bridge conducted *Tannhäuser*. Of his conducting, the reviewer says he "rather succumbed to the manifold difficulties of directing a much 'cued' opera such as this."

B156. Bates, Frank. "Festival Music." *Eastern Daily Press* (Norwich), 10 September 1924, p. 3g.

This article outlines Bridge's musical accomplishments, describing highlights such as his String quartet in E minor receiving "mention d'honour" at the international Bologna competition. His suite, *The Sea*, introduced as "the only purely instrumental work by an English composer to be performed during the [Norwich Triennial] Festival," is described by the Carnegie Adjudicators, who have arranged for its publication, as "A very striking piece of tone painting and a notable example of what, for want of a better word, is called 'atmosphere' in music." *See*: W160h

B157. Bauman, Carl. [Review of recording by the Royal Liverpool Philharmonic Orchestra]. *The American Record Guide* 41 (February 1978): 42.

Devoted exclusively to Bridge works, EMI/HMV ASD 3190 is reviewed in this article. The reviewer describes the "very lovely romanticism" of *The Sea*. *Summer* reminds him of Delius while "Cherry ripe" reminds him of Eric Coates. The reviewer calls *Enter spring* a "minor masterpiece." *Lament* is described as "the most somber work in the collection." *See*: D30a

B158. B[auman], J[ohn]. [Review of a recording by Julian Lloyd Webber]. *Fanfare* 7 (January-February 1984): 156–57.

Musicmasters MM 20026, also released under the ASV ACA 1001 label, contains works by Britten and Ireland, along with Bridge's *Elégie*. The reviewer briefly, but favorably, comments on *Elégie*. Describing it as "sadly beautiful," he recommends it as "well worth having on disc." *See*: D29a

B159. "Bechstein Hall." *Daily Telegraph* (London), 16 June 1905, p. 12g.

A review of two recitals given at Bechstein Hall on June 15, 1905. During the evening recital "a cleverly written Capriccio from the pen of Frank Bridge" was performed for the first time. Played by Harold Samuel, it was encored. The other work performed under the title "Two Pianoforte Solos" was Bridge's *A Sea idyll*. *See*: W98b, W133a

B160. "Bechstein Hall." *Daily Telegraph* (London), 9 March 1907, p. 12b.

A review of a Bechstein Hall recital of March 8, 1907 featuring works by Haydn, Tchaikovsky, and Bridge. The review highly praises Bridge's *Three Idylls*. The "work of the clever young composer," played by the Grimson Quartet, received the "tribute of a double recall." *See*: W13a

B161. "Bechstein Hall." *Daily Telegraph* (London), 17 June 1909, p. 8g.

A review of the first London performance of the String quartet in E minor. Note is made of the honorable mention awarded this work at the international Bologna competition in 1906. Performed by the English String Quartet, the work is described as having "much interesting music in it." Neither Allegro is "quite convincing" while the "Allegretto grazioso" is described as "very light and attractive." *See*: W55a

B162. "Bechstein Hall." *Daily Telegraph* (London), 19 June 1913, p. 16a.

Review of the first performance of the String sextet in E-flat major. Performed in Bechstein Hall by the English String quartet, joined by Ernest Tomlinson and Felix Salmond, the reviewer praises, in particular, the second, slow movement. The first and last movements are of a lower quality but are "full of good ideas." *See*: W60a

B163. "Berkshire Chamber Festival." *New York Times*, 29 May 1938, p. 5X, col. f.

An announcement of the upcoming Berkshire Festival of Chamber Music to be held September 21–23, 1938. Bridge's String quartet no. 4, dedicated to Mrs. Coolidge, is to be performed on the fourth concert, on the morning of September 23, 1938. *See*: W58a

B164. Bonavia, F. "Two New British Works: Bridge's Phantom Rhapsody." *Daily Telegraph* (London), 11 January 1934, p. 8d.

A review of the first performance of Bridge's *Phantasm*. Described as "immensely musical," the reviewer questions its "ultimate prospects of success." *See*: W156a

B165. "Bridge's New Work: Philharmonic's First Chamber Concert." *Daily Telegraph* (London), 19 January 1934, p. 10c.

A review of the first performance of Bridge's Violin sonata. Although the music was "burdened with complicated harmonies," the reviewer describes a favorable reception to the work by the audience. *See*: W64a

B166. "British Chamber Music." *The Musical Times* 52 (April 1911): 242–43.

A discussion of a lecture on British chamber music given at the Royal Academy of Music on February 1, 1911 by Walter Cobbett. During his talk Cobbett focused on the phantasy form as encouraged by the Cobbett Musical Competition which, as he mentions, awarded Frank Bridge second prize for the 1905 competition (Phantasie in F minor) and first prize for the 1907 competition (Phantasy in C minor). He also mentions Bridge's Phantasy in F-sharp minor, commissioned by Cobbett in 1910. It was performed for the audience. *See*: W33b

B167. "British Music: BBC Orchestra's Concert." *Times* (London), 11 January 1934, p. 8c.

A review of the first performance of Bridge's *Phantasm*. The reviewer strongly disliked the work, calling the material "undistinguished and its treatment turgid." *See*: W156a

B168. B[roder], N[athan]. [Review of record by Peter Pears]. *High Fidelity* 7 (November 1957): 84–85.

Two Bridge songs, *Go not, happy day* and *Love went a-riding* appear on this London recording (LL 1532) reviewed here. Bridge's songs, as well as the other contemporary songs on the recording, are described as "on the whole rather conservative." *See*: D36d

B169. Bronston, Levering. [Review of recording by the Allegri String Quartet]. *The New Records* 41 (August 1973): 6.
Four recordings are reviewed in this brief article, one of which is Argo ZRG 714 which contains Bridge's String quartet no. 3 and String quartet no. 4. The reviewer calls them "masterpieces—lyrical, expressive, deeply felt." *See*: D129a

B170. ———. [Review of recording by the London Philharmonic Orchestra]. *The New Records* 47 (June 1979): 3.
Of the four recordings reviewed in this brief article, one—HNH 4078—is composed of music from an early stage in Bridge's career. Particular note is made by the reviewer of the "Nocturne," from his Suite which is called "one of the tenderest, most appealing things I've heard by this composer." *See*: D56b

B171. Cecil, Winifred. "Singers and Songs." *Saturday Review* 40 (September 28, 1957): 100–102.
This article reviews several recordings, one of which is London's LL 1532. Bridge's *Go not, happy day* and *Love went a-riding* are heard on this recording. The Bridge pieces are not mentioned specifically. The author does, however, lament Peter Pears poor diction. *See*: D36d

B172. "Chamber Music." *The Musical Times* 52 (January 1911): 31.
This article briefly reports on a performance of *Novelletten* by the Motto Quartet. The work was described as "pleasant." There is mention in passing of the December 13, 1910 performance of Bridge's String quartet in E minor by the same quartet. *See*: W27c

B173. "Chamber Music: A Frank Bridge Tribute." *The Brighton and Hove Herald* 18 January 1941, p. 1f.
A review of a chamber music concert in the Brighton Art Gallery. The director, Clifford W. Musgrave, spoke at the opening and described Bridge as "most eminent as a composer of chamber music, with unusual genius for writing for strings." Miss Bannerman began the recital with *O that it were so* as a tribute to his memory. *See*: W218c

B174. C[harles], J[ohn]. [Review of recording by the Gabrieli String Quartet]. *Fanfare* 1 (November–December 1977): 13–14.
This is a review of a Decca recording, SDD 497, on which appear Bridge's *Three Idylls* and *Novelletten*. The reviewer describes Bridge as his "candidate for 'most interesting neglected British composer.'" These works he describes as having a "warmth and luxuriousness unusual in the English music of this period." *See*: D46b

B175. C[hissell], J[oan] O. [Review of recording by Mstislav Rostropovich] *Gramophone* 48 (October 1970): 610.

Bridge's Violoncello sonata and Schubert's "Arpeggione" sonata comprise Decca SXL 6426 reviewed here. The author gives a great deal of credit to the performers for the success of the work, mentioning in particular the first movement's "soaring cantilena and impassioned climaxes" and the "big climax" of the work, bowed with the great intensity of Rostropovich. *See*: D144b

B176. "College Concerts." *RCM Magazine* 1, no. 1 (1904): 12–14.

This article is a review of student concerts at the Royal College of Music from October through December of 1904 and includes Bridge's *Novelletten*. Described as interesting and clever, this work first appeared on the student concert of November 24, 1904, one which was considered by the author as perhaps "the best of the term." *See*: W27a

B177. "Comment in Brief on New Disks." *New York Times*, 22 September 1957, p. 11X, col. c–e.

Brief review of London LL 1532 on which appears Bridge's *Go not, happy day*, and *Love went a-riding*. The recording is described as an "interesting juxtaposition of songs by Elizabethan and modern composers." *See*: D36d

B178. "Concerts." *Times* (London), 22 May 1905, p. 14b.

A review of a performance by Mr. Mark Hambourg of Bridge's Capriccio no. 1 in A minor. The work is described as "extremely effective and very difficult." *See*: W98a

B179. "Concerts." *Times* (London), 23 June 1906, p. 13f.

A review of a performance by the Saunders Quartet. On the June 22, 1906 recital program six works chosen winners of the Worshipful Company of Musicians Cobbett prize were performed. No comments specific to Bridge's Phantasie in F minor are made although it was one of the works performed. Specific comments, both positive and negative, are made concerning phantasies by W. Y. Hurlstone, Josef Holbrooke, and James Friskin. *See*: W31a

B180. "Concerts." *Times* (London), 9 March 1907, p. 7f.

A review of the first performance of Bridge's *Three Idylls*. The work is described as "thoughtful and quite original in style" as well as "quite modern." *See*: W13a

B181. "Concerts." *Times* (London), 27 February 1908, p. 14e.

A review of a performance of Bridge's *Isabella*. It is described as containing four contrasting movements and as being "very fully scored." *See*: W150b

B182. "Concerts: End of the Promenades." *Morning Post* (London), 23 October 1922, p. 4f.
A review of a Promenade Concert on October 21, 1922 in Queen's Hall at which Bridge conducted his *Sir Roger de Coverley*. The work is described as one in which Bridge has taken "a friendly old tune" and "treated it with every kind of friendly disrespect. It was like slapping Sir Roger on the back so heartily as to make him choke." *See*: W163a

B183. "Concerts of Many Kinds: Past Events and Future Schemes." *Times* (London) 24 June 1916, p. 11b.
In this article the author comments on the June 17 performance of Bridge's *Two Old English songs* by the London String Quartet. He calls them "slight things, but both were worth having." Of "Sally in our alley" he says that Bridge manages to "get a wealth of harmonic variety without torturing the tune." He calls "Cherry ripe" "a most dainty contrivance." *See*: W28a

B184. "Concerts of the Week: Royal Philharmonic Society." *Observer* (London), 22 March 1914, p. 6d.
A review of the first performance of Bridge's *Dance poem*, this critic found it a "sound and conscientious piece of work." The audience, on the other hand, "was scarcely decided whether it liked the work or not." *See*: W145a

B185. "Concerts: String Quartet Phantasies." *Morning Post* (London), 23 June 1906, p. 9b.
A review of an evening recital on June 22, 1906 in Bechstein Hall which featured works which had won prizes in Cobbett's string quartet competition. As a condition of the prize, phantasies were composed and subsequently performed. Bridge's Phantasie in F minor, showing a "disposition to adhere to the sonata form" was performed by the Saunders Quartet. *See*: W31a

B186. Crumb, Rupert W. [Review of recording of Bridge's choral music]. *The New Records* 30 (October 1982): 8–9.
Bridge choral works, recorded on Pearl SHE 568, are reviewed in this article. The author provides a brief, sentence-long introduction to the songs, noting in particular, the three Tagore songs and the "impressionistic quality to their fascinating harmonies and exotic orchestration." *See*: D23b

B187. Diesterweg, Alan. "Aus dem Berliner Musikleben." *Allegemeine Musikzeitung* (February 6, 1931): 100–102.
A review of a performance of Bridge's Piano sonata. The reviewer strongly disliked both the performer's playing and the Piano Sonata itself. *See*: W127d

B188. Discus. [Review of recording by Maggie Teyte]. *Harper's Magazine* 231 (July 1965): 115–16.

This is a review of London 5889 on which Bridge's *E'en as a lovely flower* appeared. The emphasis of the review centers on Teyte's performance of *Tu n'es pas beau* from Offenbach's *La Perichole*, but here "incredible nuance, impeccable diction, complete technical accuracy, highly personal and authoritative phrasing" found in the other works are also mentioned. *See*: D28a

B189. Ditsky, John. "More Lyrita from Allegro." *Fanfare* 6 (September–October 1982): 62–64.

This article consists of reviews of five Lyrita recordings, one of which is SRCS.104. Bridge's *Unfinished symphony*, *Oration*, and *Two Poems* appear on this recording. The author briefly describes each work, also stating his pleasure in that Bridge's works "are now finally getting the chance at a wider dissemination." *See*: D86b

B190. ———. [Review of recording by the Chelsea Opera Group Chorus and Orchestra]. *Fanfare* 7 (May–June 1984): 168.

This is a review of Bridge's *The Christmas rose* on Pearl SHE 582. The author describes the work as "no masterpiece itself, simply a very attractive stage work." He also characterizes it as "more a modern musical mystery play than a conventional opera" but "*very* pretty stuff." *See*: D17a

B191. ———. [Review of recording by the English Chamber Orchestra]. *Fanfare* 8 (May-June 1985): 152.

Chandos ABRD 1112, on which Bridge's Suite appears, is reviewed here. The work is described, along with its accompanying works by Ireland, as "lovely, dark, and deep." He notes a "tone of sadness throughout" but feels it adheres to a "comforting and balanced beauty." *See*: D132a

B192. ———. [Review of recording by the English Sinfonia]. *Fanfare* 5 (May–June 1982): 293–94.

This is a review of EMI/HMV ESD 7100. The recording contains Bridge's *There is a willow grows aslant a brook* but the work is not referred to specifically. The reviewer does, however, "highly" recommend both recordings. *See*: D135c

B193. ———. [Review of performance by the Royal Liverpool Philharmonic Orchestra]. *Fanfare* 2 (January–February 1979): 159.

This is a review of EMI/HMV ASD 3190 on which Bridge's *The Sea*, *Summer*, "Cherry ripe," *Enter spring*, and *Lament*. The reviewer urges the purchase of the recording, saying that "even the ones [collector friends] whose musical tastes are most severe soon capitulate to the charms, if not the orgiastic splendors, of the music on this disc." *See*: D30a

B194. ———. [Review of recording by the Royal Philharmonic Orchestra]. *Fanfare* 5 (July–August 1981): 83.
This is a brief but direct review of EMI/HMV ASD 3190 on which five orchestral works by Bridge appear. The reviewer praises the recording. *See*: D30a

B195. ———. [Review of recording by Graham Trew]. *Fanfare* 8 (January–February): 291–2.
No specific mention is made of the Bridge songs included on this recording Hyperion A66085 entitled *Songs of England*. The reviewer does recommend the recording. *See*: D11a

B196. Donner, Jay M. [Review of recording by the Music Group of London]. *The New Records* 50 (December 1982): 8.
Bridge's String quintet in E minor and Phantasy in C minor comprise Nonesuch 71405. In this review of that recording, the author primarily discusses this particular performance. The works themselves are described as conservative with melodies and rhythms that "exist within the relatively stringent structural limitations in force in England" but are "yearning to escape." *See*: D95b

B197. Downes, Olin. "Music." *New York Times*, 19 February 1926, p. 18b.
This article describes an Aeolian Hall recital by Myra Hess. Performed was Bridge's Piano sonata. The reviewer did not like the work, describing it as "long, labored, and verbose." *See*: W127b

B198. Dunhill, Thomas F. "Bridge's New Trio." *Monthly Musical Record* 60 (April 1930): 104–5.
An analytic description and review of Bridge's newly published Piano trio. The reviewer calls the work a "vital musical expression of the highest importance." *See*: W38

B199. Einstein, Alfred. "The Siena Music Festival." *New York Times*, 7 October 1928, p. 8X.
A lengthy description and review of the Siena Music Festival. Bridge's String quartet no. 3 is described as making a "Victorian impression." *See*: W57f

B200. Elbin, Paul N. [Review of recording by Kathleen Ferrier]. *Etude: The Music Magazine* 73 (February 1955): 18.

This review of London LS 1032, a recording which includes Bridge's *Go not, happy day*, discusses the recording itself very briefly. It is noted that profits from the sale of the recordings will go to the Kathleen Ferrier Cancer Research Fund. *See*: D36f

B201. E[llis], S[tephen] W. [Review of recording by Stuart Campbell]. *Fanfare* 5 (September–October 1981): 91–92.

This is a review of Pearl SHE 545. Bridge's complete output of organ music appears here. The reviewer gives high praise to the works, calling *Three Pieces* Bridge's masterpiece in the genre. In contrast, he describes *Lento (In Memoriam C.H.H.P.)* as "without lasting value." *See*: D59a

B202. ———. [Review of recording by Julian Lloyd Webber]. *Fanfare* 5 (January–February 1982): 251–52.

The generally unfavorable review of this recording, ASV ACA 1001, which includes Bridge's *Elégie*, finds the work to be "tuneful salon stuff." *See*: D29a

B203. "The English String Quartet." *Morning Post* (London), 17 June 1909, p. 7e.

A review of a performance by the English String Quartet of Bridge's String quartet no. 1 in E minor at Bechstein Hall on June 16, 1909. Having obtained honorable mention at an International Competition in Bologna in 1906, the piece is described as "a lengthy work of undeniable merit" but as a whole it shows "too much of that modern restlessness which arrests attention without exhibiting special significance." *See*: W55a

B204. "The English String Quartet." *Times* (London), 19 June 1913, p. 10f.

A review of the first performance of Bridge's String sextet in E-flat major. The reviewer finds the first two movements the most successful. *See*: W60a

B205. "Entertainments: London Philharmonic Orchestra." *Times* (London), 24 February 1941, p. 6f.

A review of the first performance of Bridge's *Rebus*. While the work is not described as a total success, the reviewer felt that it "should be a welcome addition to the orchestral repertory." *See*: W158a

B206. Ericson, Raymond. "Tradition Shapes British Music." *New York Times*, 28 November 1982, p. 21H, col. a–f.

This review addresses ten recordings of British music, one of which is Nonesuch 71405. Bridge's Piano quintet and Phantasy in C minor comprise this recording. The writing is described as "enormously skillful and frequently of great beauty." The reviewer feels the Quintet deserves a place in the standard repertoire. *See*: D95b

B207. Evans, Edwin. "The Coolidge Chamber Music Concerts: Vienna." *The Musical Times* 68 (November 1927): 996–98.
A review of the first performance of Bridge's String quartet no. 3. The reviewer states that "probably Bridge has written nothing better." *See*: W57a

B208. ———. "Notes on the Week's Programmes: Bridge, Beck and Copland." *The Listener*, 8 January 1936, p. 95.
This article describes three works to be aired on January 16, 1936 on BBC's concert of contemporary music. Bridge's *Oration* is one of the three works. It is described as containing three principal constituents: a march, an animated phantasy, and a lyrical thread which binds the whole. *See*: W155a

B209. "Fifth Concert of British Music: Two First Performances." *Morning Post* (London), 11 January 1934, p. 5d.
A review of the first performance of *Phantasm*. Suggesting an "uneasy atmosphere," the work's architecture is described as "vague" while as a whole it had "several dramatic moments." *See*: W156a

B210. F[iske], R[oger]. [Review of recording by Peter Pears]. *Gramophone* 42 (November 1964): 239.
Five Bridge songs appear on the Argo recording (RG 418/ZRG 5418) reviewed here. The reviewer, in comparing *When you are old*, *Journey's end*, and *So perverse* to the Ireland songs, states his preference for the Bridge songs citing their "marvelous relaxed melancholy," "light touch," and great song line, respectively. *See*: D38a

B211. F[lanagan], W[illiam]. [Review of recording by Peter Pears]. *HiFi/Stereo Review* 14 (June 1965): 82.
The author of this review of English songs on Argo (ZRG 5418) describes Bridge as "in about the same class as our own John Alden Carpenter: honest and sincere enough, but rather lacking in sophistication." *See*: D38a

B212. F[leming], S[hirley]. [Review of recording by Mstislav Rostropovich]. *High Fidelity* 21 (January 1971): 93.
The author of this review of Bridge's Violoncello sonata in D minor on London CS 6649 gives the work high marks. He describes it as "a Niagara of melody" which "blossoms to enormous, impassioned climaxes." Although perhaps "a work of more flesh than bone," Rostropovich's performance gives it "real dimension." *See*: D144b

B213. F[oreman], L[ewis]. [Review of performance by John Georgiadis, Neil Watson, and Brian Hawkins]. *Fanfare* 2 (November–December 1979): 19.

This is a review of a recording, Pearl SHE 547, on which Bridge's *Rhapsody* is heard. The reviewer describes it as a "private, haunted work which demonstrates Bridge's mastery of string sonority at its greatest." *See*: D111a

B214. ———. [Review of recording by the London Philharmonic Orchestra]. *Fanfare* 2 (January–February 1979): 29–30.

Bridge's Suite, *Sir Roger de Coverley*, *Two Old English songs*, *Lament*, and *Rosemary* complete the recording reviewed here, Lyrita SRCS.73. The reviewer feels that Bridge's music for full orchestra is superior to his music for strings but feels this recording "should not be rejected out of hand for here are some good things on it." *See*: D56b

B215. "Frank Bridge's Works: Mrs. Hobday and Mr. Elwes" *Times* (London), 31 October 1918, p. 8.

A review of a concert devoted entirely to the music of Frank Bridge. Performed were the Piano quintet, the String sextet in E-flat major, and several songs: *Mantle of blue*, *So early in the morning, o*, *Come to me in my dreams*, *Where she lies asleep*, and *Adoration*. The reviewer feels the composer's strength lies in his "versatile harmonies." *See*: W36b, W60c, W172a, W179a, W211a, W223a, W240a

B216. Freed, Richard. "Bridge and Britten: Teacher and Pupil Splendidly Served by the Gabrielis." *Stereo Review* 44 (January 1980): 90–92.

The reviewer of this London recording (STS 15439) compares the compositional styles found in Britten's String quartet in D major and Phantasy quartet with Bridge's *Novelletten* and *Three Idylls*. They both share a "direct sort of communication." He feels that both composers had something to share and that both found the string quartet medium a fitting form for this communication. *See*: D46b

B217. ———. [Review of recording by the Allegri String Quartet]. *Stereo Review* 31 (October 1973): 136.

The reviewer of this Argo recording (ZRG 714) of Bridge's String quartets no. 3 and 4 describes the works as "profound, individual, and directly communicative." He calls them "major works in terms of the entire quartet repertoire." *See*: D129a

B218. ———. [Review of recording by Peter Wallfisch and the London Philharmonic Orchestra]. *Stereo Review* 39 (November 1977): 135.

The author of this review of Bridge's *Phantasm* on HNH 4042 describes the work as not sounding particularly English in any conventional sense. He notes hints of Gallic influence and evocations of early Schoenberg. He describes the work as "good enough to make one wonder why his music is so little known here." *See*: D94b

B219. From Our Special Correspondent. "Bradford Music Festival: Modern British Works." *Daily Telegraph* (London), 1 October 1930, p. 10d.

This article reviews a performance of Bridge's String sextet in E-flat major. The reviewer feels that "the Sextet exhibits perhaps better than any other work the qualities of his music we prize most highly." Mention is made of Bridge's knowledge of the medium and the fact that his chamber music, in general, is "solidly founded on the classical model." *See*: W60e

B220. Furley, Mabel McDonough. "Bridge is Guest of Detroit Symphony." *Musical America* 39 (November 17, 1923): 33.

A review of a performance by the Detroit Symphony of Bridge's *Summer* and *Sir Roger de Coverley*. A "very favorable impression" was created by Bridge's conducting, over that of the works themselves. *See*: W163b, W165b

B221. G., H. "New Music: Organ - Curwen." *The Musical Times* 81 (December 1940): 490.

A review of Bridge's *Three Pieces* for organ published by Curwen. Described as "modern" by the reviewer, he feels that with these works, Bridge "has re-entered the organ music field to some purpose." *See*: W129

B222. ———. "New Music: Pianoforte Music." *The Musical Times* 66 (August 1925): 704–6.

A review of Bridge's *In autumn* and *Three Lyrics* published by Augener. The pieces are described as "more persistently dissonant" than earlier Bridge works. *See*: W111, W114

B223. Glock, William. "Music and Musicians: Programmes." *Observer* (London), 2 March 1941, p. 11c.

Using Bridge's *Rebus* as an example of a contemporary work, the author laments the excessive programming of late nineteenth century compositions. He feels these works "represent a kind of indulgence which is a bad preparation for the appreciative effort that is needed for present day music" and encourages that "classics" be programmed opposite contemporary works. *See*: W158a

B224. Hale, Philip. *Boston Symphony Orchestra. Programme of the Twenty-fourth Afternoon and Evening Concerts*. Boston: Boston Symphony Orchestra, 1920.

Bridge's *Blow out you bugles* is listed on the April 30 and May 1, 1920 program. Works by Berlioz, Mozart, d'Indy, and Wagner were also performed. The historical notes present the origins of the Brooke sonnet, on which Bridge's work is based, and list its text. A brief biographical sketch of Bridge is given along with a catalogue of his compositions. *See*: W178e

B225. H[all], R. A[lbert]. [Review of recording by the Gabrieli Quartet]. *Fanfare* 3 (March–April 1980): 70–71.

Bridge's *Novelletten* and *Three Idylls* appear on London STS 15439 which is reviewed here. The works are described as "light in tone" with each having "a firm direction and shape." *See*: D46b

B226. ———. [Review of recording by the Tunnell Trio]. *Fanfare* 2 (January–February 1979): 30.

Argo ZK 40 is reviewed. This recording is comprised of three works by Bridge: Piano trio, Phantasy in F-sharp minor, and *Miniatures*, set 3. The Piano trio is described as "one of the most well-crafted and expressive pieces of chamber music of its day, in England or elsewhere." Phantasy is "elegantly simple in form" and the Miniatures are described as "pure *Hausmusik*." *See*: D71a

B227. H[amilton], D[avid]. [Review of recording by the English Chamber Orchestra]. *High Fidelity* 20 (April 1970): 111.

High praise is given to the English Chamber Orchestra's performance on this London recording (CS 6618) which includes Bridge's *Sir Roger de Coverley*. This work is described as an "artful (if sometimes too arty), arrangement of *Sir Roger de Coverley*." *See*: D118e

B228. Harris, Dale. "The Tragic Art of Kathleen Ferrier: Five Richmond Reissues Recall the English Contralto's Brief but Glorious Career." *High Fidelity* 23 (September 1973): 84–86.

This review of five Richmond reissues consists primarily of a tribute to Ferrier. Bridge's *Go not, happy day*, on Richmond R 23187, is not mentioned specifically but can probably be lumped together with what the author calls "folksongs and English artsongs." In these, the reviewer feels Ferrier is the least successful. *See*: D36a

B229. H[arrison], M[ax]. [Review of recording by Richard Deering]. *Gramophone* 54 (May 1977): 1717.

Bridge's *Three Sketches* appears on the Saga recordings (5445) reviewed here. The author notes the work's "careful workmanship." He mentions other recordings of works by Bridge and notes the restoration of Bridge's reputation through the appearance of these recordings. *See*: D120a

B230. ———. [Review of recording of the Delmé String Quartet]. *Gramophone* 61 (September 1983): 356.

Music by Bridge for string quartet is heard on the Chandos recording (ABRD 1073) reviewed here. His String quartet no. 2 in G minor is reviewed in detail. Among other comments, the author mentions the "beautifully flexible part-writing." The reviewer feels the other works on the recording are not on the same level as the String quartet no. 2. *See*: D52a

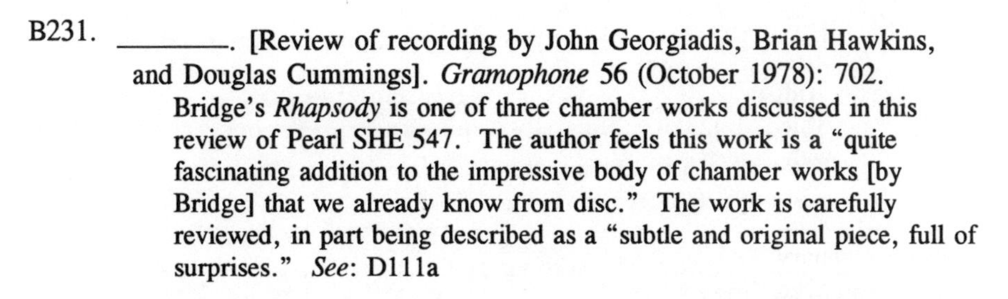

B231. ———. [Review of recording by John Georgiadis, Brian Hawkins, and Douglas Cummings]. *Gramophone* 56 (October 1978): 702.

Bridge's *Rhapsody* is one of three chamber works discussed in this review of Pearl SHE 547. The author feels this work is a "quite fascinating addition to the impressive body of chamber works [by Bridge] that we already know from disc." The work is carefully reviewed, in part being described as a "subtle and original piece, full of surprises." *See*: D111a

B232. ———. [Review of recording by the Hanson Quartet]. *Gramophone* 58 (April 1981): 1332–34.

Bridge's String quartet no. 1 in E minor is heard, with Moeran's String trio, on Pearl SHE 563 which is reviewed here. The author describes the Bridge quartet as "being among Bridge's first really personal statements." *See*: D127a

B233. ———. [Review of recording by Julian Lloyd Webber]. *Gramophone* 58 (May 1981): 1486.

Brief mention is made of Bridge's *Elégie* in the review here of ASV ACA 1001. The work is described as one of "somber loveliness." *See*: D29a

B234. ———. [Review of recording by Moray Welsh]. *Gramophone* 60 (December 1982): 729.

Eight short Bridge works comprise one side of Pearl SHE 571. The reviewer note the pieces' "exact craftsmanship, each having a well-defined character." He prefers *Mélodie* as "the pick of the bunch." *See*: D9a

B235. H[arvey], T[revor]. [Review of recording by Anne Dawson]. *Gramophone* 62 (November 1984): 639–40.

Four songs by Bridge are included on this recording (Hyperion A66103) of English songs reviewed here. His *Go not, happy day* is the only one of the four mentioned specifically and it is discussed only in regards to the performance—which the reviewer feels was too slow. *See*: D18c

B236. ———. [Review of recording by the English Chamber Orchestra]. *Gramophone* 47 (June 1969): 45.

A recording of Bridge's *Sir Roger de Coverley* on Decca SXL 6405 is reviewed here. Of the work, the reviewer anticipates that the listener "will find it a delight," describing it as "brilliantly done." *See*: D118e

B237. ———. [Review of recording by the English Sinfonia]. *Gramophone* 59 (November 1981): 713.

British orchestral works, including Bridge's *There is a willow grows aslant a brook*, are featured on EMI/HMV ESD 7100 reviewed here. The author just mentions the Bridge work, describing it as "anything but easily approachable." *See*: D135c

B238. ———. [Review of recording by Graham Trew]. *Gramophone* 62 (October 1984): 516.

Three songs by Bridge are included on the recording of English songs (Hyperion A66085) reviewed here. Bridge's *Journey's end* is singled out as one of the most noteworthy of the collection. *See*: D11a

B239. Henderson, Robert. "Music in London: Bridge and Britten." *The Musical Times* 108 (June 1967): 524.

A review of the April 9, 1967 performance of Bridge's *Enter spring*, conducted by Benjamin Britten. Although this performance was felt by the reviewer to signal a slight resurgence of interest in Bridge, he fails to be completely taken with the work. *See*: W148f

B240. H[inton], J[ames], Jr. [Review of recording by Kathleen Ferrier]. *High Fidelity* 4 (January 1955): 66.

This review of London LS 1032 briefly comments on Ferrier's artistry, mentioning specifically only a couple of songs. Bridge's *Go not, happy day*, which is heard on the recording, is not discussed. *See*: D36f

B241. Hughes, Herbert. "New Chamber Music: Mr. Bridge's Trio." *Daily Telegraph* (London), 5 November 1929, p. 8f.

A review of the first performance of Bridge's Piano trio, performed by Harriet Cohen, piano, Antonio Brosa, violin, and Anthony Pini, violoncello. Described as "patently 1929," the reviewer raises the question of the existence of the work's "real meaning, even superficial, to the composer himself." *See*: W38a

B242. J[acobs], A[rthur]. "Student Performances: Royal College of Music, December 8." *Opera* 17 (February 1966): 164.

A review of a revival performance of Bridge's *The Christmas rose*. The reviewer finds the libretto, the acting, and the work of the producer and scenic designer less than appealing but the score "is not itself displeasing." *See*: W242b

B243. Jacobson, Bernard. "British Music: The Pastoral Tradition." *Stereo Review* 43 (September 1979): 108.

The author of this review speaks briefly of the HNH release (4078) on which Bridge's Suite, *Sir Roger de Coverley*, *Two Old English songs*,

Lament, and *Rosemary* appear. Bridge, who "suffers too often from the obscuring shadow of Benjamin Britten" is described as having "a distinctively individual compositional voice." *See*: D56b

B244. ———. [Review of recording by Mstislav Rostropovich]. *Stereo Review* 26 (March 1971): 98.

The reviewer of this London disc (CS 6649) which couples Schubert's "Arpeggione" with Bridge's Violoncello sonata in D minor is surprised to find he enjoyed the Bridge more than the Schubert. He describes the tone as late Romantic with an "overripe" harmonic language at times but feels the work "displays a sense of formal logic no less powerful and at the same time considerably less obvious than his more famous pupil's tends to be." *See*: D144b

B245. J[ellinek], G[eorge]. [Review of recording by Maggie Teyte]. *HiFi/Stereo Review* 14 (June 1965): 85.

The author of this review of songs on a London disc (5889) focuses on the artistry of Maggie Teyte rather than the works performed. Her singing is described as "always tasteful, expressive, and unfailingly musical." *See*: D28a

B246. Kalisch, A. "London Concerts." *The Musical Times* 61 (December 1920): 820–23.

A review of a performance of Bridge's Suite on November 6, 1920. The work is described as containing much "admirable writing" while suffering "somewhat from over-elaboration." *See*: W164c

B247. Keener, Andrew. "Concert Notes: Chamber." *Strad* 92 (July 1981): 167–69.

A review of a performance of Bridge's String quartet no. 3 by the Hanson String Quartet on May 6, 1981. *See*: W57i

B248. Kolodin, Irving. "Ferrier, Hayes, Dermota." *Saturday Review* 39 (November 27, 1954): 63.

The author of this review of London recording LS 1032 speaks very highly of Kathleen Ferrier's performance. Bridge's *Go not, happy day*, while not specifically mentioned by the reviewer, appears here on a recording for the first time. *See*: D36f

B249. ———. [Review of recording by Peter Pears]. *Saturday Review* 48 (July 31, 1965): 42.

This is a review of Argo RG 418 on which several of Bridge's songs appear. Described as a recording with "rather narrow interest," the author praises songs by Priaulx Rainier and Richard Rodney Bennett and notes Peter Pears "constantly diminishing vocal resource." *See*: D38a

B250. ________. [Review of recording by Mstislav Rostropovich]. *Saturday Review* 54 (January 30, 1971): 54.

Bridge's Violoncello sonata in D minor appears on London CS 6649 reviewed here. Rostropovich is lauded for his enthusiasm which elevates to greater heights "a work whose sentiment is stronger than the means of the composer for conveying it." *See*: D144b

B251. L., H. St. "Music Notes: BBC Concerts of Modern Music." *The Catholic Times*, 31 January 1936, p. 11d.

The author here discusses the performance of contemporary music heard over the BBC. In particular, he discusses Bridge's work *Oration*. Conducted by Bridge, the cello part was performed by Florence Hooten. The author feels that the work "communicates something of real value, over and above the satisfaction it must have given to its creator." *See*: W155a

B252. "Last Philharmonic Concert: Miss Myra Hess's Playing." *Times* (London), 14 March 1916, p. 9b.

A review of a performance of Bridge's *Summer*. This was one of the works which provided the program with "considerable interest." *See*: W165a

B253. L[incoln], S[toddard]. [Review of recording by the Music Group of London]. *Stereo Review* 48 (January 1983): 69.

This reviewer of Bridge's Piano quintet and Phantasie in C minor as heard on Nonesuch 71405, feels, based on these works, that the revival of his music is long overdue. He notes the music is one which "holds one's attention with its power and drama." *See*: D95b

B254. "London and Suburban Concerts: Royal College of Music." *The Musical Times* 44 (February 1903): 117.

A discussion of the first performance of his Piano quartet in C minor. "His latest addition to chamber music is an excellent composition. The themes are significant and melodious; they are effectively treated, and throughout the four movements....there is displayed a lively sense of contrast." His Trio in d minor and String quartet in B-flat minor are mentioned as having been premiered in the previous year. *See*: W34a

B255. "London Concerts." *The Musical Times* 60 (August 1919): 431-32.

A review of a performance of Frank Bridge's *Isobel*. Mr. George Fergusson "sang pleasantly." *See*: W203b

B256. "London Concerts: Chamber Concerts." *The Musical Times* 53 (April 1912): 258-59.

A review of the March 18, 1912 performance of Bridge's *Two Pieces* which are described as "new and attractive." *See*: W39a

B257. "London Concerts: Chamber Concerts." *The Musical Times* 54 (July 1913): 468–69.

A review of the first performance of Bridge's String sextet in E-flat major. The work is described as "ripe, thoughtful, and effective." *See*: W60a

B258. "London Concerts: Chamber Concerts." *The Musical Times* 57 (January 1916): 30–31.

A review of a December 8, 1915 performance of Bridge's String sextet in E-flat major and String quartet no. 2 in G minor. The reviewer feels that his String Sextet "does not on the whole avoid monotony," but describes his String Quartet, performed on December 9, as "an interesting item." *See*: W56b, W60b

B259. "London Concerts: Chamber Music." *The Musical Times* 50 (July 1909): 468–69.

A review of "a new Quartet in E minor" by Bridge. While lacking "continuity and coherence of design" the work was "thoroughly satisfying." *See*: W55a

B260. "London Concerts: Henkel Pianoforte Quartet." *The Musical Times* 52 (February 1911): 117.

A review of the first performance of Bridge's Phantasy in F-sharp minor on January 21, 1911. It is described as a work of "singular beauty" although "a more strenuous climax in the middle section would have been welcome." *See*: W33a

B261. "London Concerts: London String Quartet." *The Musical Times* 57 (July 1916): 341.

A review of a performance of Bridge's string quartet arrangement of "Cherry ripe" and "Sally in our alley." *See*: W28a

B262. "London Concerts: London String Quartet." *The Musical Times* 57 (November 1916): 508.

A review of a performance by the London String Quartet of Bridge's "Bologna" Quartet which took place on October 20, 1916. It was considered a "strong feature" of the program. *See*: W55c

B263. "London Concerts: Miss Myra Hess: Mr. Bridge's New Sonata." *Daily Telegraph* (London), 16 October 1925, p. 15b.

A review of the first performance of Bridge's Piano sonata. The reviewer begins with great praise of Bridge's musical contributions. Of the Piano sonata, however, praise is lacking. He says it "seems...to incline to dourness throughout." *See*: W127a

B264. "London Concerts: Mr. Frank Bridge's 'Three Idylls.'" *The Musical Times* 48 (April 1907): 254.

A review of the first performance of Bridge's *Three Idylls* by the Grimson Quartet on March 8, 1907 in Bechstein Hall. The pieces are described as "admirably contrasted and pleasantly permeated by manly spirit and healthy sentiment." *See*: W13a

B265. "London Concerts: Other Orchestral Concerts." *The Musical Times* 82 (March 1941): 117.

An announcement of the works performed on the Beecham series of Sunday concerts from February 2 to March 2, 1941. The first performance, conducted by Sir Henry Wood, of Bridge's *Rebus* took place on February 23, 1941. *See*: W158a

B266. "London Concerts: The Patron's Fund." *The Musical Times* 52 (July 1911): 471.

A description of a June 14, 1911 Patron's Fund concert. This concert consisted of selections of the best works that had been produced at previous Patron's Fund concerts. "Songs by Mr. Frank Bridge" as well as other composers' works were performed. *See*: W198c, W230b

B267. "London Concerts: Pianoforte Recitals." *The Musical Times* 51 (December 1910): 791.

A report of the evening concert premiere, on November 4, 1910, of Bridge's *Three Sketches* performed by Ellen Edwards. *See*: W135a

B268. "London Concerts: Prize Phantasies." *The Musical Times* 47 (July 1906): 489.

A report of the performance of the six string quartet phantasies that won prizes in the first Cobbett Musical competition. Three of six were praised while the remaining three, including Bridge's Phantasie in F minor, were described as "lugubrious" and lacking any sense of humor. *See*: W31a

B269. "London Concerts: Promenade Concerts." *The Musical Times* 48 (November 1907): 739–40.

A review of the first performance of Bridge's *Isabella*. The review praises the work, saying that the composer "shows better taste in his music than in his choice of subject." *See*: W150a

B270. "London Concerts: The Promenade Concerts – Queen's Hall." *The Musical Times* 57 (November 1916): 508.

A review of a performance of the orchestral arrangement of Bridge's "Sally in our alley" and "Cherry ripe." *See*: W154a

B271. "London Concerts: The Promenades." *The Musical Times* 71 (November 1930): 1032–33.

A review of a September 25, 1930 performance of Bridge's *Enter spring*. The review recognized "sterling musicianship and fine earnestness" in the work but did not care for Bridge's "harmonic system." *See*: W148b

B272. "London Concerts: Queen's Hall Orchestra." *The Musical Times* 58 (February 1917): 82.

A review of a performance of Bridge's *Two Poems*. The work is described as difficult "for ordinary folk to understand or enjoy." *See*: W157a

B273. "London Concerts: Royal Philharmonic Society." *The Musical Times* 55 (April 1914): 256–57.

A review of the first performance of Bridge's *Dance poem*. The reviewer found it "bizarre" and closes with the hope that Bridge will "revert to the style in which he has distinguished himself." *See*: W145a

B274. "London Concerts: Scontrino's Quartet." *Daily Telegraph* (London), 16 July 1917, p. 3d.

A review of the premiere performance of Bridge's Violoncello sonata in D minor. The reviewer describes Bridge's aim as "lofty as usual," one in which "he generally hits his mark." He recommends more succinct writing. *See*: W65a

B275. "London Concerts: Wigmore Hall." *The Musical Times* 58 (August 1917): 374.

A review of a recital at which Bridge's "Sonata for 'cello and pianoforte in D minor" played a role in the "attractive programme" of July 13, 1917. *See*: W65a

B276. "London Music-Makings: Recital." *The Musical Times* 49 (May 1908): 326.

A review of the first performance of Bridge's *Morceau characteristique* and *Gondoliera* which were described as "distinguished by pleasing imagination and musicianly resource." *See*: W11a, W24a

B277. "London Promenade Concerts: New Works by Frank Bridge." *Manchester Guardian*, 26 September 1930, 16d.

A review of the first London performance of Bridge's *Enter spring*. The reviewer feels the piece is overly long but demonstrates Bridge's skill as a craftsman. *See*: W148b

B278. "The London Trio and British Phantasies." *The Musical Times* 50 (March 1909): 178–79.

Although no specific mention is made of Bridge, this article describes two of the three concerts at which two Phantasie trios, winners of the Cobbett competition, were performed. *See*: W32a

B279. M., E. de S. "String Quartet Recital." *Washington Evening Star*, 31 October 1930, sec. B, p. 6a.

A review of the Founder's Day concert of the Elizabeth Sprague Coolidge Foundation, this article focuses its attention primarily on the performers rather than the works performed. Bridge's Piano trio was performed as well as Debussy's String quartet and Mozart's String quartet in C major. *See*: W38d

B280. "M. Ravel's Works: Classical Concert Society at Bechstein Hall." *Times* (London), 18 December 1913, p. 11e.

A highly praised performance by the English String Quartet, of which Bridge was a member, in Bechstein Hall on December 17, 1913. Ravel's String Quartet in F major was played "with perfect understanding."

B281. M[acDonald], M[alcom]. [Review of recording by the English Chamber Orchestra]. *Gramophone* 62 (December 1984): 736.

Bridge's Suite appears on Chandos ABRD 1112 reviewed here. The reviewer describes the piece as "a worthwhile suite" one which "lies exceptionally well for the players" and whose "resulting good sound is itself an expression of poetical music." *See*: D132a

B282. ———. [Review of recording of songs and chamber music by Bridge]. *Gramophone* 63 (January 1986): 952.

Songs and chamber works by Bridge constitute the recording (Pearl SHE 586) reviewed here. The *Miniatures* are felt by the author more appropriate for the "Sunday afternoon family trios" for which they were written than with any "professional circumstance." The songs, on the other hand, are described as "an obvious source for the ready enjoyment of listeners." *See*: D5a

B283. McN. "London Concerts: The British Music Festival." *The Musical Times* 75 (February 1934): 170–71.

A review of the British Music Festival as a whole and some works performed during it, one being Bridge's *Phantasm*. The festival, composed entirely of modern music from one country, was not a box-office success and Bridge's *Phantasm* contributed to this with its qualities of "a quest in the wrong direction." *See*: W156a

B284. ———. "Variety in Music: And a Fine Concerto by Frank Bridge." *The Evening News*, 18 January 1936, p. 3b.

This is a review of a BBC concert on which Bridge's *Oration* is performed by Florence Hooton. The work is said to have "redeemed the concert." It is described as "full of ideas, beautifully scored for orchestra, and of special interest in the solo part." *See*: W155a

B285. "Mme. Suggia's Concert." *Times* (London), 2 December 1918, p. 11d.

A review of a New Queen's Hall Orchestra concert conducted by Bridge. Guilhermina Suggia and Gervase Elwes sang on the program. *See*: W178b

B286. M[arsh, R[obert] C[harles]. [Review of recording of Leonard Warren]. *High Fidelity* 8 (December 1958): 72.

This is a brief review of Victor LM 2266, on which Bridge's *O that it were so* appears. It was recorded in Leningrad and Kiev in May of 1958. Although the reviewer felt the engineering for the recording was good, as a whole the review was not glowing. *See*: D81f

B287. Michaels, Everette. [Review of recording by the Hanson Trio]. *The New Records* 53 (January 1986): 7-8.

This author reviews Pearl recording SHE 586 which contains songs and chamber music by Bridge. He calls the Miniatures "high class 'wallpaper'" which "fulfill their role to perfection." The songs "contrast mood and melody in a way that only the English could." The reviewer also mentions the orchestration of *Norse legend* by Bridge in 1938. *See*: D5a

B288. M[iller], J[ames]. [Review of recording by Anne Dawson]. *Fanfare* 8 (May-June): 230-31.

The reviewer highly praises the four songs by Bridge on this Hyperion recording (A66103). He calls them the works "of a *real* song writer." His music "not only 'adds' to the poems but even flatters the human voice." The author "regrets that the entire record was not devoted to this grossly under performed minor master." *See*: D18c

B289. Miller, Philip L. [Review of recording by Leonard Warren]. *Library Journal* 84 (February 15, 1959): 588.

This extremely brief review of Victor LM 2266 is one of many under the subheading "Miscellaneous Recitals." Mentioned is the origin of the recording—Warren's Russian tour—and his singing: "that of an intelligent operatic artist." *See*: D81f

B290. ———. "Two Voices from the Past—Thill and Teyte." *The American Record Guide* 32 (January 1966): 422-24.

The recording of interest in this review is the London 5889 issue which includes Bridge's *E'en as a lovely flower*. Teyte is described as being "thoroughly at home in the English songs." The Bridge work is described as "a rather mild version of *Du bist wie eine Blume*." *See*: D28a

B291. "Miss Marie Brema's Opera Season." *The Musical Times* 51 (December 1910): 789.
A review of the first performance of Bridge's five interludes to the play *The Two Hunchbacks*. They are described as "well-conceived arrangements." *See*: W243a

B292. Mr. B. "Mr. Bridge's Conducting: Mr. Sammons and the London Symphony Orchestra." *Times* (London), 18 November 1921, p. 8b.
A review of a performance of Bridge's *Two Poems* with comments more on his conducting than on the work. The reviewer describes the conducting as the "feature of the evening." *See*: W157b

B293. Moore, Edward. "London Musicians Heard in Festival of Chamber Music." *Chicago Daily Tribune*, 14 October 1930, p. 19d.
A review of the first United States performance of Bridge's Piano trio on October 13, 1930. The trio, performed as part of the Coolidge chamber music festival, was described as being "full of gaiety, sometimes bitter in its undercurrents, but full of hearty cheer." *See*: W38b

B294. M[organ], R[obert] P. [Review of recording by the Allegri String Quartet]. *High Fidelity* 23 (November 1973): 102.
In this review of an Argo recording (ZRG 714) of Bridge's String quartets no. 3 and 4, the author describes the works as "written in a richly chromatic tonal language and in an expressive, nonromantic manner rather reminiscent of Berg." Although tending to be overly repetitive, "the music is beautifully written...and contains many fine moments." *See*: D129a

B295. "Music." *Times* (London), 16 November 1910, p. 12e.
A review of the November 15, 1910 performance of *Orpheus* at the Savoy Theatre, as part of Miss Marie Brema's season. Frank Bridge conducted "in first-rate style."

B296. "Music and Musicians: Chamber Concerts." *Sunday Times* (London), 7 November 1915, p. 4d.
A review of the first performance of Bridge's String quartet no. 2 in G minor. The work is described as being written "adroitly and genially." *See*: W56a

B297. "Music and Musicians: Concerts of the Week." *Morning Post* (London), 22 May 1905, p. 4d.

A review of a performance by Mark Hambourg of Bridge's Capriccio no. 1 in A minor. The work is described as "brilliant and fanciful." Bridge was called to the platform to receive the audience's applause. *See*: W98a

B298. "Music and Musicians: Royal Philharmonic Society." *Sunday Times* (London), 22 March 1914, p. 6d.

A review of a performance of Bridge's *Dance poem*. Although the reaction of one member of the audience was hissing, this was reportedly "drowned by cheering." *See*: W145a

B299. "Music and Musicians: Royal Philharmonic Society." *Sunday Times* (London), 19 March 1916, p. 4d.

A review of a performance of Bridge's *Summer*. The work, conducted by Bridge, is described as a "charmingly coloured mood-picture." *See*: W165a

B300. "Music: The English String Quartet." *Times* (London), 17 June 1909, p. 13d.

A review of a performance of Bridge's String quartet no. 1 in E minor by the English String Quartet. The work was "enthusiastically received" and the composer was "recalled several times at the close." *See*: W55a

B301. "Music: The Henkel Quartet." *Morning Post* (London), 23 January 1911, p. 3e.

A review of the first performance of the Phantasy in F-sharp minor by the Henkel Piano Quartet in Steinway Hall. The work is described as one which "exhibited the sound and virile qualities of which its composer has previously given proof." *See*: W33a

B302. "Music in the Provinces: Birmingham." *The Musical Times* 61 (January 1920): 51–53.

A review of a performance of Bridge's *Three Idylls*. The Catterall Quartet provided a "masterly reading" of the work as well as of Beethoven's Quartet in A minor, op. 132 and Elgar's Quartet, op. 83 in E minor. *See*: W13c

B303. "Music in the Provinces: Bristol." *The Musical Times* 61 (January 1920): 53–54.

A review of a performance of Bridge's *A Prayer* on December 3, 1919. It is described as a "scholarly but not remarkable work." *See*: W89b

B304. "Music in the Provinces: Liverpool." *The Musical Times* 62 (May 1921): 365–66.
A review of a performance of Bridge's *A Prayer*. The reviewer felt the work failed to sustain interest. *See*: W89c

B305. "Music in Wales: The Siena Festival of Modern Music." *The Musical Times* 69 (October 1928): 936–37.
This article provides a description of the music performed at the annual Festival of the International Society for Contemporary Music. Bridge's String quartet No. 3 was one of the works performed. *See*: W57f

B306. "Music: London String Quartet." *Morning Post* (London), 19 June 1916, p. 4f.
A review of "some new arrangements for string quartet of old English songs," this article describes the first performance of the chamber versions of "Sally in our alley" and "Cherry ripe." The pieces, performed by the London String Quartet, were "warmly received, and the second repeated." *See*: W28a

B307. "Music: Mr. F. Bridge's Quartet." *Times* (London), 23 January 1911, p. 10e.
A review of the first performance of Bridge's Phantasy in F-sharp minor. The work is described as "written in a perfectly distinctive style." *See*: W33a

B308. "Music of the Week: Contemporary Music Centre." *Observer* (London), 13 November 1927, p. 14b.
A review of the British premiere of Bridge's String quartet no. 3. The reviewer was unable to reflect on specific favorable elements of the work but felt that "undoubtedly the work contains fine things." *See*: W57c

B309. "Music: Two Instrumentalists: Bridge's New Work for 'Cello." *Morning Post* (London), 20 January 1936, p. 8g.
A review of the first performance of *Oration* as performed by the BBC Orchestra under the composer's direction. Well-received by this reviewer, the work is described as "manifestly one of the finest things Frank Bridge has written to date." *See*: W155a

B310. "Musical League Festival at Liverpool." *The Musical Times* 50 (November 1909): 724.
A review of a performance of Bridge's *Dance rhapsody* on September 25, 1909. The work is described as "clever, and of light character." *See*: W146b

B311. "New Music: Pianoforte." *The Musical Times* 67 (April 1926): 331–33.
A review of Bridge's Piano sonata published by Augener. The reviewer, pleased with the work, suggests that attempts to understand the latest developments in Bridge's harmonic style are best done in the "Andante ben moderato" movement. *See*: W127

B312. "New Orchestral Work - Mr. Bridge's Composition at the 'Proms.'" *Morning Post* (London), 22 August 1927, p. 5f.
A review of the first performance of Bridge's *Impression* or *There is a willow grows aslant a brook*. The work receives a poor review in part because of the reviewer's feeling that Bridge "fails to communicate his emotion when he sets out to express it." *See*: W167a

B313. "A New Quartet." *Times* (London), 5 November 1915, p. 11e.
A review of the first performance of Bridge's "new string quartet." It is described as a work "of remarkable power and very varied beauties." *See*: W56a

B314. "A New Quartet: Frank Bridge's Chamber Music." *Times* (London), 6 November 1915, p. 11d.
A review of the first performance of Bridge's String quartet no. 2 in G minor. The work is favorably described as one of "unusual power." *See*: W56a

B315. "A New Year Concert: Theodore Dubois and Frank Bridge." *Times* (London), 2 January 1917, p. 5d.
A review of a performance of Bridge's *Two Poems*. The work is described as making "a very happy contrast" to the other works on the program. *See*: W157a

B316. "New York." *Morning Post* (London), 28 October 1927, p. 7b.
A review of the first performance of Bridge's *Enter spring*. Commissioned for the Norwich Triennial Festival, at which it received its first performance, the work was well received, being described by the reviewer as a "fluent inspiration." *See*: W148a

B317. N[ewman], E[rnest]. "The Week's Music: British Composers." *Sunday Times* (London), 28 September 1930, p. 5b.
A review of a performance of Bridge's *Enter spring*. It is described as "harsh in conception and unnecessarily coarse in tissue." *See*: W148b

B318. ———. "The Week's Music: Contemporary Music." *Sunday Times* (London), 19 January 1936, p. 7b.

A review of the first performance of Bridge's *Oration*. Although the reviewer acknowledges that the work is difficult to grasp at first hearing, he feels that it is a work "that musicians would like to hear again." *See*: W155a

B319. ———. "The Week's Music: Miss Myra Hess." *Sunday Times* (London), 18 October 1925, p. 7c.

A review of the first performance of Bridge's Piano sonata. The work is described as one to "respect rather than love." *See*: W127a

B320. "Norwich Musical Festival: New Tone Poem by Mr. Frank Bridge." *Times* (London), 29 October 1927, p. 10b.

This article is a review of the first performance of Bridge's *Enter spring* at the Norwich Musical Festival for which it was written. The reviewer notes that the work might have been received better elsewhere—the audience giggled during the music but applauded vigorously when it was over. The work is described as a "highly-wrought piece of orchestral design." *See*: W148a

B321. "Odd Contrasts at Festival." *Daily News* (London), 28 October 1927, p. 8d.

A review of the first performance of Bridge's *Enter spring*. The reviewer feels the piece "has little to recommend it." *See*: W148a

B322. Olsen, William A. [Review of recording by Leonard Warren]. *The New Records* 26 (December 1958): 12.

Without commenting specifically on Bridge's *O that it were so*, recorded on this Victor album (LM 2266), the reviewer cites this recording as "uninteresting" and one which fails "utterly to generate any enthusiasm." *See*: D81f

B323. Osborne, Conrad L. "Peter Pears and Julian Bream: In a Word, Musicality." *High Fidelity* 15 (June 1965): 58–59.

Two recordings featuring Peter Pears are reviewed in this article. Five songs by Frank Bridge are heard on the Argo selection (RG 418/ZRG 5418). Of these, *When you are old* is favored by the reviewer. In general, the pieces are described as "good at capturing an initial mood" but then "run into trouble when they start to move, or develop." *See*: D38a

B324. "The Pageant of London." *The Musical Times* 52 (June 1911): 384–85.

This article describes the music for the various scenes of the Pageant. Bridge's Scene 3c, "Henry VII entering London," is described as a "brilliant march-movement." *See*: W246a

B325. Passarella, Lee. [Review of recording of Bridge songs]. *The New Records* 52 (April 1984): 6.

The author of this record review discusses Bridge songs which comprise Pearl SHE 577. Not altogether a glowing review, the author calls *Tears, idle tears* the best, it being "more cosmopolitan in style," reminding the reviewer of "some of Ives' tender, less dissonant songs from the same period." *See*: D1a

B326. "The Patron's Fund." *RCM Magazine* 1, no. 1 (1904): 19–22.

This is a review of a performance of three of Bridge's songs. The "three songs of dirge-like character," *Night lies on the silent highways*, *A Dead violet*, and *A Dirge*, were all performed on a program on December 6, 1904. The author expresses dismay at these choices as "it is an open secret that he [Bridge] submitted others which were in a less depressing vein." *See*: W184a, W187a, W217a

B327. "The Patron's Fund." *RCM Magazine* 7, no. 3 (1911): 94.

A description of a Patron's Fund concert given at Queen's Hall on June 14, 1911. This concert consisted of many of the most successful works performed at previous Patron's Fund concerts. Included were Frank Bridge's *Thou didst delight my eyes* and *The Hag*. *See*: W198c, W230b

B328. "Patron's Fund Concert." *The Musical Times* 50 (August 1909): 532.

A review of a performance by Robert Chignell of Bridge's *I praise the tender flower* and *Thou didst delight my eyes*. Performed at Queen's Hall on July 14, 1909, the works are described as "excellent examples of the best modern ideals." The works "owed a good deal to their well-balanced and controlled orchestral scoring." *See*: W200a, W230a

B329. "Patron's Fund Concert." *The Musical Times* 46 (January 1905): 40.

A discussion of the second Patron's Fund concert which included Bridge's *Night lies on the silent highways*, *A Dead violet*, and *A Dirge*. These works were far from the preferred pieces on this program in this reviewer's mind. They are described as having "presented a crescendo of misery" but "were excellently rendered by Mr. F. Augry Millward." *See*: W184a, W187a, W217a

B330. P[ernick], B[en]. [Review of recording by the London Philharmonic Orchestra]. *Fanfare* 1 (January–February 1978): 18–19.

This is a review of a recording, HNH 4042. Bridge's *Phantasm* appears here. The reviewer, calling the album disappointing, describes *Phantasm* as "amorphous and rambling and of little communicative consequence." *See*: D94b

B331. Pettitt, Stephen. "Hanson Quartet." *Times* (London) 7 April 1983, p. 7b.

Bridge's String sextet in E-flat major as performed by the Hanson Quartet with Stephen Tess and Lionel Handy is reviewed here. The reviewer notes that "some of the harmonies in the faster sections recall early Schoenberg." Also mentioned is his "indisputable craftsmanship." *See*: W60j

B332. "Piano Recital – New Sonata by Mr. Frank Bridge." *Morning Post* (London), 16 October 1925, p. 6e.

A review of the first performance of Bridge's Piano sonata. Described as a "disappointment," the reviewer laments Bridge's move to composing in a "hard-minded, clashing, atonal style," and expresses his hope that Bridge will return to his past compositional style. *See*: W127a

B333. Pirie, Peter J. [Review of recordings of Bridge works]. *Music and Musicians* 26 (October 1977): 44–45.

This article is an insightful review of four recordings of Bridge works. These recordings are Decca SDD 497, Lyrita SRCS.91, Saga 5445, and Pearl SHE 541. Bridge and the works reviewed are place in their historical context and are critically discussed. *See*: D46b, D94b, D120a, D143a

B334. ———. [Review of recording of Bridge works]. *Records and Recording* 17 (August 1974): 51–52.

This article, ostensively a review of Pearl SHE 513/4, gives a great deal of background information on Bridge and his newly recognized place in history. About the works included here he gives critical comments, both positive and negative. *See*: D12a

B335. ———. [Review of recordings by the London Philharmonic Orchestra]. *Music and Musicians* 28 (April 1980): 41–44.

This review discusses two Lyrita recordings. Bridge's *Dance rhapsody*, *Dance poem*, and *Rebus* are heard on SRCS.114. His *Oration*, *Two Poems*, and *Unfinished symphony* are heard on SRCS.104. The bulk of the article is an analytical discussion of the works, placing them in their historical perspective. The works are only briefly discussed in the context of these two recordings. *See*: D20a, D86b

B336. P[orter], A[ndrew]. [Review of recording by Peter Pears]. *Gramophone* 34 (June 1956): 20.

This article is a review of Decca LW 5241 on which Bridge's *Go not, happy day* and *Love went A-Riding* appear. Calling the recording "a well-chosen anthology of British twentieth-century songs," the author describes the performance of these two songs as "buoyant and bright." *See*: D36e

B337. "Promenade Concert." *Times* (London), 8 October 1920, p. 8c.
This is a review of Bridge's Suite performed on October 7, 1920. The reviewer notes that the first movement's theme, "of which a great deal is made, does not seem quite worth it." The slow movement is described as "perfectly beautiful." *See*: W164b

B338. "Promenade Concert: British Composers." *Times* (London), 26 September 1930, p. 10c.
A review of a performance of Bridge's *Enter spring*. The work is described as "full of recollections of the manners of yesterday." *See*: W148b

B339. "Promenade Concerts." *Daily Telegraph* (London), 16 September 1915, p. 11e.
A review of Bridge's *Lament* as performed for the first time. Conducted by Bridge, the writing is described as "simple and effective," appropriately so as it was written, according to the reviewer, for "Catherine, aged 9, who, with her whole family, went down in the Lusitania." *See*: W151a

B340. "Promenade Concerts." *Daily Telegraph* (London), 22 August 1927, p. 5g.
A review of the first performance of Bridge's *There is a willow grows aslant a brook*. A favorable review is presented, this a result of the reviewer's impression that Bridge seems to have "broken away" from the "manner of the recent sonata." *See*: W167a

B341. "Promenade Concerts." *Morning Post* (London), 4 October 1907, p. 6e.
A review of an October 3, 1907 Queen's Hall concert in which Bridge's symphonic poem, *Isabella*, was performed. The reviewer laments the difficulty of recognizing coherence in the work. He states that, "As an exercise the present work is very clever, but one cannot but feel that it lacks inspiration." *See*: W150a

B342. "The Promenade Concerts." *The Musical Times* 53 (November 1912): 737–38.
A review of the first performance of Bridge's *The Sea* on September 24, 1912. It is described as "among the most individual, imaginative and pleasing of the works" performed during the recent Promenade season. *See*: W160a

B343. "Promenade Concerts, Queen's Hall." *The Musical Times* 56 (October 1915): 619.
A review of the first performance of Bridge's *Lament* on September 15, 1915. The reviewer felt that through this work Bridge has shown his ability to "express his inward emotions through the medium of music." *See*: W151a

B344. "Promenade Concerts: Sea Music." *Times* (London), 25 September 1912, p. 9d.
A review of a performance of Bridge's *The Sea*. The work is described as "vividly picturesque and full of fine feeling." *See*: W160a

B345. "The Promenade Concerts: Two English Works." *Times* (London), 24 September 1913, p. 8b.
A review of a performance of Bridge's *The Sea*. The reviewer describes the storm scene as less successful than the other sections of the work. *See*: W160b

B346. Prunieres, Henry. "The Coolidge Festival in Chicago." *New York Times*, 19 October 1930, p. 8X, col. f.
A review of the performances given at the Coolidge Festival in Chicago held in October of 1930. Bridge's Piano trio, "full of ingenuity and the spirit of invention," received "long applause." *See*: W38b

B347. "Queen's Hall." *Daily Telegraph* (London), 22 May 1905, p. 11c.
A review of a piano recital by Mark Hambourg in Queen's Hall on May 20, 1905. Bridge's Capriccio no. 1 in A minor was performed and encored. Bridge had recently been awarded ten guineas by Mr. Hambourg for this composition, which is described by the reviewer as "extremely vivacious and brilliantly effective." *See*: W98a

B348. "Queen's Hall." *Daily Telegraph* (London), 2 January 1917, p. 4b.
A review of the first performance of *Two Poems* by the Queen's Hall Orchestra. Conducted by the composer, the reviewer describes the work as "clever" while describing the composer's musical outlook as one with a "very decided lean towards modernity." *See*: W157a

B349. "Queen's Hall." *Daily Telegraph* (London), 2 December 1918, p. 2f.
A review of a Queen's Hall concert in which Mr. Gervase Elwes contributed his "fine singing" of the second performance of Bridge's "recently-produced" *Blow out you bugles*. *See*: W178b

B350. "Queen's Hall." *Times* (London), 4 October 1907, p. 7f.
A review of the first performance of Bridge's *Isabella*. Although perhaps "a little too self-conscious in his writing" Bridge "won very hearty applause" from the audience. *See*: W150a

B351. "Queen's Hall Promenade Concerts." *Morning Post*, 25 September 1912, p. 8g.
This is a review of the first performance of Bridge's *The Sea* on September 24, 1912. The work is described as a "very faithful and clever picture" of the sea. The reviewer says, "The music is descriptive, and it is also melodious, and in this combination are found the qualities that make great music." *See*: W160a

B352. R[abinowitz], P[eter] J. [Review of recording by Meral Güneyman]. *Fanfare* 5 (November–December 1981): 99–100.
This is a review of Finnadar SR 9031 on which Bridge's Piano sonata appears. The reviewer calls the work a masterpiece saying "this sonata remains one of the most shattering musical responses to World War I." *See*: D98b

B353. R[adford]-B[ennett], W[illiam]. [Review of recording by Peter Wallfisch and the London Philharmonic Orchestra]. *High Fidelity* 27 (December 1977): 80–82.
The author of this review of an HNH recording (4042) of Bridge's *Phantasm* describes the work as a major discovery. "As troubled a work as its shadowy title suggests," the reviewer expects the work to "alter an American listener's opinion not only of Bridge, but of English music as a whole." *See*: D94b

B354. "Recitals of the Week: Miss Myra Hess and New Piano Sonata." *Times* (London), 16 October 1925, p. 12b.
This is a review of the first performance of Bridge's Piano sonata. Myra Hess performs. The reviewer describes the character of the work as "elegiac." The work "uses no key signature and would no doubt be described by the new theorists as 'polytonal.'" *See*: W127a

B355. R[eed], P[eter] H[ugh]. [Review of recording by Kathleen Ferrier]. *The American Record Guide* 21 (December 1954): 140–41.
This review of songs, including Bridge's *Go not, happy day*, on London LS 1032 describes Ferrier's "fine song singing" and encourages one to purchase the recording as profits are being donated to the Kathleen Ferrier Cancer Research Fund. *See*: D36f

B356. Rees, Leonard. "Music and Musicians: The Promenade Concerts." *Sunday Times* (London), 1 October 1916, p. 4d.
A review of the first performance of the orchestral version of Bridge's *Two Old English songs*. It is described as a "quasi-novelty." *See*: W154a

B357. [Review of recording by the English Chamber Orchestra]. *Monthly Guide to Recorded Music* (January 1985): 4.
This is a review of Chandos ABRD 1112 on which Bridge's Suite is heard. The reviewer criticizes the conductor, David Garforth, saying Bridge's melodic lines need more lilt and that the "dark undercurrents" of the Bridge "need more direct emphasis." *See*: D132a

B358. [Review of recording by Kathleen Ferrier]. *New York Times*, 28 November 1954, p. 8X, col. f–g.

A very brief review of Kathleen Ferrier's Broadcast recital issued on London (LS 1032). The proceeds of the recording were to be donated to the Kathleen Ferrier Cancer Research Fund. *See*: D36f

B359. [Review of recording by Maggie Teyte]. *Saturday Review* 48 (May 29, 1965): 52.

Bridge's *E'en as a lovely flower* is included on London 5889 which is reviewed here. The author's main thrust, however, is Maggie Teyte's difficulty in conveying the essence of the German songs on the recording. But the record as a whole is described as "wonderful." *See*: D28a

B360. [Review of recording by Graham Trew]. *The Monthly Guide to Recorded Music* (January 1985): 18–19.

This is a review of Hyperion recording A66085. Bridge songs *Blow, blow thou winter wind*, *Journey's end*, and *Love went a-riding* are included on the disc. The reviewer directs his comments primarily to the performance but does describe the mood of *Journey's end* as elusive. *See*: D11a

B361. [Review of recording by Graham Trew]. *Ovation* (October 1985): 45–46.

This is a review of Hyperion A66085. Bridge's songs *Journey's end*, *Blow, blow thou winter wind*, and *Love went a-riding* are heard on the disc. Ten other composers are represented on the recording. The reviewer singles out Delius and Bridge as the two composers "who make the strongest impression." *See*: D11a

B362. [Review of recording by Leonard Warren]. *Saturday Review* 41 (November 29, 1958): 48.

This is a review of Victor LM 2266 on which Bridge's *O that it were so* appears. The author notes Warren's clear articulation on this and the other English songs. *See*: D81f

B363. "Reviews: Pianoforte Music." *The Musical Times* 59 (January 1918): 20.

A review of music sent to the magazine which includes the comments "pungent and bizarre" in regard to Bridge's *Four Characteristic pieces*. *See*: W100

B364. Rich, Alan. "Criticism Disarmed—or The Art of Maggie Teyte." *High Fidelity* 15 (May 1965): 57–58.

This article discusses the artistry of Maggie Teyte on the occasion of the release of a London and an Argo recording of her songs. The London (5889) includes Bridge's *E'en as a lovely flower*. *See*: D28a

B365. R[obertson], A[lec]. [Review of recording by Kathleen Ferrier]. *Gramophone* 32 (November 1954): 264.

Bridge's *Go not, happy day* appears on this Decca recording (LX 3133) reviewed here. This work, as well as Warlock's *Pretty ringtime* are described as "joyously sung." *See*: D36f

B366. ———. [Review of recording by Maggie Teyte]. *Gramophone* 42 (October 1964): 200.

Bridge's *E'en as a lovely flower* is heard on Decca LXT 6126 reviewed here. The Bridge work is mentioned only in passing. Overall, the reviewer is disappointed in Maggie Teyte's performance on this disc. *See*: D28a

B367. Rogers, Bernard. "Berkshire Festival, Bringing Forward Notable Works and Artists, Launches America's Concert Season Brilliantly." *Musical America* 38 (October 6, 1923): 1.

This article describes the Sixth Annual Berkshire Festival. Bridge's String sextet in E-flat major was performed on the first day of the festival and is described as a work which is "in general superbly fashioned." *See*: W60d

B368. Rosenfeld, Jay C. "Berkshire Festival." *New York Times*, 2 October 1938, p. 7X, col. a.

A review of the works that were performed at the Berkshire Music Festival. Bridge's String quartet no. 4, performed by the Gordon String Quartet, is described as containing "polytonality" which the reviewer found "difficult to assimilate." *See*: W58a

B369. "Royal College of Music." *Daily Telegraph* (London), 22 July 1908, p. 7b.

A review of the first performance of *Dance rhapsody* by the pupils of the Royal College of Music. Conducted by Bridge, the work is described as "full of colour of a familiar sort." Bridge is criticized for a lack of sense of climax, however, "his piece came off successfully enough." *See*: W146a

B370. "Royal College of Music." *The Musical Times* 49 (August 1908): 532.

A review of the first performance of Bridge's *Dance rhapsody*. The work "delighted the listeners" and Bridge was "enthusiastically applauded." *See*: W146a

B371. "Royal College of Music." *The Musical Times* 73 (January 1932): 65.

A review of Bridge's opera *The Christmas rose*, three performances of which were given in December 1931. The work was produced with "conspicuous success." *See*: W242a

B372. "Royal College of Music: Commemoration Concerts." *The Musical Times* 60 (August 1919): 429.

This article lists programs for three concerts given to commemorate the anniversary of the opening of the Royal College of Music building in May of 1894. Bridge's *Blow out you bugles* was performed on the first concert. *See*: W178c

B373. "Royal College of Music: 'Patron's Fund' Concert." *The Musical Times* 45 (June 1904): 397.

A discussion of performances of *Symphonic poem* and *The Hag* as part of the first 'Patron's Fund' Concerts. For these concerts, a result of a financial gift to the Royal College of Music, compositions were submitted and selected by Royal College and Royal Academy of Music experts. *The Hag* is described as "a weird song." "Interesting and ambitious" but "would bear condensation" is the description of *Symphonic poem*. *See*: W166a, W198b

B374. "Royal College of Music: Two Operas: *The Blue Peter* and *Christmas Rose*." *Morning Post* (London), 11 December 1931, p. 5g.

A review of the first performance, a student production, of Bridge's *The Christmas rose*. Criticized as being overly complicated in relation to the simple theme, credit is given to Bridge's production of "some very agreeable sounds." *See*: W242a

B375. "Royal College of Music: Two Short Operas." *Times* (London), 12 December 1931, p. 8a.

A review of the December 11, 1931 performance of Bridge's opera *The Christmas rose*. A somewhat mixed review, the reviewer comments on the work's originality, use of "modern harmonic colour" and use of a "rather austere style of vocal declamation." *See*: W242a

B376. "The Royal Collegian Abroad." *RCM Magazine* 5, no. 3 (1909): 86–87.

This article consists of paragraph long announcements of concerts performed by persons associated with the Royal College of Music. Bridge's "Italian" Quartet, performed during the year by the English String Quartet, is described as "a work of exceptional interest." *See*: W55a

B377. "The Royal Collegian Abroad." *RCM Magazine* 7, no. 2 (1911): 62–66.

This column lists the first performance of Bridge's Phantasy in F-sharp minor for piano quartet. It was performed by the Henkel Quartet on January 21, 1911 at Steinway Hall. On February 1, 1911 it was again performed at a meeting of the Concert-Goers Club. The reviewer says, "Familiarity with the Quartet only increases the estimate of its beauties." In addition, this column states that Miss Marie Brema's latest opera season at the Savoy was conducted by Bridge. *See*: W33a, W33b

B378. "The Royal Collegian Abroad." *RCM Magazine* 8, no. 2 (1912): 60–64.
On unspecified dates, the Motto Quartet gave two performances at Aeolian Hall. Bridge's *Three Idylls* were "very favourably received by an appreciative audience." *See*: W13b

B379. "Royal Philharmonic Society." *Daily Telegraph* (London), 14 March 1916, p. 11d.
A review of the premiere performance of *Summer*, by the Royal Philharmonic Society in Queen's Hall. The work, conducted by Frank Bridge, is described as containing "nothing to startle one." Bridge is described as a composer who "can mix his colours very skillfully for a small orchestra." *See*: W165a

B380. "Royal Philharmonic Society: Chamber Concerts." *Times* (London), 19 January 1934, p. 12b.
A review of the first performance of Bridge's Violin sonata. The reviewer comments on the "brilliantly constructed Scherzo," the only movement that "condescended to immediate attractiveness" and the work's "laboured climax." *See*: W64a

B381. "The Royal Philharmonic Society: Queen's Hall." *The Musical Times* 57 (April 1916): 200.
A review of a performance of Frank Bridge's *Summer* on March 13, 1916. It is described as an "agreeable and dainty" work. *See*: W165a

B382. S., M. M. "Chamber Music: The Royal Philharmonic Society's Chamber Concerts." *The Musical Times* 75 (February 1934): 174.
A review of the first performance of Bridge's Violin sonata on January 18, 1934. The reviewer found it an example of Bridge's "mature style." Bridge was called to the stage after the performance of the work. *See*: W64a

B383. S., P. A. "The Royal Philharmonic Society." *The Musical Times* 64 (May 1923): 352.
A review of a performance of Bridge's *The Sea* by the Royal Philharmonic Society on March 22, 1923. The work is described as a "remarkably vivid four-movement Suite." *See*: W160d

B384. S., R. [Review of recording by Kathleen Ferrier] *Musical America* 75 (January 1, 1955): 30.
This brief review of London LS 1032, which includes Bridge's *Go not, happy day*, describes it as a "splendid cross-section of British song in the past century." The warmth and beauty of Ferrier's tone is mentioned as well. *See*: D36f

B385. Shupp, E. E., Jr. [Review of recording by Geoffrey Tristram]. *The New Records* 48 (April 1980): 14–15.

This review of three recordings includes Vista's VPS 1051 on which is found Bridge's *Organ pieces*, book 1. The reviewer is impressed with the program on this record and refers to *Organ pieces* as "quiet" and "beautiful." *See*: D87b

B386. *The Stage Year Book*. (1921–1925): 121.

In this book, *Threads*, for which Bridge wrote the entr'actes, is listed as one of the plays of 1921. Characters and corresponding players are listed, as well as opening and closing dates. *See*: W248a

B387. "Steinway Hall." *Daily Telegraph* (London), 23 January 1911, p. 8e.

A review of the first performance of Phantasy in F-sharp minor. The reviewer criticizes the work as containing beautiful ideas which "are presented so discursively and with so little logical coherence that the interest of the listener is not maintained at full stretch." The reviewer finds Phantasie not "up to the standard of his best work." *See*: W33a

B388. Stinson, Eugene. "Modern Music Seeks Grammar for Expression." *Chicago Daily News*, 14 October 1930, p. 9h.

This article reviews works performed in Chicago's Simpson Theater as part of Coolidge's Festival of Chamber Music. Bridge's Piano trio is described as "a very effective piece of work." *See*: W38b

B389. Stone, Kurt. [Review of recording by Peter Pears]. *The Musical Quarterly* 51 (October 1965): 725–27.

The author of this review of an Argo disc (ZRG 5418), while questioning the use of the broad title, *Twentieth Century English Songs*, calls it "an unusual and pleasant addition to the repertory." Bridge's, as well as Ireland's songs, are described as lacking "the uniqueness of personality and invention that transcends geographic and historical confines," yet "within these limitations it is eloquent, sensitive, beautifully composed, and always pleasant to listen to." *See*: D38a

B390. "Success is Scored by String Quartet." *Washington Post*, 31 October 1930, p. 5d.

A review of a performance of Bridge's Piano trio. Mrs. Cohen's piano performance is described as "masterly." *See*: W38d

B391. "Symphony Concert at Queen's Hall: The Art of the Conductor." *Times* (London), 28 October 1918, p. 9c.

A review of a "new orchestral work" by Bridge entitled *Blow out you bugles*. It is described as "well constructed and quite convincing music." *See*: W178a

B392. T., F. "New Bridge Sonata: R. P. S. Chamber Concert." *Morning Post* (London), 19 January 1934, p. 16e.
A review of the first performance of Bridge's Violin sonata. The reviewer expresses disappointment with this work in comparison to Bridge's earlier chamber music. He describes the Violin Sonata as lacking spontaneity and charm. *See*: W64a

B393. Tarsrey, Charlotte M., "Bridge, Braslau Register Triumph." *Detroit Free Press*, 2 November 1923, p. 2e.
A review of the first of two performances by the Detroit Symphony Orchestra of Bridge's *Summer* and *Sir Roger de Coverley*. Conducted by Bridge, the reviewer prefers the latter which is described as a "rollicking impetuous tumult of sound." A brief description of Bridge as conductor is also given. *See*: W163b, W165b

B394. Taubman, Howard. "2 Concerts Close Capital Festival." *New York Times*, 15 April 1940, p. 20e.
A review of the first performance of Bridge's *Divertimenti*. The reviewer felt the work and Bax's Octet, also performed on the concert, "offered almost no musical sustenance" aside from technical interest. *See*: W9a.

B395. Thompson, Herbert. "The Norwich Festival." *The Musical Times* 65 (December 1924): 1112–13.
This article describes the concert performances at the Norwich Triennial Festival including that of Frank Bridge's *The Sea*. *See*: W160h

B396. ———. "The Norwich Festival." *The Musical Times* 68 (December 1927): 1124–26.
This article reviews the 1927 Norwich Triennial at which Bridge's *Enter spring* received its first performance. The reviewer feels the piece lacks programmatic qualities but that it "commands respect" when viewed "simply as music." *See*: W148a

B397. Thornton, H. Frank. [Review of recording by the Chelsea Opera Group Chorus and Orchestra]. *The New Records* 52 (June 1984): 10.
A brief but direct review of Pearl's recording (SHE 582) of Bridge's *The Christmas rose*. The author calls it a "highly agreeable, if not very exciting, work." *See*: D17a

B398. ———. [Review of recording by Meral Güneyman]. *The New Records* 49 (September 1981): 14.
Two recordings are briefly reviewed here. Finnadar's SR 9031 contains Bridge's Piano sonata. The reviewer describes both recordings as "unusual piano works," and feels Bridge's sonata "sounds indebted to Scriabin." *See*: D98b

B399. ________. [Review of recording by Peter Pears]. *The New Records* 33 (October 1965): 13.

Five of Bridge's songs, on Argo RG 418, are reviewed here. They, with four songs by Ireland, are described as "pleasant and rather unadventuresome." The author singles out Bridge's *So perverse* as one song which he doesn't care for. *See*: D38a

B400. Tiedman, [Richard]. [Review of recording by Peter Wallfisch and the London Philharmonic Orchestra]. *The American Record Guide* 41 (January 1978): 16–18.

The author of this review of HNH 4042, on which Bridge's *Phantasm* appears, presents a brief discussion of the change in style his music underwent after the First World War. He describes *Phantasm* as "a fascinating and enigmatic score." *See*: D94b

B401. T[rimble], L[ester]. [Review of recording by the English Chamber Orchestra]. *Stereo Review* 25 (July 1970): 93.

In this review of London recording CS 6618, Bridge's *Sir Roger de Coverley* is described as "a delightful, unpretentious work." *See*: D118e

B402. Vroon, [Donald R.]. [Review of recording by the Coull Quartet]. *The American Record Guide* 53 (May–June 1990): 51.

In this very brief review of ASV CD DCA 678 on which Bridge's Piano quintet appears, the reviewer describes the work as having "considerable charm." *See*: D97a

B403. W. "Norwich Festival: Second Day - Morning Concert." *Eastern Daily Press* (Norwich), 31 October 1924, p. 9c.

The last work of the morning concert, Bridge's *The Sea* is described as showing "a highly imaginative mind" and "is very cleverly scored." The reviewer mentions some "weird harmonies" as well as "pleasant melody." The work, conducted by Bridge, is acknowledged "with due applause." *See*: W160h

B404. "War Works at Symphony Concert: A Lusitania *Lament*." *Times* (London), 16 October 1916, p. 11e.

A review of a performance of Bridge's *Lament*. The work is described by the reviewer as having "immediate and intimate appeal." *See*: W151b

B405. W[arrack], J[ohn]. [Review of recording by the Allegri String Quartet]. *Gramophone* 50 (March 1973): 1701–2.

Bridge's String quartets no. 3 and 4 are discussed in this review of Argo ZRG 714. The works' historical context is described at great length for a review. The author stresses the importance of this

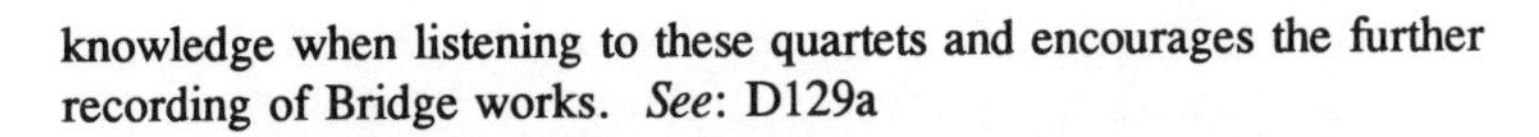

knowledge when listening to these quartets and encourages the further recording of Bridge works. *See*: D129a

B406. ———. [Review of recording of Bridge vocal and orchestral works]. *Gramophone* 60 (August 1982): 261.
This is a review of Pearl SHE 568 on which selections of Bridge's vocal and orchestral music appears. The majority of the author's comments are directed toward *Isabella* which he feels has largely been ignored. He describes it as a piece with "all the craftsmanship and the clarity of instrumental texture which were to mark Bridge's music." The other works on the album are briefly mentioned. *See*: D23b

B407. ———. [Review of recording by the Gabrieli Quartet]. *Gramophone* 55 (June 1977): 69.
Two Bridge works, *Novelletten* and *Three Idylls*, appear on the Decca recording (SDD 497) reviewed here. Coupled with two works by Britten, the reviewer uses this opportunity to discuss "where much of the contact lay between Bridge and Britten." *See*: D46b

B408. ———. [Review of recording by the Hanson String Quartet]. *Gramophone* 60 (January 1983): 836.
Bridge's String sextet in E-flat major and Phantasy in F-sharp minor appear on Pearl SHE 570 which is reviewed here. Brief background information is presented for each work. The Sextet is described as having an "easy, lyrical flow which never loses its impetus," while the Phantasie demonstrates that Bridge was "a master of unusual forms." *See*: D96d

B409. ———. [Review of recording by the London Philharmonic Orchestra]. *Gramophone* 54 (April 1977): 1542.
Bridge's *Phantasm* and Moeran's Rhapsody trio comprise Lyrita SRCS.91 and are reviewed here. The author describes *Phantasm* as a "remarkable work, one of potent atmosphere and clear, strongly felt logic." *See*: D94b

B410. ———. [Review of recording by the London Philharmonic Orchestra]. *Gramophone* 55 (April 1978): 1714.
This article is a review of Lyrita SRCS.73 which is devoted entirely to orchestral works by Bridge. The author discusses at length his Suite, describing it as "beautifully scored, with an understanding of string sonorities that sprang from Bridge's own practical knowledge of orchestral playing as a violist of distinction." The other works are more briefly but still favorably discussed. *See*: D56b

B411. ———. [Review of recording by the London Philharmonic Orchestra]. *Gramophone* 57 (November 1979): 809.

Bridge's *Dance rhapsody*, *Dance poem*, and *Rebus* are heard on Lyrita SRCS.114 reviewed here. An "excellently planned group of three of his orchestral pieces" the author commends the orchestra for their performance—Bridge is "no easy composer to conduct." Each work is thoughtfully discussed with the reviewer finding *Dance rhapsody* the least successful but nonetheless a rewarding piece. *See*: D20a

B412. ———. [Review of recording by the London Philharmonic Orchestra]. *Gramophone* 57 (January 1980): 1141.

Three orchestral works by Bridge comprise the Lyrita recording (SRCS.104) which is the subject of this review. His *Oration* is described as "beautifully constructed," written "in the nature of an orchestral tone poem with cello obligato." The *Unfinished Symphony* and *Two Poems* also appear on this recording. The latter is described as having "the lively ingenuity of Bridge's most relaxed manner." *See*: D86b

B413. ———. [Review of recording by the Music Group of London]. *Gramophone* 57 (June 1979): 66.

This is a review of Enigma Classics K.53578 on which is found Bridge's Piano Quintet and Phantasy in C minor. The author prefers the trio, calling it a "splendidly energetic work." *See*: D95b

B414. ———. [Review of recording by Eric Parkin]. *Gramophone* 57 (November 1979): 874.

The author of this review of Unicorn RHS 359 discusses briefly the revival of interest in Bridge as seen in the recordings available. The Piano sonata heard on this record is described as a "bitter, tense work." Bridge's more "relaxed side" is evident in the other works on the album. *See*: D16a

B415. ———. [Review of recording by the Royal Liverpool Philharmonic Orchestra]. *Gramophone* 53 (May 1976): 1749–50.

This is a review of Bridge's orchestral works found on EMI/HMV ASD 3190. The author calls this a "well-chosen survey" in which each of Bridge's three compositional periods have representation. A very insightful and detailed review, the author calls the following three works masterpieces: *The Sea*, *Summer*, and *Enter spring*. *See*: D30a

B416. ———. [Review of recording by the Tunnell Trio]. *Gramophone* 55 (February 1978): 1419–20.

A recording devoted to works by Bridge, Argo AK 40 is reviewed here. The author commends Argo's "balance and choice of works." He places the works in historical context and describes each in some detail. *See*: D71a

B417. W[ebb], S[tanley]. [Review of recording by Christopher Herrick]. *Gramophone* 52 (October 1974): 737.

The author writes a glowing review of this Vista recording (VPS 1001) of organ works. Bridge's Adagio in E major is described as "a beautiful Adagio based on a rising theme announced on his own instrument—the viola..." *See*: D102i

B418. ———. [Review of recording by Geoffrey Tristram]. *Gramophone* 55 (November 1977): 868.

This review of Vista VPS 1051 contains only passing mention of Bridge's "rarely played" *Organ pieces*, book 1 which appears here. The author feels that the disc is "well worth a hearing" and isn't displeased with the sound of the electronic organ of Christchurch Priory heard here. *See*: D87b

B419. Westrup, Jack A. "Frank Bridge's New Concerto: Inspiration from War." *Daily Telegraph* (London), 18 January 1936, p. 10d.

A review of the first performance of Bridge's *Oration*. The solo part of this "imaginative and deeply sincere work" was performed by Florence Hooton, whose part was "without any wanton display of virtuosity." *See*: W155a

B420. W[iser], J[ohn] D. [Review of Bridge works on Pearl and Chandos]. *Fanfare* 7 (May–June 1984): 166–68.

Bridge songs and string quartet music, as recorded on Pearl SHE 577 and Chandos ABRD 1073, respectively, are reviewed in this article. The Pearl recording is described as a "miscellany, particularly as to quality." Although displeased with the performance, the reviewer enjoys String quartet no. 2. The less well-known quartet versions of the shorter pieces on the Chandos recording are also discussed. *See*: D1a, D52a

B421. ———. [Review of Bridge works on Pearl and Nonesuch]. *Fanfare* 6 (January–February 1983): 124–26.

Here the author reviews Pearl SHE 571, Pearl SHE 568, Nonesuch 71405, and Pearl SHE 570. He observes both "magnificent music and music-making in this lot, as well as some routine things." Each work is given careful and thoughtful criticism. *See*: D9a, D23b, D95b, D96d

B422. ———. [Review of recording by the Hanson String Quartet]. *Fanfare* 7 (July–August 1984): 145.

This is a review of Pearl SHE 563 on which Bridge's String quartet no. 1 in E minor appears. The author describes the work as "an harmonically lush, lively, and effectively scored piece." In addition, he notes that "the music improves rapidly with acquaintance." *See*: D127a

B423. "Yesterday's Concerts: British Music and British Artists." *Morning Post* (London), 14 July 1917, p. 9d.

A review of the first performance of Bridge's Violoncello sonata in D minor in Wigmore Hall. The work is described as falling "under the heading of 'modern romantic'" and its performance is appreciated by the reviewer. *See*: W65a

B424. "Yesterday's Concerts: The Grimson Quartet." *Morning Post* (London), 9 March 1907, p. 5c.

A review of the Grimson Quartet's Bechstein Hall recital given on March 8, 1907. Bridge's *Three Idylls* was performed for the first time. The pieces are described as "delicate impressionist sketches of a light and fantastic nature." *See*: W13a

Appendix I: Alphabetical List of Compositions

Numbers following each title, e.g. W40, refer to the "Works and Performances" section of this volume. The H. Number column refers the user to Paul Hindmarsh's numbering. This numbering, first used in his *Frank Bridge: A Thematic Catalog*, is used by the Royal College of Music Library as a finding guide to their manuscript holdings.

H. Number	Title
90	"?", W93
11	Adagio ma non troppo, W94
57	Adoration (voice and orchestra), W173
57	Adoration (voice and piano), W172
77	All things that we clasp, W174
53b	Allegretto, W1
82	Allegro appassionato, W2
59	Amaryllis, W3
112d	Arabesque, W95
24	Autumn, W66
110	The Bee, W67
8	Berceuse (orchestra), W140
8	Berceuse (piano), W96
9	Berceuse (voice and orchestra), W175
8	Berceuse (violin and strings), W141

92 O weary hearts, W84
119 Two Old English songs (piano duet), W122
119 Two Old English songs (string orchestra), W154
119 Two Old English songs (string quartet), W28
180 Oration, concerto elegiaco (violoncello and orchestra), W155
180 Oration, concerto elegiaco (violoncello and piano), W29
56 Organ pieces, book 1, W123
106 Organ pieces, book 2, W124

98 The Pageant of London, W246
158 Pan's holiday (voices and piano), W85
158 Pan's holiday (voices with piano and string orchestra), W86
16 Pensees fugitives I, W125
53a Pensiero, W30
123 Peter Piper, W87
55 Phantasie in F minor, W31
182 Phantasm (piano and orchestra), W156
182 Phantasm (two pianos), W126
79 Phantasy in C minor, W32
94 Phantasy in F-sharp minor, W33
15 Piano quartet in C minor, W34
49 Piano quintet, W35
49A Piano quintet (1912), W36
160 Piano sonata, W127
1 Piano trio in D minor, W37
178 Piano trio (1929), W38
101 Two Pieces, W39
63 Three Pieces for organ, W128
190 Three Pieces for organ (1939), W129
43 Three Pieces for string quartet (1904), W40
64 Three Pieces for string quartet (1905), W41
163 The Pneu world, W42
112a-c Three Poems, W130
118 Two Poems, W157
140 A Prayer (chorus and orchestra), W89
140 A Prayer (chorus and organ), W88
13 The Primrose, W220

74 The Rag, W43
191 Rebus, W158
35 Two Recitations, W221
176 Rhapsody, W44
26 Rising when the dawn still faint is, W222
108c Romance, W131
45 Romanze, W45
68b Rosemary, W159

20	Scherzettino, W132
19	Scherzetto, W46
19A	Scherzo, W47
6	Scherzo phantastick, W48
100	The Sea, W160
54a	A Sea idyll, W133
23	Serenade (orchestra), W161
23	Serenade (piano), W134
23	Serenade (violin/violoncello and piano), W49
155	Sir Roger de Coverley (orchestra), W163
155	Sir Roger de Coverley (string orchestra), W162
155	Sir Roger de Coverley (string quartet), W50
137	Sister, awake, W90
68	Three Sketches, W135
130	So early in the morning, o, W223
61	So perverse, W224
42	Song cycle, W225
5	Sonnet, W226
48	Souvenir, W51
164b	Speak to me my love, W227
104b	Spring song, W52
157	A Spring song (voices and piano), W91
157	A Spring song (voices and string orchestra), W92
109	Strew no more red roses, W228
3	String quartet in B-flat major, W53
187	String quartet movement, W54
70	String quartet no. 1 in E minor, W55
115	String quartet no. 2 in G minor, W56
175	String quartet no. 3, W57
188	String quartet no. 4, W58
7	String quintet in E minor, W59
107	String sextet in E-flat major, W60
93	Suite, W164
116	Summer, W165
30	Symphonic poem, W166
62	Tears, idle tears, W229
173	There is a willow grows aslant a brook, W167
65b	Thou didst delight my eyes, W230
151	Threads (orchestra), W248
151	Threads (piano), W247
124	Thy hand in mine, W231
146	'Tis but a week, W232
129	To you in France, W233
181	Todessehnsucht (Come sweet death) (piano), W136
181	Todessehnsucht (Come sweet death) (string orchestra), W168

Appendix II: Chronological List of Compositions

Numbers following each title, e.g. W40, refer to the "Works and Performances" section of this volume.

????	Miniature suite, W118
1900	Three Dances, W8
	Une Lamentatione d'amour, W15
	Piano trio in D minor, W37
	String quartet in B-flat major, W53
1901	Adagio ma non troppo, W94
	Berceuse (orchestra), W140
	Berceuse (piano), W96
	Berceuse (voice and orchestra), W175
	Berceuse (violin and strings), W141
	Berceuse (violin/violoncello and piano), W4
	Coronation march, W143
	If I could choose, W201
	The Primrose, W220
	Scherzo phantastick, W48
	Sonnet, W226
	String quintet in E minor, W59

1902 The Hag, W198
Trois Morceaux d'orchestre, W152
Pensees fugitives I, W125
Piano quartet in C minor, W34
Scherzettino, W132
Scherzetto, W46
Scherzo, W47
Valse intermezzo à cordes, W170

1903 Autumn, W66
Blow, blow thou winter wind, W176
Con moto, W5
The Devon maid, W186
A Dirge, W187
E'en as a lovely flower (voice and orchestra), W191
E'en as a lovely flower (voice and piano), W190
Go not, happy day, W196
Mazurka, W17
Moderato, W120
The Mountain voice, W213
Music when soft voices die (voice and piano), W214
Two Recitations, W221
Rising when the dawn still faint is, W222
Serenade (orchestra), W161
Serenade (piano), W134
Serenade (violin/violoncello and piano), W49
Symphonic poem, W166
Where e're my bitter teardrops fall, W238

1904 Cradle song (voice and piano), W180
A Dead violet, W184
Elégie, W10
Fly home my thoughts, W195
Harebell and pansy, W199
Lament (voice and orchestra), W205
Music when soft voices die (mixed chorus), W83
Night lies on the silent highways, W217
Novelletten, W27
Three Pieces for string quartet (1904), W40
Romanze, W45
Song cycle, W225
Souvenir, W51
Violin sonata, W63

1905
- Adoration (voice and orchestra), W173
- Adoration (voice and piano), W172
- Allegretto, W1
- Amaryllis, W3
- Capriccio no. 1 in A minor, W98
- Capriccio no. 2 in F-sharp minor, W99
- Dawn and evening (voice and orchestra), W182
- Dawn and evening (voice and piano), W181
- Etude rhapsodique, W104
- Fair daffodils, W192
- Lean close thy cheek against my cheek, W207
- Norse legend (piano), W121
- Norse legend (violin and piano), W26
- Organ pieces, book 1, W123
- Pensiero, W30
- Phantasie in F minor, W31
- Piano quintet, W35
- Three Pieces for organ, W128
- Three Pieces for string quartet (1905), W41
- A Sea idyll, W133
- So perverse, W224
- Tears, idle tears, W229

1906
- Come to me in my dreams, W179
- Dramatic fantasia, W103
- Dramatic overture, W147
- Far, far from each other, W194
- I praise the tender flower, W200
- Three Idylls, W13
- My pent up tears oppress my brain, W216
- The Rag, W43
- Rosemary, W159
- Three Sketches, W135
- String quartet no. 1 in E minor, W55
- Thou didst delight my eyes, W230
- Valse Fernholt, W61
- The Violets blue, W235
- Where is it that our soul doth go?, W239

1907
- All things that we clasp, W174
- Gondoliera, W11
- Isabella, W150
- Love is a rose, W208
- Music when soft voices die, with viola, W215
- Phantasy in C minor, W32

1908 "?," W93
Allegro appassionato, W2
Dance rhapsody, W146
Dear, when I look into thine eyes, W185
An Irish melody (string quartet), W14
Miniatures, set 1, W21
Miniatures, set 2, W22
Miniatures, set 3, W23
Morceau characteristique, W24

1909 Hilli-ho! Hilli-ho!, W77
O weary hearts, W84

1910 Cradle song (violin/violoncello and piano), W7
The Two Hunchbacks, W243
Phantasy in F-sharp minor, W33
Suite, W164

1911 Coronation march (1911), W144
Mélodie, W19
The Pageant of London, W246
The Sea, W160

1912 Columbine, W101
Country dance, W6
Easter hymn (SATB), W68
Easter hymn (voice and piano), W189
Isobel, W203
Lullaby (violin and piano), W16
Meditation, W18
Minuet, W119
O that it were so (voice and orchestra), W219
O that it were so (voice and piano), W218
Organ pieces, book 2, W124
Piano quintet (1912), W36
Two Pieces, W39
Romance, W131
Spring song, W52
String sextet in E-flat major, W60

1913 The Bee, W67
Dance poem, W145
Strew no more red roses, W228

1914 Arabesque, W95
Love went a-riding (voice and orchestra), W210
Love went a-riding (voice and piano), W209
Three Poems, W130
Where she lies asleep (voice and orchestra), W241
Where she lies asleep (voice and piano), W240

1915 Lament (piano), W112
Lament (string orchestra), W151
Two Poems, W157
String quartet no. 2 in G minor, W56
Summer, W165

1916 For God and king and right (voices and piano), W71
The Graceful swaying wattle (chorus and piano), W74
Lullaby (voices and piano), W81
Two Old English songs (piano duet), W122
Two Old English songs (string orchestra), W154
Two Old English songs (string quartet), W28
Peter Piper, W87
A Prayer (chorus and organ), W88

1917 Four Characteristic pieces, W100
A Fairy tale, W105
Miniature pastorals, set 1, W115
Thy hand in mine, W231
To you in France, W233
Violoncello sonata in D minor, W65

1918 Blow out you bugles (voice and orchestra), W178
Blow out you bugles (voice and piano), W177
Three Improvisations, W110
The Last invocation, W206
Lay a garland on my hearse, W79
Lento (In memoriam C.H.H.P.), W113
A Litany, W80
Mantle of blue (voice and orchestra), W212
Mantle of blue (voice and piano), W211
Morning song, W25
A Prayer (chorus and orchestra), W89
Sister, awake, W90
So early in the morning, o, W223
Variations on Cadet Rousselle, W234

1919	Fair daffodils (revision), W193
	For God and king and right (voices and orchestra), W72
	The Graceful swaying wattle (chorus and string orchestra), W75
	Into her keeping, W202
	Lantido dilly, W78
	Lullaby (voices and string orchestra), W82
	'Tis but a week, W232
	The Turtle's retort, W137
	What shall I your true love tell, W236
	When you are old, W237
1920	The Hour glass, W109
1921	In the shop (piano), W245
	In the shop (piano duet), W244
	Miniature pastorals, set 2, W116
	Miniature pastorals, set 3, W117
	Threads (piano), W247
1922	Day after day, W183
	Evening primrose, W69
	The Fairy ring, W70
	Golden slumbers, W73
	Hence care, W76
	Pan's holiday (voices and piano), W85
	Sir Roger de Coverley (orchestra), W163
	Sir Roger de Coverley (string quartet), W50
	A Spring song (voices and piano), W91
1924	In autumn, W111
	Three Lyrics, W114
	Pan's holiday (voices with piano and string orchestra), W86
	Piano sonata, W127
	Speak to me my love, W227
1925	Dweller in my deathless dreams, W188
	Goldenhair, W197
	Journey's end, W204
	The Pneu world, W42
	Vignettes de Marseille, W138
	Winter pastoral, W139
1926	Canzonetta (orchestra), W142
	Canzonetta (piano), W97
	A Dedication, W102

	Graziella, W107
	Hidden fires, W108
1927	Enter spring, W148
	String quartet no. 3, W57
	There is a willow grows aslant a brook, W167
1928	Gargoyle, W106
	Rhapsody, W44
1929	The Christmas rose, W242
	Piano trio (1929), W38
1930	Heart's ease, W12
	Oration, concerto elegiaco (violoncello and orchestra), W155
	Oration, concerto elegiaco (violoncello and piano), W29
	A Spring song (voices and string orchestra), W92
1931	Phantasm (piano and orchestra), W156
	Phantasm (two pianos), W126
	Todessehnsucht (Come sweet death) (piano), W136
1932	Violin sonata (1932), W64
1934	A Merry, merry xmas, W20
1936	String quartet movement, W54
	Todessehnsucht (Come sweet death) (string orchestra), W168
	Viola sonata, W62
1937	String quartet no. 4, W58
1938	Divertimenti, W9
	An Irish melody (string orchestra), W149
	Norse legend (orchestra), W153
	Sir Roger de Coverley (string orchestra), W162
	Threads (orchestra), W248
	Vignettes de danse, W171
1939	Three Pieces for organ (1939), W129
1940	Rebus, W158
1941	Unfinished symphony, W169

Index

About the Author

KAREN R. LITTLE is Assistant Head of the Dwight Anderson Music Library at the University of Louisville.

Recent Titles in
Bio-Bibliographies in Music

Anthony Milner: A Bio-Bibliography
James Siddons

Edward Burlingame Hill: A Bio-Bibliography
Linda L. Tyler

Alexander Tcherepnin: A Bio-Bibliography
Enrique Alberto Arias

Ernst Krenek: A Bio-Bibliography
Garrett H. Bowles, compiler

Ned Rorem: A Bio-Bibliography
Arlys L. McDonald

Richard Rodney Bennett: A Bio-Bibliography
Stewart R. Craggs, compiler

Radie Britain: A Bio-Bibliography
Walter B. Bailey and Nancy Gisbrecht Bailey

Frank Martin: A Bio-Bibliography
Charles W. King, compiler

Peggy Glanville-Hicks: A Bio-Bibliography
Deborah Hayes

Francis Poulenc: A Bio-Bibliography
George R. Keck, compiler

Robert Russell Bennett: A Bio-Bibliography
George J. Ferencz

György Ligeti: A Bio-Bibliography
Robert W. Richart

Karel Husa: A Bio-Bibliography
Susan Hayes Hitchens

Ferruccio Busoni: A Bio-Bibliography
Marc-André Roberge